Nutritional Diversity: An Abstract of All-Natural Human Optimization

Revision V

Cinco de Mayo 2023

Written by Brandon Eisler and Edited by Dr. Tabinda Nasir

Just as nature takes every obstacle, every impediment, and works around it--turns it to its purposes, incorporates it into itself, so, too, **a rational being can turn each setback into raw material and use it to achieve its goal. - Marcus Aurelius**

About the Author

Born in Albuquerque, New Mexico. After Honorable discharge in 2008 he would already be making an award-winning movie and several two-story apartment buildings in Philadelphia after attending one year at Temple University on the GIBILL. A "Whirwind Blackhole (this book's final chapter)" would then land him in Panama put through immense tortuous PAIN and then; blasted through space and time in a wild connect the diet dots ride to unlocking a dynamic playbook of health and fitness performance; a discovery that could revolutionize human health, ecological health and nutritional security on this planet, and also social-cultural health, is faced with "mission impossible" after mission impossible and continues to ride through on what he claims is our natural intended diet that we don't eat.

By the time he was 13 years old, he had visited much of the United States. By the age of 17, he had established renowned dance clubs. For these venues as well as his work in the media, he was later admitted into the music halls of fame of Philadelphia, Pennsylvania, and Albuquerque, New Mexico. He enlisted in the US Navy to serve in Operation Iraqi Freedom in 2005 as a star member of the Carl Vinson Strike Group. For the final two years before his honorable discharge, he served as a Damage Control LPO head instructor.

He also discovered his "Nutritional Diversity" systems and abstract approaches to life through his devout dedication to God and goodness. As a result, he began to see that this eating strategy, which he later began to refer to as "Nutritional Variety," was improving every illness it came into contact with, including ulcerative colitis, mental

trauma, and physical performance in every case and category. He has since been working with the diet now a decade and has been published in United Nations Food & Agriculture journals, as well as being the basis for new scientific studies in many applications such as carbon capture and climate change discussions, and PTSD therapies for Veterans. A nightmare of a life has realized robust solutions to many of the world's issues, proposing new compartmentalized communities that exist in a more nature-harmonious form with permaculture agriculture systems as the central concept and using the MMPI2 test to disqualify unethical management, using a structure of experience-oriented seniority in management and single-issue digital voting to ensure community success.

This book describes in many ways the seriously 'set-up' life one (or many) would have if they can pull off the organization and possibly innovation to have this diet model on a regular basis. Small groups can come together and should be able to enhance and secure some kind of portion of a small farming economy or their own farm.

Editor's Note

Dear Readers,

As the editor of this book on Nutritional Diversity, let me take a moment to thank Brandon Eisler, our primary author and researcher, for his effort and commitment. His study of plants, herbs, and permaculture has been crucial in developing a thorough manual on how to consume a variety of nutritious foods to obtain nutrient diverseness.

The book is interspersed with Brandon's study on plants, herbs, and permaculture, stressing the variety of nutrients that can be found in these foods and how they can be included in our meals to enhance our general health. He imparts his knowledge on sustainable agriculture and how it may benefit the environment and human health, highlighting the significance of a diverse diet.

As the book's editor, I would like to express my sincere gratitude for Brandon's efforts. This book is the result of his unwavering commitment to the subject and his extensive research and writing. His work has compiled the most recent findings and thoughts on nutrition and health, providing a useful and inspirational manual for achieving optimum wellness.

We are happy to have had Brandon Eisler as our primary contributor and researcher because it is obvious that his work has been a labor of love. His dedication to this endeavor has been unshakable, and we are sure that his research will significantly benefit those who want to increase the variety of their diets and their general health.

I'm also hoping this book will motivate you to transform your life for the better by combining the ideas of dietary variety, physical fitness, and gastric health. We are convinced that this book will become a vital tool for anyone looking to enhance their health and wellness thanks to Brandon's study and our team's efforts.

Sincerely,

Dr. Tabinda Nasir,
BDS, Bsc. Medical Researcher

Acknowledgment

My special thanks to my Dad, I would want to express my sincere gratitude for his constant support and inspiration. His confidence in me and willingness to offer advice and support at every turn have been priceless. The writing of this book would not have been possible without his love and support. I may not even be alive had he not been in my corner throughout this. I have hung by a thin thread through out several chapters of this actual journey and athlete's will understand when I say, it is through "Big Pain" that I write about what I have found to be a big gain. Furthermore I have many to thank, My Uncle Bo Yancy living through your death has been a rocket ride, and adventure of love, and of OVERCOMING, learning and growing. My friends Carolina Romero, Mickey Kennedy, Mikhail Ioffee, Micheal Dichioria, Dr. Ricky, Jonanda, Craig.S, Mr. Bruce Hill, Mr. Lee, Holly Weaver,, Mr. Killa Jeremy Page, Shawna Lovato, Justin Ismond, Joseph & Alana Bliss, Jessica Housand Weaver, Regina Gonzales, Tina Trebino, Mayo Aragon,
Dr. Jennifer Daniels, Richard Nichols, Mike Lopzonski, Harry
Goodheart, Manuel Sanjur, Rob Allen, Dave Hepburn, Micheal Duncan, and a few others for your honest and unwavering support and /or interest in this stuff, my success, through some of my toughest times. I have to thank Joe Rogan, Mike Tyson and Even Brettin, Tom Bilabeau, Wes Watson, Patrick-Bet David
Valuetainment, Zach Bush, Tucker Carlson, Candace Owens, Dr, Romani, Batel Skater, Dr. Grundy, Koncrete Podcast, Andrew & Tristan Tate, Dana White, Sad guru, the Church of Jesus Christ of Latter Day Saints, Islam, The Seventh Day Adventist Church, Next Level Soul Podcast also friends Mr. Wolf, Mike Hines, Andrew Hyde, Sam Meager, Ramiro Salceda, Sterling Thompson, Allan Bollinger, Sebastian Leblanc for helping restore my IQ and faith in humanity to be honest. I want to thank my little one for her videos at age 14, they may have saved my life then. I will have to thank pain and problems cause without them I would have never needed this, or found these rare gems within it. I have to thank OVERCOMING,

because without that we stop living, and become stuck. Those named here, will

all likely be stalked and harassed by Jerry Springer people for the rest of their life - To the new level of humanity in our age; the Nutritional Diversifist: Good Luck!

Table of Contents

NUTRITIONAL DIVERSITY 10

Revision 'V' 10

Stomach Nutrition 32

Digestive Culture 40

Introduction to Nutritional Biodynamics 44

Working Together, in Rhythm 60

Hydration 65

Proteins, Carbohydrates & Fats 79

Love 87

Physical Food States 94

The Core Principles 109

The Food Tour 125

Fitness Training 208

Cross Training 212

Nutritional Diversity Application 220

Increments 221

Go with Your Gut 231

Get on the cutting edge today! 246

ABSTRACT 247

METHODS 252

DISCUSSIONS: 253

RESULTS: 257

Continuation 260

ABSTRACT 261

METHODS 262

INITIAL RESULTS: 267

Mandatory Fitness Component 268

Business Models..278

Carbon Conversation..292

iReferences...300

NUTRITIONAL DIVERSITY

AN ABSTRACT OF ALL-NATURAL H UMAN OPTIMIZATION
Revision 'V'

Introduction:

Humans were not created with manuals. We ought to have, though!!!

It's possible that we misplaced it or that someone hid it -if so it would be what we call a "narcissist," in this text who would have done something so limiting to our experience, and they would do it "limit, deceive and to control." I suppose that Yoga, is one there are others, and that any expansion on them is something that is left up to us to recreate and rediscover.

Here is an attempt at solution that continuously produces

strong human optimization in the face of diet confusion, agricultural misinformation, and diet authorities that are directly responsible for the global health crisis and ecological catastrophe that is truly much more intense and ongoing than most realize.

Because of this scientific research, underprivileged

individuals and troublesome youth have a fantastic opportunity to become more than healthy (human optimization), to enhance the lives of those around them, and to realize their full potential. The most important nutritional notion is presented in this literature, and it is a trip on which anyone, at any moment, can set off. The theory demonstrates a connection between obtaining food from a new type of farmer and farm (permaculture), from the wild also; extremely varied special

consumption, and obvious improvements in one's physical, mental, digestive, recuperation, and immune system.i

Nutrition described here needs a whole new source and supply chain. If humans hadn't previously shown up with spears and fire from alien spaceships, we would have evolved to this stage through a nutritionally diverse diet. By this reasoning, agriculture and bowls of rice are de-evolutionary diets that would have followed. These days, our animals consume varied diets that can be improved in the same ways as ours if done correctly. This should be the overarching concept that unites everything.

Along with producing enough calories, one significant and frequently disregarded challenge in agricultural and food systems is to offer an adequate diversity of nutrients, which are essential for a healthy life. According to Zahra et al. (2022), Adequate nutrition is essential for growth and development and can protect humans against both infectious and non-communicable diseases. ii Continuous monitoring of their food consumption is necessary to ensure that they are in the best possible nutritional condition. At least 51 nutrients must be present in sufficient, continuous levels in a human diet.

Dietary diversity has long been recognized as important for adequate nutrient intake but the concept of nutritional diversity has yet to be integrated into planning and assessments of agricultural and food systems and policies. The primary criteria used to evaluate the efficacy of agricultural systems, according to IAASTD (International Assessment of Agricultural Knowledge, Science and Technology for Development 2009), are crop yields, economic output, and cost-benefit ratios. Providing enough diversity of nutrients, which are necessary for a healthy existence, is a crucial and sometimes ignored difficulty in agricultural and food systems, in addition to supplying enough calories.iii

As a former Chemical, Biological, and Radiological Warfare Defense

Instructor for the United States Navy, I discovered that this country's equatorial location and weather patterns offer a safe haven from disasters like "nuclear" winter because contaminants will move back up to their respective pole, northern or southern hemisphere. In other words, the Earth would begin again from this point if a major disaster such as an explosion or asteroid strike were to occur. Because of this equatorial relation Panama enjoys some of the highest crop yields in the world. Ofcourse this can always change if the polar shift theory was to happen.

The athletic and health performance study is ongoing here in the tropical growing bridge of diversity, the beautiful Republic of Panama. The first three revisions of the athletic science were tailored

for troubled youth because this just loudly seems like the perfect alternative occupation for our troubled youth. Funding foreign wars while we have all these children poor? We need tree replacements and we should pay these kids to do it and advance our knowledge of the ecological wonder system we have been gifted here. "Guerrilla Permaculture:" (Revision II, Brandon Eisler) was used in Addressing the Climate Change & Poverty Nexus, a coordinated approach by the United Nations Food & Agriculture Organization (FAO), to the 2030 Agenda and the Paris agreement. One year later the text has become a bit clearer, as has the diet formulations and diet science itself (Revision IV 2020). Then three years later (current revision) things have very much progressed in testing, we have been able to offer this diet solution to a much broader scale and get some video testimonies as we were advised to, along with really heighten the stack of amazing case study information for this team to move forward to the next-level with. There is a long way to go, however looking back we are far ahead of everyone else and now there is enough of us that people are starting to learn from one another far outside of our realm.

I have done my best to update and edit the document(s), and evolve the science. The great thing about this ecological journey is we have infinite time to learn this. No one person will learn it all, and we likely take another 100 years to really get our head around "ecology."

Brian Faith in his book "Encyclopedia of ecology" describes "Permaculture" proposes pragmatic methodological principles to create autonomous, resilient, and equitable living spaces".iv

After fifty 'permacultures' over a near decade of doing this, I am making in this revision an effort to have something presentable about the diet concept potentials and some hot points on cultivation and harvest.

Holmgren (2002) has defined 12 principles of permaculture design. These principles are: (1) observe and interact, (2) catch and store energy, (3) obtain a yield, (4) apply self-regulation and accept feedback, (5) use and value renewable resources and services, (6) produce no waste, (7) design from patterns to details, (8) integrate rather than segregate, (9) use small and slow solutions, (10) use and value diversity, (11) use edges and value the marginal, (12) creatively use and respond to change. v

This ecology is the most super computer thing that has ever existed or will ever exist and we are pro's at damaging it?

In the interim, this is the ideal time for those selected young people (regardless of their real age) who somehow end up running with a strong heart and powerful vision to set up a solid operation for putting high diversities of excellent nutrition together for themselves and their loved ones. Furthermore, the push to focus on the troubled sector of youth in society is very much a need of our sustainability, and the working design for improvement in this sector that is; our future is currently unsatisfactory.

The largest jump in web stats any of this information has had to date is when I told a friend of mine from my home area how this system could be used to produce a variety of products, make their team the strongest team out there and hide certain ~~crops~~ they may not want found. Northern Mexico visited our site about "Guerilla Permaculture" (a theory and experimentation system that seeks the enhancement of our ecology via a unique human-to-naturenurturing program, is a contemporary work aimed at overall personal and ecological health with new climate-change awareness technical efforts.) viin mass traffic numbers for the next year. India, China, Russia, Canada, Costa Rica, Argentina, Panama, follow as largest traffic sources. Our largest steady traffic source in the United States is Northern Virginia, for some reason, followed by Florida – however these are more likely stalkers that I have had, the main point here is almost zero American interest for this English-only (at this time) text.

I don't know what could possibly be more important now than supporting young people today, except supporting our ecology.

If we look at nature we will notice that all living things from virus to vulture survive and procreate enough to fulfill their special duties to the greater cycle of life. In the face of all the human disrespect, destruction and abuse they forgive us and attacks on our populations are minimal compared to what is deserving. Maybe we can take that hint and forgive some of the young people that would absolutely fall in love with gardening and creating the unimaginable ecosystems of the future.

In the past two years since the last Revision the other thing that happened was a XPRIZE vii1 a company that organizes international contests to conserve the environment. Competitions like "Carbon Removal," which sought to remove carbon from the atmosphere, and "Feed the Next Billion," a protein-focused quest for better and more plentiful food production, both sought to feed the world's population.

We might refer to our plan as "Ecological Enhancement." according to their justification "Excess carbon is an

____

1

excellent opportunity to reforest and repair the damage we have done."

Right now, I want you to get up and do something it will take only one minute. Go outside and shove your hand into the natural ground in a spot that you will promise to plant in. Exhale with the purpose to plant and promise the ground that you will keep setting aside some time each day to learn more about it. Ask the topsoil to prepare itself for such a shift.

Welcome what we call 'natural dynamics' and the only reason we must explain it here is because most people in modern age don't even get this far. If you can get this far, you have separated yourself from the pack – which is also insane. The concrete Jungle has been fun, but are we missing something? The balance that a relationship with nature provides is clear, and drastic. Many who take this step will soon loose themselves and become extremists, 'nature-freaks.' Arguably this is actual, valid "consciousness," taking over whats been taught.

To the degree this promise of earth time is applied a degree of peace, happiness, intelligence and courage (true consciousness?) will manifest in the entity of the originating intention. I have cited

several studies in the references however just trust me, keep it up and you will be able to find a point of appreciation you will thank me over and over for.

I totally believe that young people can get a working base knowledge (on living their best life, and on growing the best things) through an intensive class or time with an elder who has done many things and many of them already have this education from their elder. Many already know about moving high-quality consumables to high quality buyers in a similar network to what they may already know with the illegal plant-based businesses out there. We can really convert would be "criminals " (as incorrect a statement as that is to begin with) into the planet loving and saving ecological force we truly need. This strong youth are our future heroes or we have failed them no doubt about it. As I troubled youth myself I can't help to try to develop also an idea of social rehabilitation through this. In 2014 from one of the first revisions of this and my connections to Northern Mexico, so many fields were converted to permacultures and so many people diversified into nutritional produce! For that year we recorded all the web traffic, as it spread throughout Mexico. The species of production in a permaulture as as vast as the permaculturist wants to have.

The diverse nutrition concept outlined here helps a lot with this metaphysics stabilization also!

I will never forget hearing the howler monkeys (Panama) from the tree line above a hill that muffled the chainsaw behind it down below. For a week they cried I thought maybe and elder passed, until the dramatic howling continued and so I walked and machete my way out there and over the large hill, to find the other side of it completely cleared of primary forest (Revision IV).

The howler monkeys that used to be on our small permaculture experiment here on Island Colon, Bocas del Toro, Panama once every 30 days or so, are now here full time. Because of this same type of human deforestation.

The majority of deforestation here is the poor selling the wood to the rich. The guilty parties are obviously in complete ignorance of the karmic destruction of their own soul (?), their

own destiny and their own potential by this completely unnecessary and murderous extremism. They continue to stumble around where ever good people lack their needed natural edge and allow it, bringing us all closer and closer to hell (?). We have no conscious agreement with one another and we have no common education about how to harvest without killing (plant) and harvesting in a functional balance. The collective realization that our previous practices were wrong and that this is the natural way to fix the damage, -and that it also convinces the control freaks of the world that we don't need their solutions that will lead to our total enslavement even more.

Through seriously diverse experience I can say that for me

Karma is real, it is a word for a cosmic truth also somewhat described by Isaac Newton when he said "what goes up must come down." If one does something deserving of reward they

will rise, it is a dependable science. The thing we notice in

natural study is that it is dependable because of thousands of failed attempts where one got through. Don't expect one good motion to do anything at all, however thousands of good motions are a guarantee for advancement. The versus is true, and you'll notice the level of dedication and consistency a liar has.

This nutritional plan is so powerful it has the power to revolutionize human life and experience in several ways.

- Human physical health & performance
- Human mental health & performance
- Human cultural health & performance
- Human spiritual health & performance

Let's call these the "five fists (Kung Fu says start with five focuses of attack) of nutritional diversity." You see our ecology should consist of all these dynamic factors in our minds, they all work together and if you corrupt one the wheel becomes wobbly and it just gets worse. We don't admit it but we have undying faith in natures intelligence to balance out our bad behavior. We do not realize   the exponential potential in reversing our neglect, and nurturing a complete 'ecology' that is full and enhanced to optimal performance.

I have had a reoccurring dream that came to be well into my training from the natural teacher, that we could be living in completely different reality. The dream is right there within our grasp. A massive cultural re-direction. The actual solution to the problem the narcissists want to use to further their control-freakism. They refer to the valid issue as "global warming" or "climate change." Their solutions however are far from valid.

What is obviously a correct nutritional, cultural and ecological direction is also potentially and probably our best economical savior as well.

The work if done in this permaculture methodology, is valuable, most dependable and potentially bio-nuclear work that can be done anywhere in the world. The ultimate natural product and non-toxic medicine sellable to the upper echelons of society If you're not going to do the permaculture yourself, which is very needed, then support someone who does and eat right.

Just putting together, the highly diverse permaculture sourced diet is invaluable. 1- you get this nutrition for yourself, 2- you no longer consume the toxins and 3- you can share the program with others who can even pay a percentage of your pantry - a process that can easily grow into a small business.

Your own Garden of Eden or the best attempt by the designer, and, a place where true happiness, health, strength, stamina, quickness, dexterity, balance and ultimate attention to detail is cultivated. A natural blend you want your strongest youth to grow from.

Carnivore dieters and meat eaters would argue "I don't need to do this." What I say to that is our animals eat a nutritional diversity diet too. I also say get your running shoes on we are going to do some experiments and see if what vegetation I give you makes you perform better or worse. Either way we can assume with my permaculture nutritionally diverse beef, and goats raised by my instructions are going to top out what you are buying.

We know there are three distinct point in the spectrum of liver chemical production one being of a meat only diet, another distinct production is from a mixed meat and vegetable diet, and another from a vegetable only diet. "I want it all," is a scary statement usually and we will get into that more, however in the case of liver

production chemicals, and long as our method is using all natural, top-shelf ingredients wouldn't we want a full spectrum of production?

I have tried to invite Dr. Shawn Baker, and a few other noted "carnivore dieters" to do some experiments here in Bocas del toro, and I still want to do something-like that even though I have done solid months at carnivore concept and introduced plants and gone full switch also, already on my own.

The fix all. We can see the best animal and human performance in every situation by watching any species, including monkeys, ants, and pretty much anything else! This is no doubt the human diet of the future because it's the ideal one. Invest in permaculture or existing permaculturist's today! Dumber than the animal in this instance, we keep nourishing ourselves with a slave diet that we continue to tune our pulse to—killing the earth covertly through the pollination system.

This diet could be the leveling factor against antibiotic-resistant

bacteria(s) concerns, about this bacterial breed made stronger by strong antibiotic medicine. If you can eat more, you can take more in the way of biological essence. It seems to just be new levels of strength here for everybody each year that passes with this system. We have been turning people around in three days' time and have a few high dollar clients now that are coming on the regular.

Antibiotics are no doubt revolutionary biological understandings that present huge advantages. Like all thing in nature, just when you think you understand it there is another layer to the onion. The more advanced position meta-culturally is that of a 'student.' We don't know everything about antibiotic substance, potential combinations, natural

enhancements and variation to production – which should be a forefront priority in science. Antibiotics will likely soon be obsolete replaced by a natural substance or combination,

crisper adjustments or stem cell therapies that enhance the system's ability to deal with challenges and resistances.

David Shenk is his book "The Genius in All of Us" mapped out genetic changes happening through behavioral decisions and environmental conditions. Most never noticed this pinnacle shift in science where junk DNA (80% of the material once tested) is no longer cut right out of the Petri-dish but recognized as the most important part of the gene expression. We can thank major Academia (narcissistic construct, narcissistic industrial complex).

If we want to see the needed balance in this world ever, we should empower it with the formula for sustainably and a path to wild, natural and unbound freedom. Nature heals those who have been hurt and hurt people don't need to hurt people.

It wouldn't be that difficult to implement a new land enhancement plan, especially in the present. There is no other option but to act. Do it right now. Begin by composting. It wouldn't be that difficult to implement a new land enhancement plan, especially in the present. There is no other option but to act. Do it right now. Begin by composting. Drop off buckets as for the organic, clean stables (near a stable is ideal), and visit a location with a lot of chop. Use mattress coverings and plastic covers that are tossed on top of many little ones. You are off to a wonderful start with just a few visits, the necessary vaccinations, and a few months.

Those who are behind bars make excellent candidates for reforestation, therefore we shouldn't overlook them.

'Poverty is the worst form of violence.' — Mahatma Gandhi

These tougher individuals will serve as the best ushers of a new paradigm focused on optimal performance in the true athletic spirit. A tougher upbringing will result in a tougher fighter in the battle of life; therefore, build your groups wisely and treasure your protectors because you'll need them.

We can carry that idea right to the garden also, as the number 1 essential premise of this science which is: All biology flourishes against resistance.

Funny thing is that no one will actually recognize that once these sites are constructed, they will be the most valuable places on planet. This is true of all the magnificent homesteads still standing today. Who should also help out a tough guy or two – undoubtedly the correct ones, most vital thing.

To the extent that a person applies the science, however, doing so will gradually and concretely bring about miraculous transformations in every part of their lives. The inner cause is found both within ourselves and nature. Distressed youth are ideal for implementing this new approach to health into our culture and launching the first wave of small businesses and production models that provide their communities with significantly improved nutrition.

We must acknowledge how the political, cultural, financial (however revolting that is), mental, and physical abuses caused by societies organized under an excessively large umbrella that is now collapsing on us and itself causing the damage are being perpetrated against our young people in too many ways.

Giving them better food could be a good answer to this part.

To completely advance as a culture we must no longer leverage over one another in such a rich culture of domination, but in lighter culture of commutable "fair-share" culture where there are no payments to institutions on transactions. It sounds like the world is coming up with this.

The answer to most of this separation with nature, and crossing the line against nature, we will find is 180-person encampments   or enchantments - depends how far you want to go with it.

These villages are policed from within, are like minded and when they get big enough they split into two, each with sufficiently spaced and adequate domains for their future growth. African and other tribes came up with these numbers a long time ago. Civil positions are not that complicated and can be done as extra jobs ten to twenty hours per week. Simply by leaving the urban patch of cancer on the skin of the globe, the cost of life of these people economically goes far down. The potential risk of starvation in a logistics or viral pandemic like the one we just had is slim to none.

Think about this could even be verifiable and transparent voting situation for the overall Empire. We know the majority of small "district" will be, and we can easily audit that at any time.

Agriculture needs to be completely re-started anyway, and in learning from previous mistakes we need to be sure the new methods contain heart and soul again, which brings us back to motivating youth development centers to become involved. This should not be violent and abrupt, but slow and subtle in the right direction how all other nature grows and repairs from damage. To try to make a swift change will surely kill those trying to make it, this natural time in things is not a fight that can be won.

The timeline's passage through the COVID-19 point is a harsh wake-up call that may represent nature's response to human interference with her. If so it was an effective idea being that manufacturing is shut down (Revision IV), logistics affected substantially and so on. I'm inclined to believe that this is a tactic used by control freaks who have chosen to use every available lever while feigning concern for others—a narcissistic control strategy in and of itself.

We now know with complete security that biological and chemical poisoning of the population will come from the major institutions that have outgrown their sustainable size limits to a whole new level in sickness. History is repeating, this is not a learning body. The control-freakism that is going on here is something we little people just don't have a concept of. The COVID experience has shown us we must look to new places for health undeniably (Revision V).

In order for us humans to have the best Nutritional Diversity diets, we need a diverse amount of people creating new diverse all-natural and organic agriculture installations also known as "permacultures." There at these sites we need to cultivate genuine love. Love for each other and love for nature.

We need these biologists everywhere and we need them becoming experts on the species in which they propagate and selected for their own nutrition sources. We need to stop mistreating our species and discover new practices for raising ourselves that don't result in such high levels of escapism and agitation as they did yesterday.

Even without the new dietary recommendations that are now guaranteed through years of extensive testing improved results in every case of every type of performance for the better, cultivating

this nature-culture can heal trauma and anger issues much more effectively than other treatments.

Weakness, susceptibility to disease, and even the creation of disease

—as we have observed right here for more than 70 years with the

"Panama disease" that affected the banana plantations here and elsewhere—are all results of our sheltering, domestication, and extreme modification of the natural system, or separation from the natural process. Now, why do we believe that we can live in a way that harms other biological life?

One came to the realization that the most protected among us are the weakest, least skilled, and most prone to illness via rigorous diverse experience.

Growing a sufficient quantity of better food for yourself or your community and knowing how to use it more shrewdly are two of life's most empowering experiences, almost to a fault. For instance, you might be learning about a model right now that allows for enough diversity for plant-based work to be done for ten hours in the sun without any issues.

Wouldn't it fit justly that testosterone and all correct chemical production within the body is firing on all pins at this point of fullspectrum nitrification?

Consuming that diversity, you loved and grew while it is still alive and won't die may create and give intake and that plant may create something it knows you need. Would that also make sense?

These is some science behind that idea. Three types of reasons have been put forward to justify current concerns about threats to biodiversity. First, biodiversity provides us with a number of natural resources that lead to the production of use values, whether as food, new pharmaceuticals, genes that improve crops, or organisms that perform biological control. Second, it is intricately linked to human well-being for aesthetic, ethical, cultural and scientific reasons. Third, it contributes to the provision of ecosystem services that are generally not accounted for in economic terms, such as primary and secondary production, plant pollination, climate regulation, carbon sequestration, the maintenance of water quality, and the maintenance

of soil fertility. It is this third category of potential impacts of biodiversity which gave rise to the emergence of the biodiversity and ecosystem functioning area: could biodiversity loss alter the functioning of ecosystems, and thereby the ecological services they provide to humans? viii

The machine killing of the plant and soil life is not necessary. It is a

"narcissistic construct," a term from German artist and scientist, Kia Karlberg's "Anti-Narcissism "science and philosophy. I have keyed onto this science published interestingly the same exact day as

Revision IV (April 23, 2020) was published but one year later (April 23, 2021) and even more significant day that publishing the Revision where I and 10 friends made and published videos for a young person who was robbed of having people in her life was turning 18. That child was killed off actually no part of her left was anything of what she was.

Most tragic thing I think I will ever see. In my ten years of trying to move forward, and even optimize what's really crazy is how many times we come back to narcissistic hold-ups. All this potential so many times, but someone has to dominate, the pride factor is so stroked today people can't be team players. This is how the good people loose. If we can all be as selfish as those at the top they stay there,   toxic agriculture persists, health crisis persists and now logistics crisis food shortage, political sabotage of existing supplies rather than intelligent transition. This chaos simply allows the small to fall further and the top of financial chain to rise to more leverage than even before.

It is quite the story of how this dynamic nutritional testing and discovery came to be - one day I will bang it out on the keys, if I live long enough. This revision (V) intends to have a start at that.

"The root of all problems is narcissists." It's actually true. If we didn't have evil intending folks running the money system, money itself wouldn't be so bad. The thing is we agreed to use money thugs make, and we never removed them from that position. Now-we inter-generational thugs who are ready to the bigger clamps on society than Daddy demon did.

New plant consumption and organization itself also requires a certain amount of adventurousness that is somehow enhanced by troubled roots. Diamonds under pressure. They sure can cut through it all.

I was standing next to a mountain and I chopped it down with the edge of my hand. - Jimmy Hendrix

For now, the priority of delivering the core of the discoveries from the nutritional study, in a (1) smart and (2) careful way, that is in the forefront. These feelings of responsibility also push me in the direction of troubled youth because I care about a youth troubled, and that I was one of the most troubled young people you ever saw.

sssss

This keys on the importance of leadership, are outstanding in the implementation of the science. I want to start the whole presentation of this, with a speech I give usually full of profanity and eloquently timed. It's called the "hook it up speech." Easy thing here. You hook up a fruit tree the tree hooks you, up right?

Great fertilizer takes time to make, lots of ingredients the best, it is investment.

Try something new. Realize we are sick. Realize we will not heal ourselves that we need nature to do it, and it will do it if we access it the right way.

Hook up your farm volunteers, your plants, your animals, your neighbors, your community. Hook them up. Don't do it unless it has a hook something the .... up in there. There is no point in doing something wrong, it is a temporary do that will need to be redone right.

You know I remember when we would see a guy who had to sell on the road receive more money than he was asking for, this is a classic New Mexico move called "charity wrapped in dignity." A phrase and practice long gone today. This gets you respect on the street, and you knew the extra little money comes back times a million in other ways.

The category of moves this move falls under is called "class." Another word non-existent today.

Somehow, we have chosen for ourselves to be a Gerbil wheel of relearning that do it right the first-time lesson, all the time! It's been a century, and beyond that, we continue to want to re-learn that lesson.

Readers will find that in every step of the way of experimentation over our last 8 years here in Panama, unveils that the antidote to all of human societies ailments and the next step in our evolution is likely the change in our diets from 4-24 soft food species to 60-200 different robust and non-toxic natural species regularly.

In nature we can break down the Carnivores diet routine in a given microclimate of residence to the neighborhood of 60 items including the separate organ counts. Omnivores have been observed over and over again, in the neighborhoods of 120 to 270 different species in their natural jungle diets in one residential micro climate.

This natural method will inherently render the modern agriculture system obsolete and knock out every other domino in the line to planetary salvation.

From the current, unfortunate story in modern agriculture one will gain an understanding of the damages to pollinators that is being done by pesticides and modern agriculture chemicals, how to create cancer and health crisis across the majority of human life, and create a technological codependency. That is about the one authentically constructive accomplishment our current biological story offers.

We need to look at the root cause of this problem.

By WEEDING OUT NARCISSISTS we will see toxic agriculture go away, the acceptance of company and big institutional damage to health will dissipate and in combination with the science of Permaculture we can turn completely around. Ultimately at least separated from all involvement with narcissists (who never stop attacking good people) life could finally become a utopia. See 'Guerrilla Permaculture' for an impressive model and furthering of the concept.

If an issue or toxin like glyphosate or a narcissist directly affects you, and you are smart enough, and disciplined enough, you will make the change, and other dominoes around you will also begin to fall. This is our physics. However, in contrast if there is lack of strength and intelligence or the toxic dose is too high; the subject will get obliterated emotionally, physically, mentally, financially, and spiritually in the end. Truly it must be seen this way, and it likely IS this way

Modern men have a real trouble here, we have not developed enough in natural ways and too much in unnatural ways we have a culture where the gardeners of men all want mono-crop people.

Allot of this also has to do with the lack of intuition, something nature teaches better than any other instructor, and ability to detect lies

To accept lies, liars or tell them or be one is to join the disease, the corruption, is to support the degeneration of biological life (which is totally honest for the most part), and the spiritual body, and ultimately could lead to the total destruction of both.

So, as well as mentioning Anti-Narcissism (Kia Karlberg) as a genius staple to optimal doctrines, I should mention the MMPI Minnesota Multiphasic Personality Inventory test (II) and the new Eye Detector Lie Detector, as valid tools in detecting good/honest or bad/dishonest people. Since the last revision (IV) we all have gotten a good dose of televised education of these tools and the tragic phenomenon in cluster b or narcissistic disorders (Heard vs. Depp).

These bright realizations namely about diverse performance nutrition, Guerrilla Permacultures, and the importance of 'AntiNarcissism,' are very dark realizations also in the way that hard things must be done in order for the rest of us to thrive. Get this idea through your head since it will be the focal focus of all your efforts to improve yourself. There are many men who advocate staying wild and such things. Great nothing in the natural consumes rotting matter. Nonetheless, rest assured that once or twice a year, we can go out drinking and return a week later with tales, recollections, and crazy antics. For me, focused momentum—which tends to spiral out of control on its own—is more significant than the other kinds of craziness, and I can usually go for good three years without interacting with it.

To get a full-spectrum or adequate amount of supportive nutrients for top performance I have found through an intensive study that eating in the area of 85 different food species, breathing, stretching and exercising regularly in a cyclic day-rhythm provides for the most

drastic increases to the quality of life at any age (that I have

discovered so far). These increases are normally in the 20-40% range for healthy individuals and have gone up to the 400% range in under a month with certain unhealthy individuals.

This diet would help stem cell therapies work better. We have worked with and interviewed many stem cell patients in Panama City, and

In this book I outline a full range of specific daily plant species that I have worked with and that can help others quickly get into a sufficient range of nutrients. The book is a principle guide to where

I am now 8 years later and gives a great foundation for individual efforts and work that can take this all to the STARS.

Applying Nutritional Diversity's regimens and doctrines is a sure way to see progress in every part of your life.

The information presented here essentially conveys a message from nature and wild animals that can be discovered by everyone via sincere and devoted plant research. I try to make it a fun read for a biology, diet

and plant-based book, and it truly is something from the pages of the Hitchhikers Guide to the Galaxy in the extreme rocks and rolls, through grooves in the record rarely played onto the dynamic and powerful master control dimensions right in front of us,   completely ignored. These factors have been realized in the course of the last ten years, in an intensive and dynamic study in the rain forests, diverse micro-climates, and jungles of Panama, Costa Rica and beyond.

This revision contains the following main sections;

Human Performance Fuel, Bio-dynamic Nutrition, Food Tour,

Next-Level Physical Training, Importance of Character in Growth, Anti-Narcissism, and Toxic Culture The ROOT of toxic food, and every other evil toxin.

Business Models; a starting place for those who are ready to divorce what is and be what's next.

Along the course of our study since 2012, we have seen this Nutritional Diversity Science play its role in successful diabetic treatments, ulcer forming colitis treated, severe depression treated, sexual function restored, arthritic conditions improved and alleviated completely confidence restored and athletic and mental performance enhanced in every case. We have seen young and old alike free themselves on permaculture farms and in this way not comparable to other treatments, environments, or on other diets or medicines. While a few doctors are in the study circle here in Central & South America over the last few years, we are NOT doctors. I hold no license of any kind, and you need to take responsibility for your health and what you put in, around and on your body, with the utmost importance.

These areas contain some of the last concentrations of biodiversity, and because of corporate and governmental interests, they are constantly being attacked and defended. It is crucial that Nutritional Diversifists understand their connection to nature and their profound regard for these elders.

The core doctrinal factors of this new diet type have been realized only just in the last 5 years of this study, and interestingly, no other nutritional information seems to hold this in-depth key to health and performance. Welcome to the cutting edge. The doctor of the future will no longer treat the human frame with drugs, but will rather cure and prevent disease with nutrition". Thomas Edison's contemplation may come to fruition if the nutritional revolution continues in its current course. Two realizations have propelled the world into a new age of personalized nutrition: (i) food can provide benefits beyond its intrinsic nutrient content, and (ii) we are not all created equal in our ability to realize to these benefits. Nutrigenomics is concerned with delineating genomic propensities to respond to various nutritional stimuli and the resulting impact on individual health. This review will examine the current technologies utilized by nutrigenetics, the available literature regarding nutrient-gene interactions, and the translation of this new awareness into public health.ix

Stomach Nutrition

The stomach is a marvelous and intricate organ that grinds the food that powers our bodies. Even the least attractive morsels can be turned into essential nutrients in this bubbling pot of acids and enzymes, which acts as a gourmet cauldron. The stomach needs the proper fuel to operate at its best, just like any other machine. The key to realizing the full capacity of this magnificent organ is a wellbalanced diet consisting of nutrients, foods high in fiber, and regular meals.

You are now a part of a living, breathing science that is developing both an idea in your head and the micro-biome, a culture of digesting bacteria in your gut. Several nutritionists now refer to the gut as a second brain, suggesting that it may actually be more complicated since it communicates with so many other bacteria and microorganisms. Though they, along with agricultural experts, are to blame for our current health catastrophe, don't pay attention to diet experts.

Food Fundamentals such as those laid by Paracelsus, Philipps Theophrastus Aureolus Bombastus von Hohenheim, known to many as the "father of chemistry and the reformer of materia medica," also as the "Sword of Medicine," it is the dose of any said consumable, that declares it a toxin or an aid, and that all-natural foods had the potential to be both – is important foundational knowledge when getting into nutritional diversity stlye dieting.

Most modern dieters' whether Vegan, Vegetarian or omnivorous, have no idea what the effective doses of the vegetables and other foods they eat are, smart calculations certainly do not recognize vegetables in the grocery store are as toxic as they are nutritious.x

Today we partake from the 'tree of knowledge' proudly and more specifically in technological knowledge The doctor of the future will instead use nutrition to treat and prevent disease rather than administering medications to the human body.

If the nutritional revolution continues on its current path, Thomas Edison's idea might materialize. The world has entered a new era of customized nutrition as a result of two realizations: 1. food can offer benefits beyond just its inherent nutrient content, and 2. humans are not all created equal in our capacity to experience these benefits. The goal of nutrigenomics is to identify how the genome is predisposed to react to different nutritional stimuli and how this may affect a person's health. This review will look at the nutrigeneticists' present tools, the literature on nutrient-gene interactions, and how this new understanding is being applied to public health.xi

Now with the recent discovery of things such as the Pestalotiopsis Microspora (a type of endophytic fungus that can eat and break down polyurethane. xii Originally discovered in 1880 in fallen foliage of common ivy (Hedera helix) in Buenos Aires, In Hypericum 'Hidcote,' (Hypericum patulum) shrubs, it also results in leaf spot in Japan.xiii also found in the Amazon rain forest, that eats plastic we start to have examples of this.

Another ecology that fuels us rather than the world is that of the stomach. Stomach Nutrition refers to nutrition that goes down the human throat into the human stomach. This is a primary nutrient intake method for animals and humans, and breaks down into the following subcategories; Water, Plants, Animals, Digestive Culture "Microbiome," Food States, Increments, Cleansing Operations.

Many things are accessible to us naturally, but we are emotionally and culturally cut off to the majority of them because we believe that our technological knowledge will triumph over our natural abilities.

According to the ND diet study, the initial source of stomach ingredients should come from permaculture farming models and should include at least 60 different species. The upper limit is yet unknown. Up to 115 different species diets have been evaluated, and

they are far more effective. For weaker systems, a digestion mechanism must be developed over a period of weeks at the 30-60 specie starting place realization. Sixty is the starting place for the younger, stronger, omnivorous physiological system. The practice of experimenting with ferments and beverages like kombucha (is a fermented, lightly effervescent, sweetened black tea beverage that is popularly drank for its alleged health benefits.) xiv xvis centuries old and appears to open the door to the intake of even more foods. Developing strong subcultures is a crucial and vital component of the science of a diverse diet.

Watching the Jaguar, the leaf cutter ant, or one of the many primates in the nutritious, liveliest tropical environment, where they require the strongest system to survive, it is obvious that each eats significantly more than what I have determined to be a reasonable starting point for a modern human stomach. Most likely, this is a result of our intergenerational domestication, which intensifies with each generation.

The natural authentic survivors of the top performance model (the one that sustains the entire globe, nature) all retain a relationship with the main frame that produces and builds senses and skills that resemble those we were said to have ourselves by legends passed down to children in New Mexico. We don't have any such connection. We view nature as personal barriers that we may use to obtain paper and heat.

It is painful to go over these introductory steps, and also to cover them. We are too separated.

I did a series of survey's using farming students from Europe,

Australia and North America, finding that people today eat from between 6 and 24 different species to a minimum effective dose (enough of the food for its essence to work strongly in the system) a good number below my minimum sufficiency findings. The diets featuring numbers closer to 24 are usually from better financed households.

Certain doctrinal factors have been realized from this study that just can't be argued with, and across the board, the results have been recorded and duplicated time and time again. I will go over them as they come up in respective sections of this ND Diet application manual text. Moreover, a number of nutrients are necessary for optimum stomach health. For instance, sufficient vitamin B12 intake is required to produce hydrochloric acid, which is essential for the stomach's ability to break down food. Also, a stomach's immune system might be weakened by deficits in vital nutrients like zinc and vitamin C, which increases the chance of infection.xvixvii

It's curious how frequently the need to avoid massive Academics has come up and how the convolution of nutrition knowledge by this "culture of specialists" has been at nuclear-like levels for so long. A mistake that results in blunders and excessive time wasted is what I have come to refer to as the "direction of dissection." Unlocking the actual potential of nutrition may depend on seemingly little details like the revelation that black pepper increases the intake of the spice turmeric.

I highly encourage all to start finding combinations both in the garden and in the stomach and relate or combine them to your senses and abilities with a good focus, to achieve the most conclusive results with your nutrition. It gets deep, confusing and on another level but you will get it more and more as the practice continues.

The deepest of plant experts will be familiar with stories such as that of Makkah Nootka medicine man, xviiiwho believed in song to heal plants and humans, and used breath (Seminole) and song, to initiate the healing process in biology.

Yet the practice of natural dynamic or a bio-dynamic [R. Steiner] life is unheard of and unknown. The creator of the biodynamic farming method, Rudolf Steiner (1861–1925), was a well-known philosopher and scientist in his day who rose to fame later in life for his "anthroposophical" spiritual-scientific method of approaching knowledge. Steiner realized, long before many of his contemporaries, that if western civilization did not start to develop an objective awareness of the spiritual realm and its interaction with the physical world, it would eventually destroy itself and the earth. Practical holistic breakthroughs have been created in a variety of disciplines, including education, banking, health care, psychology, the arts, and not least, agriculture, thanks to Steiner's spiritualscientific approaches and insights. xixThe Seminole song science has been there for a long time now.

There are interestingly supportive results that came out of the Cleve Backster set of testing that indicated "breath & nutrition, together" was measurable to affect the plants nervous response up to 100 feet away. In short, we can scientifically say that, breath is a communication well received from, plants. We can say similarly for music and song.

The Steps to Success. Let's get practical for a moment.

Firstly, permaculture farm should be found. You might not be

familiar with this term, but it refers to a rapidly growing underground movement that began more than 40 years ago. There's probably one nearby. The second step to success is to increase the variety to at least sixty different items per day or per week, focusing on including as many hard foods as you can. Keep in mind that they cannot be from contemporary agriculture or the supermarket. Bring your belongings here to load up on the chemical causes of today's health issues.

Once you have this nutrition, you can start to explain to people what you are doing, have them buy in and start to obtain your

nutrition for free, and proceed towards creating a life off this

nutrition. People that are focused, strong, and disciplined are the same ones who can succeed in anything.

You should undoubtedly have your own interests in work and the arts, but among those who live under the sun, these passions ought to be stable. Today on your own, start to study leaves and plants yourself, visit these farms and ask them to study there - two birds with one stone, two purposes, learning the food and getting the food.

This two or more purposing is actually selection requirement in the Permaculture doctrine. Funny right? We live in mono culture society yet optimal agriculture depends on zero singular functions.

Later on, you can certify with Nutritional Diversity (www.nutritionaldiversity.com through an online course, or whatever other new more diverse, higher-minded nutrition certification entity comes to being) to ensure quality production for your own, the customer, and offer to buy a steady supply of what they can provide. For now, study the site a bit each day.

Certain species may grow well together but adversely not ingest well together so just know that growing together is not always an indicator of a good digestive combination. Work with what you can, do whatever it takes, grow your own (the Best way), and get your diversity up! I will talk about other food sources in this section, but permaculture or verifiably organic farms are the ideal place to start. Also, most permaculture farms will be open to growing specific new things for you.

People always ask me how I work out like such an animal in the gym or on the track, but the most effective trick in my athletic toolbox right now is eating this very diversely. We have been able to toss the shovel and the machete in the scorching sun from 5 am to 8 pm thanks to this discovery, and we are incredibly grateful for it.

What negative effects can be anticipated is a frequent query from beginners? (who frequently make mistakes).

Inappropriate pairings, such as ginger and cassava, or the simultaneous consumption of two different types of carbohydrates, can have unfavorable side effects, including weight gain and energy depletion.

A proper diet, it seems, can be most simply achieved by consuming one species at a time all day long. These outcomes are significantly mitigated if a few fundamental principles are understood and followed.

Increased hair and nail growth, higher hair density, increased pheromone production, increased bowel movements, increased fat loss and lean muscle growth, improved sleep, and killer training sessions are all common advantages. Creative ability increases and we have seen the diet play a role in the treatment and healing of many issues now to include diabetic treatments, ulcerative colitis treated, severe depression treated, sexual function restored, arthritic conditions improved and alleviated completely confidence restored and athletic and mental performance enhanced in every case. While a few doctors are in the study circle here in Panama over the last few years, we are NOT doctors. I hold no license of any kind, and you need to take responsibility for your health and what you put in, around and on your body, with the utmost importance. I have my story and my findings, and you can do your own research, and or slow-going, careful experimentation on what I say.

"Fight off all sickness, all depression and optimize yourself using this simple switch. Grocery store produce is loaded with chemicals, so sourcing new nutrition, new growers, or growing your own is your biggest task here. This convenient food source also narrows your spectrum of diversity which is the health biggest mistake. After learning more about the natural foods we should be eating, and cultivating, everything in a grocery store begins to look insane. It's the root of the health crisis!!"

The next chapter in your own ND diet study, is to find out which species work well together, work well for you and which ones may be slowing things down a bit.

So many nutritionists today are confused. They study in what I refer to now as "the direction of dissection." This is the wrong way, we need to be studying in the direction of diverse combination.

We don't require study papers explaining why seeds grow; if we do produce these pages, which are largely useless for our purposes, they are likely to be inaccurate regarding the characteristics of organic living forms. Unfortunately, we still lack that accuracy in organic sciences.

We need to know things like turmeric and black pepper do for one another, support and help each other in the system - as a diversely combined effort.

A few intriguing formulas that appear to serve as functional guidelines for combining have been discovered by us, and they have given us access to a highly   effective performance edge. There are indications of many more formulas, and with so many varied formulations, our grasp on proper nutrition will become even more firm. If you think of a per-workout formula, it is similar in concept we are simply going a bit further and going after the natural stuff. I have never done hormones (test or HGH), however I have known

many who have and I notice it causes fairly interesting sidesymptoms and I do think that with the refinement of this all-natural pursuit, much great, more balanced results are in store.

A free health presentation July 18th this past year (2018), by "The Real Truth About Health" which really showed the connection between our diets, and some of the problems and issues on our globe. Statements like "doctors know nothing about nutrition," and "if we go by the USDA food pyramid we will perish," were some of the opening statements made by these doctors, in a presentation on the latest scientific findings on proven benefits to your health from a Whole Food Plant-Based Diet panel participant; M.D, Pamela A.

Popper, Kim A. Williams,

MD, MACC, FAHA, MASNC, FESC, Ph.D., N.D., T. Colin Campbell, Ph.D., Caldwell B. Esselstyn Jr., which claimed to be the new current diet "truth."

There was no mention of diversity, permaculture or modern agriculture chemicals. There was mention of whole plant-based food consumption models stopping and regressing several diseases.

Digestive Culture

There is as digestive culture of life that builds up in the stomach over the day week and the month and the year, the lifetime, constantly improving itself as time goes on in relation to the minimum effective amounts of Nutritionally Diverse intake, that assists the body in food uptake. This very important nutritional factor is very overlooked by health, nutritional and fitness concentrations in most human health or fitness sciences. Diverse organs, enzymes, and microorganisms, together referred to as the digestive culture, interact intricately during the digestion process.

We must have understanding of fundamental components of digestive culture and how they contribute to preserving the body's general health in this response.xx

Popularly this digestive culture has been named the gut microbiome. If we look at the universal principles in nature we can assume that, this culture and mix of species, should be robust and diverse like the strongest cultures in biology we see. The basic idea of this whole concept is that with a more full-spectrum and robust microbiome, more robust performance is possible. The digestion of complex macromolecules like proteins, lipids, and fcarbohydrates into more easily absorbed forms is one of the digestive system's main jobs. Beginning in the mouth where the amylase enzyme begins to break down carbohydrates, this process continues in the stomach where pepsin and hydrochloric acid combine to break down proteins. In order to digest fats, carbohydrates, and other nutrients, the small intestine subsequently takes over and secretes a range of enzymes like lipase, sucrase, and lactase.xxi

A healthy inner digestive culture that also has been referred to as the 'microbiome' an inner gut ecosystem, the garden of the gut, that is made up of friendly micro-flora (good bacteria) that reside in our intestines and keep us healthy and strong.

The tougher this army of gut-stuff the more food we can digest, more effectively and efficiantly. The more powerfully our hormones and enzymes xxiiare produced. The gut is the motor of the body, and rich dynamic fueling is the key to optimal performance.

According to Ayurvedic theory, poor quality food and inconsistent eating habits can create a dullness to the upper gastrointestinal intestine, which, if uncorrected, will result in further deviations from overall health. Ayurvedic medicine is one of the oldest known forms of medicine and it uses natural plant-based medicines - food is medicine.

The thing that this and other ancient doctrines of incredible worth are missing today, that they were likely not missing then is the point of high diversity.

Being such a core basic, there was no need to write it.

Is this what you are reading now? A simple replay of the history of Mosha (Moses) who freed the slaves through knowledge of how to really eat the "mana," all around provided by the Earth? Sickness and afflictions would not be suffered so violently with this highly diverse, proper diet. It is merely educational or lack of education that we suffer most sickness.

Nutritional Diversity dieting with a high diversity of living food sources can supply a heavy arsenal of healthy bacteria for this

microbiome. A mix and complex of compost or fertilizer or any other biological medium is this way — most rich and effective with more diverse ingredients. The dose of ingestion of a substance is the determining factor of whether the substance will behave as a remedy or toxin. Too much water is a toxin. There is a dose for all elements. Small amounts of toxins help build digestive strength and internal tolerances (strengths/resistances). Inside of a larger diversity toxin have less effect — the solution to pollution is dilution. Moreover, the gut microbiome plays a role in immune system control, vitamin synthesis, and stopping the proliferation of dangerous bacteria in the gut. According to studies, changes in the gut microbiome can cause a variety of health problems, such as obesity and inflammatory bowel disease as well as irritable bowel syndrome.xxiii

More so, eating bad food leads to unhealthy, bad food cravings. Cyclic activity is also a basic lesson taught by nature. One bad food creates a feedback loop, since the poor food choices are driven by the cravings which reinforce the digestive dysfunction – it's not hard to snowball people into terrible health quickly. Athletes know one weekend of pizza will cost them a week in training. Same with drinking, guys who go out on the weekends get much less results in the gym. You can have best of both worlds if you take the time to cultivate higher discipline and consciousness levels and even be the designated driver for a few friends who don't command as much respect in life as you do.

Given all the health and growing potentials available here in Although Panama has great promise for its nutrition, it currently serves as a morality tale for how toxic information, misguided culture, and ecologically sound practices may trump good health. The issue is poor diet instruction, careless public food ingredient choices, and highly profitable farming techniques.

Should this digestive gut garden be the literal master control to our quality of life and performance ability? Don't we want to cultivate the most incredible gut garden ever imagined?

How are we going to do it? Nutritional Diversity my friends.

Nutritional Diversity. It can get dynamic.

Introduction to Nutritional Biodynamics

Biodynamics can be understood as a combination of "biological dynamic" agriculture practices. "Biological" practices include a series of well-known organic farming techniques that improve soil health. "Dynamic" practices are intended to influence biological as well as metaphysical aspects of the farm (such as increasing vital life force), or to adapt the farm to natural rhythms (such as planting seeds during certain lunar phases).

Understanding the deeper aspects of nutrition, and nature doesn't just make a more qualified 'nutritional diversifist' but also allows the cultivation of a more dynamic connection to the food.

Rudolf Steiner Biodynamic Agriculture Lecture Series is the starting place for this. He also founded a system of organic agriculture, now known as biodynamic agriculture, which was one of the first forms of modern organic farming. A fundamental tenet of biodynamic agriculture is that food raised biodynamically is nutritionally superior and tastes better than foods produced by conventional methods. This is a common thread in alternative agriculture, because other ecological farming systems make similar claims for their products. Demeter, a certification program for biodynamically grown foods, was established in 1928. As such, Demeter was the first ecological label for organically produced foods xxiv

Use what you have, if dear stomach is unavailable, use the closest thing for example. That said today you can get dear anywhere and here in Panama they are even in the city on Ancon hill, the old U.S. Military Complex where Admirals and other big wigs of that occupation once lived. The examples are just that and experimentation is encouraged, and it is through these very experiments and practices of natural production that we will continue to enhance our performance abilities.

Consumption of salt, pepper, and saying "thank you" to one's food and drink has actual, established benefits. (Misurauro Emotto, Cleve Backster) xxv

As this connection to biodynamic nature and gut microbiome grows the practitioner becomes more and more aware of the potential I am trying to describe to you now, that when we eat optimally all the way our performance potential goes off its current map. Once investigators try a level of it for a few days it's an undeniable improvement in mood, sleep, stamina, creative performance, etc. Over years the improvements come little by little, but they do add up and can certainly be handed to another (taught).

To write a doctrine of advancement for troubled youth, I should have been one, right? To write how to get tough I should be tough right? To say "work on yourself," I should be working on myself, right?

To tell you I am getting amazing health and performance results from eating off permaculture food supplies in more a diverse relation to the rest of the animals in the wild, I should really be experiencing them, right? Well I put my name on it anyway, it is here for you to do what you want with. Clearly you will have to find for yourself to really know what it is.

Ayurveda, the before mentioned Ancient system of medicine through food, that predates written history has six core principles one of which being Astrology and we have scientifically found this a serious importance to human optimization, like rhythms and like the tides, likely the drummers of them, to go with the current is much easier than to go against. But to learn to go with the current it turns out for us these days anyway; the twentieth century human culture could be a difficult one to ask do try. The age of control freaks from the top to the bottom.

If man has equal valid destiny in peace and happiness he won't control anything. Control is fear is stress, we don't need it. If it is not what is needed all by itself simply keep looking for the position. You will not change something into what you need.

In my practice with the initial tribe of diversifists that have been working out a knowledge of this (in infancy), that have worked with this idea of exchange with a more natural, complete nature the most difficult thing by far was learning to catch the rhythm. Seasons is one thing, and there is much more charm and grace that can be unlocked by learning that the lunar cycles and how different days are best for different practices and performances.

To be able to know this, and live in a synchronicity with this cycle and its advantages and disadvantages day to day, gives great advantage in knowing one's environment (Tzun Zu, Art of War) xxvi . For example, 'Manguante' is when the bamboo is best harvested also chopping and clearing is best done, and the difference is very real. So, the indigenous are counting for 6-8 days from the full moon and these days they will chop. Chopping at this time one may feel like a Samurai. However, chopping at other times, one may feel like they are the worst blade sharpener or the weakest man that ever lived. Chopping is one practice but everything from harvesting, to planting, to skin care, and hair care, and dental work have known

lunar positions that are best for procedure, produce and performance.

All biological life is 70 percent water, and the tides are affected by the lunar cycle, and so is the water (and other things) within.

Lunar-based scheduling is a primary attention in the "bio-dynamic" philosophy and science, there are plenty of powerful reading factors available in the Nutritional Bio-dynamics planning curriculum, but for starters lunar cycles is the chunk to get your head around.

It's hard to figure out but the advantages are significant enough that it should be covered. Ancient populations knew these factors and had calendars that mapped these cycles.

Diet investigators should be advised that it will take time for this all to click, but stay applied and it will happen. Different people react in different ways to the spikes in all-natural, non-toxic, fuller-spectrum nutrient consumption. When done right, it produces, high, or a highlevel of energy, and some people get the tingles.

Over modern time, the introduction of harsh antibiotics (as a constant), pasteurization, and processed foods, along with a lifestyle of constant stress inside of extreme convenience, has damaged our inner ecosystems, and that could include generational genetic dysfunctions according to the findings within Epigenetic sciences.

Even the great Louie Pasteur was coming to the conclusion that environment should be used to build the immune system before ever contacting a disease which at that point it would defeat on its own in his final years. Homeopathic medicine is this very principle of taking something toxic [again – toxicity and remedy are in the dose] to build the immune system and make it more robust.

Geographical diversity could answer this call adequately also, further supporting my theories that loosing Nomadic regularity could be our largest mistake. What would cause this? Agriculture would. What would fix this?

Becoming hunter gatherers again. What's the difference here from "paleo dieting?" Somehow in years of criminology, zoology, anthropology, and the billions of nutritionists never realized the key is in the diversity.

Today chickens and many other animals are raised in cages that do not allow movement, are drugged unconscious and grown as abused bags of meat that never really move. I was in shock at the first time I had a field raised chicken. I mean talk about super-food.

What sort of epigenetic changes are happening to each generation of chicken's produced this way? What is happening in our digestive zone, in our control center for our bodies with this nutrition versus a free-range chicken loved by every age group and several other animals.

There is a genetic link between the Jurassic T-Rex and the common chicken. Could this type of abuse be what reduced them in size and made them a domestic food for human beings?

An unbalanced internal environment can cause weariness, poor health, early indicators of relapse, an ineffectively functioning digestive system, and ultimately disease and death. In contrast clearly, it is the tract of digestion in which happiness and quality of life depends on the most.

Today humans are more undernourished by narrow diversity range and chemicals and over-stressed by passionless work and confusing media than ever. We are starting to neck and neck with torture timelines of the middle ages almost. I will site Chemotherapy and Corporate Prisons as my best examples and when you really look into them you will find hell.

An Angel that has been in my life lately, has had to harp on me, even on the diet to focus, that focus is the most important leg to success. I write this text for others, let me tell you I need constant reminders myself. This is also why keeping a small well-groomed circle of like-minded company is so important.

At this time the planet suffers incredible, fires and pollution and ecologists worry that many species are going to start going extinct in an apocalyptic fashion. I brush up and edit this first revision to be published on major outlet channels during the COVID-19 pandemic. This text is the total solution to ALL OF IT. The virus is so much less powerful; should this doctrine be implemented and that goes for every evil we deal with today.

It is time to repair the garden of Eden and the gardens in our guts.

This nutrition thing is so dynamic we don't begin to scratch the surface of it. The performance we could have, the ecology we can garden and grow, and be the most intelligent pollinators and ecological creators, we could really have more awesome stuff than James Cameron's Avatar movie.

Much energy is expelled digesting meals, so you want to pay attention to increments, pay attention to maintaining a good digestive culture that can burn through the tank quickly and most importantly pay attention to your body, fatigue, nausea, and other symptoms that will come with a bad digestive culture.

Learning to go by your own metabolic speed limit without over fueling or running out is more or less an art.

When food is not digested and expelled quickly it becomes toxic, and provides clear avenues for multiple illnesses.

Eating whole foods like avocado, papaya regularly can help digest more, and more efficiently. Avocado is less likely to be sprayed in cultivation although washing both of these fruits has been recommended by health authorities around the world regularly for a list of reasons.

Ultimately a complete transition away from all grocery store produce is what we will need to accomplish victory in our mission both planetary and as individual roots of our quantum existences. There are as many plant essences as there are plants, and slowly and carefully, just as a plant grows; we can cultivate knowledge of each one.

In my experience each specie I have worked with over the last eight years has told me one thing, I barely know these florae. I still have so much to learn about each one. That is a great thing about the field of growing the most valuable goods; you will never learn it all, it will never get boring.

On the farm, learning never stops. The other day I observed the tree I tied my horse to while we camped under the night, growth spirited all of a sudden, the only of many of her kind in that area, had

suddenly sprouted. The stimulation, manure, company, increased CO2, and pressure must have been the cause. Did my horse start throughout the night and pull on the tree, generating a significant amount of soil movement? You notice how dynamic everything is?

Largely ignored in microbiome study today, is the possible function of fungi, and a mycology of the stomach. Mycology is a huge part of my focus now, and for the last year most of my research has been in mushrooms and fungi.

An old school remedy known as kombucha could help digestion happen more efficiently. It uses a culture known as a Symbiotic Culture of Bacteria and Yeast (SCOBY). A syntrophic mixed culture, generally associated with kombucha production where in anaerobic ethanol fermentation, anaerobic organic acid fermentation, and aerobic ethanol oxidation to acetate all take place concurrently along an oxygen gradient. This stuff helps digestion and uptake of nutrients go faster, which means you can consume more using it. Xxvii

This is an example of mycology workings in the human digestive system. Fungi is the next frontier of diverse eating no doubt.

Sour Kraut is another traditional and familiar grown fermented culture.

The leaf cutter ants (two genera Atta and Acromyrmex) of this region can lift twenty times their own body weight. They take pieces of leaves, and mind you, leaves from a Nutritional Diversity of plants, back to their incredible nests and they cook up a Fungi on them and that is what they eat. According to modern scientists, next to humans, leaf-cutter ants form the largest and most complex animal societies on Earth. Their level of organic and chemical mastery has been realized on several fronts.xxviii

What dynamic understanding do they have I wonder?

I need not mention they construct no non-biodegradable structure, and keep with them the ability to re-establish.

Simple digestion experiments on your own, can help to make a mind to stomach connection.

You might try eating carbs alone. Then proteins alone, in different sittings. This could promote a more direct uptake, that weightlifters who take protein supplements are familiar with. Perhaps one can instruct the body to eat carbohydrates and proteins more precisely by timing pre-workout and post-workout meals.

Typically, a focus on protein occurs after exercise, for recuperation and to enhance strength and muscular development, while a focus on carbohydrates usually comes before exercise. In order to maintain energy and prevent the lag in carbohydrate digestion, several popular nutritionists now advise eating proteins before and carbs after exercise. Those stacking on weight will eat more carbs, and those person's leaning out will eat less overall. This part is universal.

Later on, I will talk more about getting to know foods and plants. As important as understanding and developing your strong digestive culture is, connecting your thoughts to your stomach is a big advantage.

Table grace might have involved more than you had anticipated. You are ignorant. I mean, you didn't back then. Knowing how water behaves and how it stores its structure helps to train the organisms that surrounds it.

It will obviously take some effort to learn to know each of the 30– 60 species you start with in this diet venture on an individual basis, but I am convinced that it will much benefit the ultimate diet plan. I've seen it a lot already. A high level of knowledge is not necessary to achieve the fuller-spectrum of results if someone shows them, but the best ND Cook that learns the right way in a fullness that includes the rightful journey, is going to really be on the next level here. In other words there is a learning curve, it is next level food prep, and there is a value to that! I want to consume this diet, and I know many others do too, and if someone has an interesting menu, or even ND menu items – I am there!

I must recommend personal responsibility in this, as many claim to be good with things, and this is not something to play with. Especially with ferments cultures, wild foods, new foods there is real danger in doing something you are not sure about and did not learn fully, the right way. But this why you learn to be careful, pay attention to detail, go slow (rule of thumb) and take things seriously. These natural lessons, or lessons from nature work wonders on life.

I could suggest that if one were to focus on each object individually, each pixel of their field of vision the moment they entered a new room, when they were walking down the street, etc. with the intention of accelerating how quickly they saw everything, it might help them put together complex dynamic nutrition. It has a ninja training vibe to it. Everything regarding optimal farming and optimal health is going to sound like ninja training due to our extreme domestication in modern culture or the lack of a yearly two-month intensive training and diverse intake maintenance module. There is additional ninja training in the backstory to the narrative.

Those who practice nutritional diversity should be wary of any method that is initially too difficult or complicated to complete. Put an emphasis on novel species, reliable sources, and maintaining a stable, diversified mix that supports high productivity.

Stress is said to kill you. I hear it all the time. It is true however it is the stress that you are rebuilding muscle with, it is stress that you are building character with, it is stress that you are building mental fortitude with. Constant stress without recovery from stress would not be good.

Stress management can be aided with specific herbal supplementation and physical practice such as meeting simple daily exercise requirements. Recovery depends on nutrition and rest, and these functions and fuels can be enhanced through knowledge, experience and strategic practice!

Stretching out for 20 minute and 20 minutes of breathwork can create a large decrease in daily stress both to the skeletal muscle and other internal systems. Ignorance Kills the Soul. - Immortal Technique

Stress is a killer. One of your biggest enemies, and the one you should most, "just let go of "

Could it only be that through this type of pain gauntlet this type of information that unlocks our true destiny and potential is achieved?

On the farm I am ablse to more easily get it all into a rhythm which is another sign that the farm is integral to life, or at least a certain amount of space per person is integral to life. If you think about that for a minute it actually solves everything.

Not to mention the Nutritional Diversity that has healed me of my trauma. My traumas counterpart.

Massage is another dynamic growth property although I am largely unfamiliar myself. All major athletes will tell you that it is a major help, and a friend back in the Military days told me it added whole seconds to his run times.

Today in culture we call it massage but this is example of ND diet principle #1 All biology grows against resistance, and that is metaphysical and physical both at least for metaphysical that are attached to biological permanents.

What if we try beating his legs with a stick?

Again, it really is best to go and learn from nature. This nutrition thing is so dynamic we don't begin to understand how biology

decomposes, and also how it stays strong. But we have a whole bunch of ideas on it. All of them are wrong, except maybe one.

In the most bio-diverse concentrations of life on this planet; mainly in the still existing rain-forests and jungles we can observe easily and clearly over a matter of weeks, that all these billions of organisms and micro-organisms work together in a biological artistry.

Along this observational path which is also referred to as natural meditation, observation of nature and pondering, deeper independent thought and focus on rivers, waterfalls, and vines sets in like a download way more advanced than anything you might get for the previous attention to detail exercise.

You see things you could not before, you hear things you could not before, you smell things you could not before. Thoughts based in these elements begin to emerge and it's certainly clear that there is something very serious and healthy about everything there.

Just like a person can hit the gym two hours and not work right and not get any results, and another can work right and transform, person can walk right by a permaculture and not know the difference between it and any other patch of dense nature. This is normally what you hear. "Where is it?" I remember saying it myself. It helps to know things. Knowledge is power. In this diet there is a lot to know – which means there is also a lot of power!

The basic idea of eating natural greens fresh from the leaf, and fish fresh from the river are quickly and clearly taught as a primary way for life to exist.

At this point in the voyage, people start to split into groups according to terms like fresh, prepared, raw, fruitarian, vegetarian, etc. Good food is cooked. Man has developed the use of fire for objectives that are in our best interests in terms of releasing various nutrients and enhancing our ability to digest nutrition. With the exception of a pure carnivore diet cycle, cooked greens always make up a sizable component of my meals.

This nature teaches me mostly that I must eat a large diversity of foods.

There is not any reason to assume that we know better than this nature, or we ourselves are more powerful than this nature.

What the hell is monoculture? What the hell was that notion, anyway?

When do we not even need to be aware of digestive culture, the significance of biodiversity, or how much more capable we may become as individuals by using it?

Back to basics shall we. Back to basil.

If we are living a basic, natural life, as nature can swiftly teach anybody of us who seeks its guidance, then it is obvious that in order to progress in this life, we must be respectful, courteous, and appreciative. One of the simpler teachings, it will take place rapidly.

People who embrace diversity and actually do so in their daily lives are more likely to share their experiences with others, to change over time, and to come up with the most amazing ideas and thoughts they have ever had. This is unquestionably the case in contrast to people following any of the trendy diets available at the grocery store. The important idea is that "we are better humans when we are better nourished" - most potently in this "NUTRITIONAL DIVERSITY" approach. Whether this is a question of our own imagination, or access, or both, or lots more, could be debated.

Different than those in the cities and towns a 'nature boy' would come out of natural in a timid, jumpy, sneaky, observant untrusting and ready for anything candor. They would move differently, because the natural environment everything is always sneaking, attention to details is important, going slow and careful is the way to survive.

In the city people are not quite as the natural nature to live and love and survive and let live, and more a crab-in-the-barrel nature to cut others down, control them, step on things and be angry at a fast pace.

These principles are right in front of us in striking contrast. The city is not dynamic, there is no diversity either. The concrete jungle of no living things and everything that is living in them is sick regardless of whether or not they know it or not one doctor will diagnose it.

It is as if we built the city with the sole purpose to disconnect, domesticate and deceive those who live there - to own them. It is where you buy your mono crop goods all shiny beautiful and toxic. The word town itself is an acronym of to-own. They live in the toown.

"Any intelligent fool can make things bigger and more complex... It takes a touch of genius - and a lot of courage to move in the opposite direction." -Albert Einstein

Heated, strained nutrition such as teas, and coffees can be high in acid and upset the PH and the digestive culture.

Alcohols are extreme concoctions that produce a large range of negative effects on the body, loss of control and including the killing of the digestive culture. Alcohols let the demons in, it's been long time known as Spirits for just this reason. Too many throw their life away for this stupid error.

While it may be fun to dance with devils from time to time, the damage inflicted on one's life and the lives around that person for doing so is always clearly seen and measured.

Simply following the leads of our cousins in the trees, will have you on the right trail.

Refined sugars, alcohols and fluoridated or chemically treated refined salts, prescription or non-prescription drugs, and harsh extracts can also damage or pollute this culture of life. They don't employ any of the refine, extract or ferment. We can classify all of these extracts' pharmaceuticals, and sugars as extremities.

We need to watch out for extreme people, extreme process, extreme deception. Extreme behavior extremity all together and thinks balance. Our thoughts and our microbiome our natural and the outside world nature are connected.

Cancer, diabetes, high blood sugar, etc., are all extremity or lack of balance.

How to get the best balance? By ADDING DIVERSITY. Create best genetics? The same.

The leaf cutter cooks a fungus using a diversity of leaf material, the bee and the flower makes a honey from a diversity of flower pollen.

Darkness, light and pure water are each 'keys' to life.

Diversity, a light cycle, a dark cycle, and water makes life. Got it.

Decomposition employs small amounts of fermentation, honeys and fungus. Its process is speed up by elevating the number of diverse ingredients. So here is a balance point.

If you don´t think life comes from death, throw some dead stuff out in the yard, and watch the life come in.

Selfishness and selfish decision-making will kill you and turn you into a black hole when it collapses. With the help of biblical jargon, the phrase "soul loss" for temporary pleasures might be used to explain this perfectly.

This is an example of actions creating reality. It could be considered both a conversation in metaphysics and thought as well it could be described in scientific activity and results. In time and technological advances, the two read outs will be one in the same.

Alcohol, sweets, and inactivity all contribute to sickness, the loss of life, and eventual transformation into what we refer to as the "walking dead" here. The Walking Dead is similar to "death on the shelf," in that it appears to be alive but is actually very much dead (grocery store produce.) They are all poisonous. Each of them has the potential to poison a genuine living person who still has their spirit.

Long-term happiness and empowerment come from selflessness. There are countless real-world routes and examples that can be seen, explored, and experienced. You could argue that in today's world, even learning the basics of dynamic understanding counts as great wisdom.

Its real that human settlement size is the root of most problems today next to money. I will get into great detail about sustainable space requirements.

These dynamic principles in Darkness, light and pure water are each 'keys' to life. No matter how metaphysical or hocus pocus they may be to the 'owned,' are scientifically duplication.

I used to work out with a couple guys that would drink alcohol every weekend. They would always complain they would not get the results I would. I would tell them constantly " stop drinking!"

Coffee is every morning in every movie and TV show. Alcohol is every night. Cut these two out, and your off to the races. People do not realize how impactful this consumption is. A free man with no chains other than nutrition is going to be several times stronger than someone in t-own.

The quick high, the quick escape, the chemical aids, we get great outside results, and pay for them on our insides and our children our most important things pay for them too.

Overcoming addiction to things like sugars has been one of our modern life's greatest challenges. The chemicals out there such as refined sugars and certain mass-produced alkaloids might as well be called black magic. The social and metaphysical poisons in our modern lives may as well be called voodoo.

Another dynamic voodoo is the epidemic sized, "Ultimate form of Child Abuse -Dr. Phil" now known as Parental Alienation.
    xxix All these dynamic attacks are very effective at weakening the human beings involved.

Interestingly and an introduction to what I call Nutritional Dynamics, helping someone else get their gut micro biome in check, is a great way to realize new revelations about micro biomes and human health in general. Help people, help life – it is the most powerful way to help self.

Working Together, in Rhythm

Nature demonstrates how we all rely on one another and the wider life cycle in order to exist. Each of these life cycles appears to be part of a larger history of cyclical vibrations, revolutions, and comprehension.

Prior to us by thousands of years, plants and nature held information and skills that could help you and I reach new heights of potential.

Interestingly they communicate with each other one way through fungi, and certain tests have indicated they have a telepathic mode of communication and of interpretation. You may need some good digestive computer parts inside yourself to be communicated with by them or to possibly assert your higher level of existing.

The balance and interdependence among the various elements in the natural world allow it to function in a rhythmic manner. This pattern can also be seen in how nutrients are distributed among various diets. Each nutrient in food has a unique function in the body, and they all interact in intricate ways. It can be helpful to us to tailor our diets for the best possible health and wellbeing if we understand how these nutrients are interconnected.

The interaction of vitamin D and calcium is one instance of how nutrients interact with one another. Calcium cannot be utilized correctly if vitamin D levels are insufficient, which is necessary for calcium absorption in the body. Low vitamin D levels have been linked to an increased risk of osteoporosis and bone fractures, according to studies.xxx

In this world of dense nature, hearts beat, memories are made, intelligence advances, these things we refer to in English as Love and

Desire play their roles, while sites, smells, and sounds affect our life and give us our own interpretations of life itself.

"No one is useless in the world who lightens the burdens of others." Charles

Dickens

"Everything good that ever happened to me that actually helped, came through helping other people." Danny Trejo

On the brink of cultural evolution new theories of the age start to show spirituality as a science, or the two being one in the same now finally connected, such as the new book title and phrase "bio centricity," which claims consciousness is the basis of science as we know it.

Emotions were never really explained to us in our nuclear age of airplanes and space travel. We are above emotional or spiritual pursuits, largely because we are under their control still. Most won't admit or acknowledge this, or may not be capable of realizing it yet.

Many times, when one person is angry other people die. This story is a classic tale, as I write this I possess anger towards certain individuals to the point that if they were to appear near me at any time, I don't think I could stop myself from the brutal attack that most surely would ensue in auto pilot.

The researchers concluded that the synergistic effects of the elements in these foods were probably what caused this diet's protective effects.

Each nutrient in food has a unique function in the body, and they all operate together in intricate ways. It can be helpful to understand how these nutrients interact in order to tailor our diets for the best possible health and wellbeing. The essential nutrients and nutritional synergy for optimum health can be provided by include a variety of nutrient-dense whole foods in our meals.xxxi

There is an ant somewhere in the world, an electrician told me, would go in a line march straight into a fly wheel on air conditioning units and die. So, for that area the company had to make a social machine with a different operational part for the function. Some sort of accidental signal on another plain of feeling, was being imitated by the machine.

As a matter of fact, we must be able to create more rhythmic cycles that include advantages like the mind-muscle connection, muscle memories, and dexterity built one on top of the other in the world of limitless potential that is the biologically hosted mind or consciousness. This is because modern science does not currently describe digestive culture. Physical activity according to all the studies so far has the biggest, by far, impact on the gut micro-biome.

So, the physical activity of helping people and helping nature plays a role in our own health?

Social culture should be an important fixture progressive rhythms and cycles. Our social culture is not, it is a monotone slave culture with little vibrancy and very dulled taste compared with its ancestry.

A true human student of nature, observes these potentials and the ultimate human disciplines out there, then test them, and put these types of knowledge into their own personal helpful religious practices or rhythmic routines that they know help balance out their lives.

So, there are numerous instances all around us that can either improve or ruin our lives. Humans obviously have freer will, a greater Intelligence, and better self-awareness. However, we have a "new cool culture" where it's possible to harm ourselves, each other, and its "hip" to be somewhat stupid because of pop cultural guidance and the influence of celebrities and idols, at least that's how it feels to me.

It depends on a person's intelligence whether or not they want to listen to such stupidity because these stories are told by tails between ears.

A greedy black hole club of control freaks who want to spread their disease to as many people as possible are to blame for all of the unjustified persecution, tax issues, war, and hatred that exist today. The primary origin of both good and terrible things is a desire to reproduce.

How many stories are we going to go through of people chained and persecuted for doing good things? Whoever helps these people in these real stories?

Today we stamp out good and celebrate the bad ...

The checks and balances are absent. We have a PEA that is neither urgently necessary nor DEA (Drug Enforcement Administration). As our aggressive segment of the population, which would stomp out an enemy, sits in a tiny cage doing nothing, we are constantly at war. We are hesitant to question the status quo.

You can reform it, but Buckminster Fuller(was an American architect, systems theorist,

writer, designer, inventor, philosopher, and futurist), asserts that you must replace it. This applies to us even though societal policy makers might not think so, and we always have guerilla permaculture as a backup.

Let the old you stay in the cocoon of the past. Today rebirth who you really are, who you really want to be. Give yourself a new name if it helps, you will certainly be a new person, on the new diet, and there is a new adventure waiting for that guy. Leave the other guy in the cocoon.

Today we stamp out bad and celebrate the good ...

Back to natural.

Anyone who has spent a couple of weeks in the jungle knows when a frog or a lizard dies there is an army of little guys that will devour or carry off the carcass in a matter of hours or minutes. They will equally take care of a human who dies unattended in the Jungle in the same way nearly just as fast. They have death sensors. They are biological removers of potentially harmful rotten material within the larger life cycle.

We build this wonderland of life in our stomachs when we eat healthy and natural Nutritional Diversities. A small microcosm of biological stuff that works together with the body and helps digest food and ensure optimal intake into cells. We build it really great over a month of really nutritionally diverse stuff, and no consumption of alcohols and coffees or other high acid foods or extracts which kill it off, or provide it with unnecessary obstacles. Now that it's built we are free and we are high enough to see the truth over all the obstacles that have blocked it.

To get back into nature's rhythm will take celebrating the good again, and expelling or converting all the bad.

Digestive culture like human culture like plant culture, permaculture, etc. all things, needs water. Much more water in fact than you were taught to drink in grade school. Hydration is key to performance, and these days no one is sufficiently hydrated. Nor salted.

Hydration

Water comes in amazing amounts of different forms and states. It's microscopic physical structure changes and water receives, light, vibration and influence.

Hydration and water delivery to the cells is increased with more green living plant consumption. This is very important for athletically inclined individuals and people trying to heal and recover.

Water diversity would be the best form of overall water supply for a residence, and specific water sources, like municipal water and wells close to factories, should be more carefully examined.

The most crucial element in your existence is water; it comes in first place. Water will be a main topic in my final revision of this study of the biological art of Gods, which I inadequately described in this work, with numerous pages devoted to it. For the time being, let's take a quick look at what's crucial regarding water before moving on to a wider supply and variety of buildings and treatments.

So much to talk about here. Hydration is master key to all life. We humans are made mostly out of water and we cannot live without it. If a human body or any other biology for that matter has no water, it has no life. Water should be our priority, and yet most water consumed today is not good or even close to acceptable by the new standards in this most correct diet text of our lives. That being said,

I am not young enough to know everything. – Oscar Wilde

Water comes in various forms and states beyond ice, water and steam.

Dr. Masuro Emotto showed that water responds to emotion, intention and interprets and translates so many types of energies inside and outside of the body. Water is dynamic and complex and her structure is easily changed. Be like water my friends. - Bruce Lee

Salt frequently improves the ability of water to connect electrically. I recall an experiment my father and I performed as children in which we added salt to water and utilized the mixture to show how to close a circuit using a battery wired to a nail dropped into it and a light wired to a nail on the other end of the container.

At this age, experiments like this are crucial to comprehending the real chemistry that is right in front of us and available to everyone. Today, very few people have any knowledge of chemistry, which is unfortunate because if they did, the golden bull and the small green paper would appear to be much less precious and interesting.

For someone who wants to consume and own a wide variety and range of healthy, miracle waters, finding sources and collection methods as well as filtering and nurturing water can become a fulltime job. I believe that focusing on achieving good filtration and fantastic water structure for you and your family using a few conditioning models, techniques, or products like an ozone generator is the most critical thing you could do right now.

The EPA tested city water sources around the country and discovered some startling facts about the widely dispersed water supply.

The diversity of the water is what you're aiming for. There are several sources, preferably none of which are city or commercially bottled sources. Excellent options include springs, rain collection, distilled, and mountain top fresh.

Mountain fresh means your high up, where the chances of contamination or slim. Springs are abundant, if you know how find them and how to dig. Distillers now are easy to get and fast to distill.

I combine spring and rain in a huge tank at the ND Island site. I want to add a few additional sand filter tanks, or 4" PVC sections, with various mineral rocks, and even clear portions if I can find them with openings for sunlight. A river channel with an insect screen that is open to the elements would be a fantastic flowing body of water.

Perhaps a little coconut tank where we can add avocado pieces or other items as we choose and add more oils if we choose. If one uses their creativity, they can come up with a lot of improvements—another powerful tool for creating an ideal existence...

The one atom of oxygen is a companion to the two atoms of hydrogen, which are found in water in its liquid form. Water covers 71% of the surface of the globe, 95% of which is in the oceans. A very little portion of the one to two percent of this water that is in the ground is used by people and other mammals. After hydrogen

and helium, oxygen is the third most plentiful element in the universe by mass.

We only need a small amount of oxygen to breathe because too much oxygen would cause everything to burn up and continue burning until it was gone. The oxygen in the atmosphere is perfectly balanced. The same principles apply to how oxygen functions in humans, although certain crucial.

Without proper exercise, breathing practices and stretching practices these pathways can become obstructed, clogged, corroded and in need of repair, until dead completely. The atmosphere has 78% Nitrogen.

Oxygen is a chemical element symbolized by an 'O' and the atomic number 8. It in the family of the chalcogen class on the periodic table and is a highly reactive non-metal oxidizing agent that forms oxides with most elements as well as other compounds.

The remedies to these issues, as well as those involving fat reduction, candida, and the removal of other toxins, may be found in proper or excessive oxygenation. We use oxygen like the flame does, and if that process were to stop, we would "not be breathing." Everything can be converted or reduced in large part depending on how much oxygen is present and how quickly it can be delivered through any available channels, if any

.

Water comes in various shapes and sizes, is the greatest moving element on earth, and is the universal element since it can take on any form. A person with a deep intellect will inevitably study and obey the water. Beings that can be observed but lack this interest or awareness in their surroundings are examples of the idle, consumer intelligence that frequently results in the creation of trashy environments as well as trashy physical and metaphysical systems.

The human body is 99% water when it is conceived. The human body is then 80% water when it is a born as a baby. The body is then 50% water when it is old with wrinkled skin.

Naturally water comes up from the ground fresh. Barbados, is very fresh, a Caribbean island completely comprised of surfaced, dead reef, which purifies the water, and whose rum is famous for being fine to take daily without hangover effect. Sewage systems for houses were traditionally a hole drilled down 30ft. Barbados is famous for some of the clearest waters around.

Spring water is good water usually and the earth should regrettably separate surface plastic fibers and other impurities from their various levels before they may return to the sea. Mountain water exhibits the most balanced PH and is regarded as life water.

According to "Bruce Lee" to mimic water in physics, is the ultimate physical art ability, and what he as a martial, physical, body artist himself strived to achieve this ability, "to be like water."

Dr. Masaru Emoto's research was furthered by Victor Enusian, xxxii who looked at how radiation affected water. He discovered that the structure itself changed and adopted a pathological wave that was incredibly far outside the region of radioactive contamination. Increases in the suicide rate were observed in the "structure change zone," along with other detrimental neurological impacts. He is aware that the brain is composed of 85% water and that this new pathological order of the water will be useful for something only when combined with other structures rather than radiation. Emoto

has also demonstrated that ice crystals made from water blessed by a Zen monk look so much more beautiful than those exposed to messages of hate. Xxxiii

In the particular cases of the radiated water, science paints the scenario that the new water structure meets the brain plasma water structure and has an immediate conflict, ultimately the person is removed of most sentiment, to include the will to live. So, the structure of the water in us is very important.

Heavily chlorinated, fluoridated, plastic fiber contaminated, heavy metaled and whatever else structure components of the water most commonly taken today in both bottles and city water supplies, can't be expected to produce much better results than the radiated stuff.

U.S. and many other centrally distributed, large city water plants around the world, have been tested to show some alarming substances. As the word and the knowledge spreads, people become more and more interested in the very important endeavor of finding themselves a way to clean that up.

I want to clean it up for myself also and convey the message to loved ones about how important the water we consume is, that includes a few recommended home water solutions.

Just like with the ND Diet, there is a sourcing issue, and if we can get a great source there is no need of so many costly devices.

Where we get our water from is the starting place of importance, and how we care for that water we get is next.

Today with centrally distributed city water supplies, a few different home water solutions should be applied, at each home especially for drinking water.

Water in U.S. homes, and homes around the world has turned out to be at many times contaminated, with serious contaminants such as heavy metals, microfiber plastics, harsh chemicals, even pharmaceuticals and caustic sediment matter. The most important thing to health is water, and there must be somethings residents can do clean it up for themselves and for their loved ones.

"Built into my world of convenience, I stand for the city water service to put a high amount of chlorine in the water for sanitary purposes which then goes into and all over my body each day.

I have to get to work and do some meaningless task, and I don't have time to read this piece on water, I need to get ready and jump in my shower that kills my skin each day, every day, of my whole life to the point that I don't even realize it (but it is the easiest test), and likely my insides could show signs of the same.

I go on day in and day out ignoring the fact that I drink chemicals I can smell coming from the top of my glass. Could the chemicals themselves have something to do with the lackadaisical manner in which I let myself consume poisons both from my tap and my local grocer?

Before pharmaceutical substances were discovered in tests carried out by the United States Environmental Protection Agency, which revealed that there existed positive results for several drugs in all 50 samples of the study, conducted across each of the 50 states, it may seem like a far-

fetched question or an exaggeration of a simple sanitary function. Most of the drugs found their lower blood pressure, with the exception of carbamazepine, which is used to treat epilepsy, schizophrenia, and bipolar disorder.

Everyone who exercises maintains a high-pressure tolerating system because to the intensely high blood pressures they experience throughout their periods of exercise, hence it is debatable whether high blood pressure is symptomatic of a health concern. It may be argued that using medications to lower blood pressure is similar to sedating someone, which is technically what one could say it does.

I want to raise the quality of the water in my life and the lives of the people I care about because it is the most important resource for my family.

In our world of convenience, where most people don't do anything for themselves, you may hear terms like "reverse osmosis, multistaged," and "xxPSI, x"PVC," but don't worry; finding someone to assist you with this stuff should be simple. Most poor fellas will be familiar with these terms because they cannot afford to hire someone else to do this work for them and have learned to do it themselves, and for $20 are more than willing to help you.

He helps you, and you help him, you know. We're on the go now, there we go.

"I own them all if I offer a game, and they all play it. I've issued money for the current game, and I'll offer rankings for the following one. The combination of unnatural leverage between all of you, provided by me, is the key to both of them. The Devil in me.

For urban drinking water it is recommended best that a gravity counter-top best water filter be used anyways. They are little more in price as the other in-line filters but historically produce the cleanest filtered drinking water when it comes to the city supply. It won't get all of the harsh stuff that may be there even then.

The field install system traditionally is not that complicated. A series of sealed tanks can be set up one with rock, one with sand, one with charcoal even, on to the final holding tank where water draws into the system. Sometimes people after this before the tap will put a few string filters which usually do good to pick up the micro sediment stuff. If your system is spring water, or roof collected, a little bit of the sediment may even be good for you.

Whatever which way, it is time to stop ingesting the chemicals primarily chlorine and fluoride. I would like to stop showering with them too. That may just be me.

There has been one product that has stood above the rest in the removal of the chemicals and that is the gravity fed, Big Berkey Water Purification countertop system with fluoride filter add-on.

Next in this counter-top gravity line of hot stuff I recommend is the Nikken PiWater system. I work with both of these systems, and the primary differences are Nikken's attempt to imitate a prime water structure using hand-picked elements and information from around the world in a plastic case that allows light to enter, whereas the Big Berkey is stainless steel in construction, and is the United States' most popular solution. Depending on what divine water information you may be looking at, in wanting to work on your water more you can juggle the two or do like me and get one for home, and one for office.

A multi-stage inline system that filters water for the entire home is also reasonably priced. With one of these, the water entering into toilets, showers, and air coolers will all be cleaner. I advise installing one in the home or flat for between $250 and 850. Next, there is the under-sink

inline system, which is effective for a few taps that people wish to use to get cleaner water without having to wait for it to cycle through gravity filters on the counter. Some businesses provide a wonderful shower filter that attaches directly to the shower line, stays in line, and filters the water coming from the shower.

Water Ionizer, is what many medical patients prefer and using this device which is rather expensive the user can make both more acidic and more alkaline water adjustable to their preference and based on their supply. There is a lot of arguing about this but ionic charges likely do play some part.

Then of course the frontier way to know your good is to boil the water. Some say distilled is the way to do it, that is all a whole other conversation, very deeply described in the complete ND Diet text. I have seen some permaculturist's' throw a rock or two or a few into the pot while cooking water, believing that it helps re-mineralize it, especially when rain collected.

Evaporation, in the sun, with an open, possibly cloth or   screen covered,   container   is   a   great   way   to   see   that chemicals separate from the large body of water.

A spring in a city is also likely contaminated I know arsenic was

present in underground dessert aquifers where I am from, there have been brow-raising radiation tests there also. In a place where much

of the National Weapons developments and tests are made to include the first nuclear bomb building, where the dream team of scientists operated, I guess this should not be so shocking.

I remember posting to social media, a result about radiation leakage and I was amazed at the comments, saying things like "I wonder how long it will take to see effects," and other comments that spoke to the lack of seriousness in our culture. This not caring attitude is behind pollution and contamination and clearly an optimal human will care more about these things. Why we don't seem to care is another conversation.

Don't   be   like   everyone   else,   take   the   time   to   get   some water solutions into your home. All of these home water solutions are better than nothing, with your city water supply. Ultimately another source would be better here companies have started selling the large 5-gallon waters harvested from spring sites for $5.00, and many people pay that, it is a good business. The city water supply is the one that most needs home water treatment. Certain U.S. city water taps have been found from toxic to flammable and I can only imagine what the effects must be like sitting down here in pretty Panama, where I still have to go through the motions to get good clean water in my cup. Anything centrally distributed like this is inherently open to being poisoned and hurting a lot of people.

Certain individuals myself included, notice and believe in the science class idea that chemical separation and then evaporation of a lesser substance will take place in an open container. Refrigeration, cold or heat may play their part if they exist but over time in any condition the lesser substance should move to the top, and be the first to evaporate.

We used to fill glass bottles with water and place them in the sun for a bit, then move them to the fridge hoping that this process would be quickened. Along the way I met a man who explained to me that he would put a lemon, a lime, a leaf of mint, and a quartz crystal into a glass picture and place in the sun. He said with honesty that he

found it to be a more fulfilling water. Sounds a bit ludicrous and far-

fetched. Low   and   behold, I was able   to   discover

a great deal of evidence of evidence tremendous back up these claims. In the market for water purification, there are even advertised items with inbuilt UV lights. My friend believes that when he

drinks this sun tea with hibiscus flowers, it helps him stay more hydrated. Could it be that the process took time and attention, at least in part??

Distillation is a heavily debated process regarding drinking water, but it is pure water technically. Andrew Norton Webber, says distilled water has helped him retain several youthful qualities and achieve health from an episode of sickness, and many other agree. Certain schools of thought caution that the mineral-less water may help remove toxins, but help remove from the body some vital elements also. Rain water also gets the mineral leaching criticism, and over time drinking from a rain water tank, and not entering the sea, one could start to feel this maybe, although it could be something else.

In my humble experience my best water days were some from mountain spring, some from rain collection, some distilled and all filtered to some degree, and many servings of water treated with many different treatments, such as adding a few orange slices. Most water recommends in our mainstream education recommend far too little water consumption, while our military training is more correct, and that water up, never have yellow coming out.

Nutritional Diversity, key principles are my guiding light in this water respect also, and that is; a diversity of the best sources, and structures available is best for optimal human performance.

Somewhere in this crazy complex journey (I fail as of now to bang out on the keys in a complete story) of mine, I found the work of Dr. Masaru Emoto, who photographed flash frozen water crystal structures, and spawned the practice of thanking, playing music for and praying to water. Thank your water. I thank mine. If you look at this research you will too. If you think about this long and hard, realizing that we ourselves are three fourths water, and the plant's and living essences around us all have one thing in common and that is water; you too will see from the good doctor's very recent research, that an attitude of gratitude will overcome most of the issue.

While Masaru's critiques are plenty-full, anyone who has been around snow, has seen these shapes before, even if their skepticism is out of balance with trying to hear about Mr. Emoto's hippy ideas. Just listen to nature, ask God and try it out see if it helps you to feel differently.

Mr. Emoto offers a highly duplicated on YouTube way to find the same type of results using some damp rice in three different jars treating one harshly and writing the word hate on the glass with a sharpie marker, the next in a different area of your space write love, and treat it each morning with a hug and a kiss, the third don't write anything, don't pay it any mind, ever. This particular experiment reveals each time reflectively a terrible moldy cancer on the ignored, and slight moldy cancer on the hated and the best condition on the loved. Obviously make sure all the rice is the same, and clean and the jars are clean.

Permaculture and Nutritional Diversity are food production and nutritional intake systems mainly about plants, and growing and nurturing life in a symbiotic relationship with ourselves and the biology around us. Our study finds the plants produced by modern agriculture, mono-crop systems to be toxic and less than adequate nutrition for humans, contributing to the malnutrition of humans and the mass killing of millions of pollinators all over the planet that are necessary for all biological happiness and survival. The decline in interest in old fashion healthy farming, and the rise in interest in all industry including agricultural, the rise of the age of chemical cures are all solid math behind the decline in human health and the rise of human health crisis.

Through years of domestication, we have lost an edge in our immune systems, and in our physiology overall. This makes it exiting to study wild plants.

Through the use of sane cultivation methods that have existed several times throughout our human cultural history we can quickly re-achieve more correct farming and robust production.

We have many times produced thousands of known species in cyclic waste disposal and food production intelligence's, all of which are now not present in time, and are badly needed again in a bold shotgun approach hastily organized across the water filtering, food and air producing mechanism we depend on and call "our world." Going back to the stronger less domesticated species of plants and foods, is a great idea and is sort of a double-upgrading to the quality of foods taken in.

Wild plants are in abundance, they are strong, they present new tastes and starting out you'll likely want to cook most of it. I must say though today I enjoy routinely fresh smoothies all the time all day, fresh with wild tropical plants and have been doing so now for five years.

Proteins, Carbohydrates & Fats

I now specify a ratio of 10% raw drink or eaten before 90% cooked at a volume of five times the amount of protein consumption, whether it's wild food or food you raise. Frequently, I top cooked leaf dishes with 10% fresh leaf. High protein leaves are quite appealing to vegetarian nutritional diversifiers in particular. There is a theory that leaves with darker green or darker hues may contain more protein.

Protein play important roles in regulating gene expression, antioxidative responses, neurotransmission, and immunity. They are major metabolic fuels for the small intestine to maintain its digestive function and protect its mucosal integrity. Therefore, based on new research findings, protein should be taken into consideration in revising the classical "ideal protein" concept and formulating balanced diets to improve protein accretion, food efficiency, and health in humans.xxxiv

Growing your own nutrition is the way to grow what you need specifically. One valiant hypothesis that comes from plant study has been that with the right diverse materials in the microbiome, the right dynamics as far as the decisions made by the farmer, and the relationship of being the gardener of their own food could trigger the cultivars or wild species to produce special made nutrition just for them. Could be far-fetched but there seems to be some evidence out there that gives this idea, namely the entire Rudolf Steiner work of "Biodynamic Agriculture."

Animals includes all walking creatures for the purposes of this manual. Again, a diversity of parts, and of species is what we are going after with animal nutrition.

We eat fish, chicken and cow meats usually around the world, we don't find lamb, goat, and other meats as much and populations of humans before us ate most of the red blooded, fish or fowl stuff they could their hands on. Rabbit, certain fish, certain fowl, goat and lamb I have seen become very procreative on the small farm.

Bats and rodents are known sustainable foods, wild and easy to catch through primitive trap technologies for several populations. Insects are great foods for others, and certain amphibious or serpent foods are also popular culture dishes.

Dietary diversity has been associated with a number of positive health outcomes, such as a decreased risk of chronic diseases, enhanced cognitive function, and increased immune system performance. A balanced diet that includes a range of foods from several dietary groups, such as fruits, vegetables, whole grains, protein-rich foods, and healthy fats, is advised by the World Health Organization (WHO).

Micronutrient deficits are common in many parts of the world and can be addressed by eating a variety of foods. For instance, iron deficiency affects a lot of individuals and can cause anaemia, lethargy, and cognitive impairment. People can lower their risk of anaemia and increase their iron status by increasing their intake of leafy greens and red meat. Obviously, a certain amount of experimentation has gone into, these different animal food types, but red meat seems always soluble and highly nutritious to humans in any dose. There is not highly toxic species of mammal in this category as exist within the plant kingdom. White meat follows just behind as far, as an across the board edible animal food source.

For this reason, and others, I checked out and tried some things mentioned in the new red meats diet craze, I ate more of the redblooded organs, and some of the benefits from red meat consumption realized by the "Carnivore diet," movement and switching it up to red meats only for a while to see how it went. Large groups of people have claimed to have restored their fertility, overcome incredible health feats using red meat, and some using an only red meat diet.

Paleo-nutritional studies indicate, the hunter gatherer likely practiced an advanced herbal-ism in wait for an animal catch. He had no large mono/culture which means naturally he would have eaten more of a diversity, and this is always missed in paleo diet information. In harsh, nature -adapted paleolithic time periods, the time between catching fish or animal was not long. There was many more animals and fish also during this time.

I would like to encourage the farming of new animal food types, or old ones rather but re-modernize them. New chicken varieties, not the commercial ones, rabbits, meadow dogs, nuicke (small species here about the size of rabbit), quail, pigeon, certain insects and maybe those to make robust foods for the rabbits, in a nice little cycle of nutrition building. For purely production reasons, leaving lists of other reasons unmentioned, it makes the most sense to raise animals, living a full and free life. Turning ten percent of it free at adolescence could be a helpful practice for this world.

Most important factor with new farms, is giving the animal a just and loving life. We all need to farm again even our red meat, and I provide even urban farming models to do so. No living animal should reside in their own feces. There must be a way to move the animal or the feces.

As an introduction to food dynamics, keep in mind that the less

domesticated species makes the best meat since it has the best physiological system and was happier as a result of its greater freedom. Because of this, every conscientious new agriculture enterprise should take the lead in the campaign to preserve endangered species.

The most concerned nutrient in fitness today, is protein. There is a lot of argument about animal proteins. There is a lot of abuse in modern day animal farming. There are many other essences of these animals that are very important, and they are not sufficiently considered by most diet science.

As a standard, for a fit person, Nutritional Diversifists should be shooting for one gram of protein for every gram of body weight. Certain programs maybe go for half a gram, or a gram and a half or two grams depending on the goal. Then you want 5x any non-plant derived protein amount in. I know it sounds crazy, but this is what is optimal for a routine regime standard; take in five grams of diverse (the minimum of 30-60 different species to start) plant matter for every gram of protein. This is why you have to leave the grocery store alone also, this would have you full of chemicals. I like to see my diet receiving most of its proteins from animal products, and

plant matter and less from supplements although the first supplement (other than the ND Starters supplement) I recommend to new gym heads is protein.

The impact of carbohydrate intake on athletes' endurance performance was published in the year 2021 issue of Sports Medicine. According to this review study, eating carbohydrates while engaging in endurance exercise can enhance performance by giving the muscles another source of fuel. The scientists think that activities lasting more than 90 minutes may benefit the most from consuming carbohydrates while exercising.xxxv

What do you know, the next doctrinal factor regarding animals and meats is, diversity? Get a diversity of them. Get the organs, eat those, make a broth with the bones, drink that, make a soup with the brain (keto lovers delight). Find yourself some good loving small farmers, and ask them to farm some stock specifically for you. Work with them on the care and foods the animal receives, visit that animal as often as you can and as the intro to Nutritional Dynamics; take a real hold over your health.

The carbon forming parts of meat primarily red meat when cooked also present a new form of healthy nutrient. At the same time raw meats (healthy of course) also offer their raw nutrients which cover slightly different digestive grounds. There is a range of nutrition in the preparations of the meat. There is information on the web, that warn against this material as a carcinogen, but many of the experienced and intelligent nutritionists I have spoken with have found themselves leaning towards the food in a state closer to general carbon being a plus versus a minus.

Nutritional Diversity Science very much came from in part, the study of other animals and insects in the biological cycle of life. I have made it a doctrinal

I have taken up the study of the local animal here in and around Panama City, known as the Nuike, which is like a small prairie dog, and also the jaguar. The Jaguar hunts over 85 known species for survival, in Panama where despite being smaller than South Carolina is home to more than 10,000 varieties of plants and more than 1,500 different types of animals. It is the last land for the jaguar, a marvel and sacred animal of human cultural interest with records dating back to 500 B.C.

In the dedicated study of Nutritional Diversity Science which is natural inclined and seeking to be a complete look at edibility and uptake of all forms of biological nutrients I land in a new study site near Panama City where deer, several new species of monkeys, a hand-picked ecological scenario featuring many imports dating from the time of the canal's construction are featured, as well as a plethora of these small prairie dog-like guys known as the nuicke.

I stayed there about 5 weeks in this hill known as Ancon.

In one small hill that was formed a top of rubble and garbage waist that could date back to 1881 this small rodent like animal has been a "Delicious" barbecue item already and has terrible overpopulated the area making gardening very difficult for residents. I have been using the Premier companies electric fence, and I know automated systems very well from my time in the Navy working with Fire

Fighting agent mixing systems and I have used these tools in combination with my discovery of strong species for a strong ND diet plan to design urban automated systems garden plans that keep these guys out and allow for Nutritional Diversity food production at the home level very easily, and very productive.

I have some good experience with chicken farming, and with goat farming a bit. I feel that I near mastered chicken farming, and surely, we were producing more eggs, and the most nutritious chicken meat than our neighbors. I attribute the success to genetics, portability of chicken housing establishments and nutritionally diverse insects.

I was near exited to work with a nutritionally diverse dog and maybe a horse food mix, but that opportunity was deleted by a total

narcissist ex CEO of a pharmaceutical company who was making their decisions in fear and fighting with their extreme selfishness about working in or with the unknown, and was not courageous enough to stand up to a low paid local staff who felt threatened by new talent. I tell you, you must build a strong team, with a zero narcissist factor or there is only so far you will go in your endeavor. An open minded culture that works as a team and gets behind the star players, this we know from athletics and sports is a must-have structure to win!

I tell people over and over that at the end of the day we make decisions in love or in fear, and we need to be experts at being honest with ourselves in analyzing those decisions. When and if we make decisions in fear we are best to stand up without fears of looking weak or anything else and go back and iron that mistake out with a new decision in love and courage. To get to a place that has not been reached before you will need to do something that has not been done before! Big risk is what makes big reward. Remember this. Comfort is killing the whole deal. Maybe the horse and dog food will come down the line, and that is surely not dependent on one person's fears of loves. I don't need to be the one to create it either, here yet another opportunity exists for someone else to make their name in the future of health, wellness and optimization.

I took the nudge of initially disappointing circumstance as an opportunity to venture yet again into a new place. Close but new, in the geographical diversity focus which narrowed my sights in on the two wild creatures for selection.

Another of the narrowing experiences was seeing my good friend who was also my Uncle's good friend' who met me in the new geographic region of around the oldest city in the America's with a newspaper in his hand pissed off about the government titling and selling of more of the Jaguars last corridor which exists today as a small part of Costa Rica and a larger part of the smaller land mass known today as the Republic of Panama.

This Panama portion of the corridor has been under attack several times, including recently when human indigenous residents were forcefully pushed out for the making of another hydro dam' that sells its power to neighboring countries. Yet another good friend of mine Richard, covered this in a video that got the attention of Vice

HBO productions who also did another video. Regardless of the humanitarian and ecological protection outcries and exposure the damn was constructed and recently finished.

The last times Vice was here it was to ignore the great logic of an inspirational program and turn into a reality tv rating oriented hollow piece that fell away quickly, missing a hugely important opportunity to show sustainable life trials without that kind of

contamination. The time before that was about the sloth and the secretion of a miracle cancer curing substance on sloth skin.

How do all these proteins, fats, food chemicals, gas molecules, solids and water all work so well together? Let us now talk about master chemistry.

Love

How does your state of being internally and the state of being in which you combine into yourself, affect your food? How do these dynamic physical and emotional characteristics function in you?

Which brings us to the love element, the most dynamic and powerful element in the health and nitrification of animals, plants and humans.

Photosynthesis itself is arguably a chemical process set in motion and possibly maintained also by love itself. Food, rest, water and love is the defines the nurturing of a human.

The hellish modern profit production systems of today produce an abused animal and plant, fed chemical concoctions, and hormonal altering substances that transfer to the person eating it. The pain, the suffering, the outright torture of certain "produce" is so absent of love, its a wonder how the process has gone on virtually unquestioned to long.

The caged or toxified abuse is transferred, the anger and resentment are transferred, the chemical releases and metaphysical imprints are all transferred and the abusive nutritional elements are taken into the system and used as supportive material by a highly adaptable organism that can live on garbage known as the homo-sapiens, or human being. To eat this food and force yourself to be happy and loving is 100% a strength building operation.

That is one food model. One of millions of dynamic degrees and options of how we could get food.

The Vegan diet movement and others have been extreme protesters of any animal consumption and understandably so in the face of such abuses. Little do they know some of the worst abuse is plant, and pollination insect abuse from current plant cultivation methods.

This does not change our physiology or evolution based in or towards animal consumption or not in animal consumption (I know this is arguable) and it does not change the benefits of the dynamic factors created from practices loving our food.

Many Vegan's don't realize that soy farms are much worse than cow farms to the overall ecosystem. By combining the two, we are one step in the right direction.

Vegans should love Nutritional Diversity Science, it's harvesting techniques and permaculture-like growing methods where plants are never killed in harvest.

Outside of most Vegan understandings is that plants do differ from animals in many ways namely that we can harvest parts of them and not kill or hurt the plant much, leaving the plant alive and taking only a portion of it as harvest.

Soy fields don't operate this way. Large machines and airplanes kill all the pollinators, torture the plants then kill the plants, then the plants are preserved through various means for various amounts of time as they transport to shelves in major outlets.

Money, money money manufacturing.

If we say thanks to plants and pay attention to bio-dynamic principals, we may be granted by the plant a whole new pallet of nutrients as return thanks.

Not so many from the Vegan, plant food enthusiast community I have interviewed know about the Backster tests either, that show us the slaughter of plant is recognized in the plant, who likely gives itself a nutrient decreasing shock before death.

There is a library of other dynamics like this unknown to the modern diet communities.

Most vegans and vegetarians and humans on this planet still as I type this eat from insane vegetable torture and slaughter fields (monoculture, modern agriculture systems) they know nothing about.

The nuicke rodent seems to be very interested in plant material and certainly the stuff we like just the same as rabbits. I wanted to try a series of composting and trapping operations here around the small creatures and I would like to observe more on their spectrum of consumption. I think I recently saw a few of them up at Bluff Beach in the Isla of Colon, in Bocas del Toro.

Studying one new popular wild predator and one popular wild prey each year with a very population spirit here, both carnivorous and omnivorous will be very important to human nutritional principle realizations going forward.

Love in the wild has a rare form to us, raw and brilliant courageous and at times able to form new levels of existence or growing. Love is bundled with many other elements.

In human and in animal life, fear is a part of survival too. It is the job of the animal to come up with a perfect balance of both metaphysical and physical nutritional elements in a self-sustained manner.

Folks who like to play with fire procedure more testosterone and human growth hormone naturally. The fearless are chemically more fearless after deciding to be more fearless and facing their fears.

A domesticated animal feels no fear. I am not saying to run around scaring your livestock but on my mountain top, the animals are ready for anything. Who knows what name their master gardener will take on what day and what rhythm or vibe that guy has going on then.

Essentially this animal plays a divine role during its lifetime, and will provide the best nutrition as a food.

We as a human are currently in a life-threatening struggle to find this balance of domestication versus wild nature ourselves and the most apparent and applicable solution of learning from our nature that

has been here long before us is consumption. In other words, you are what you eat.

It is with the realm of possibility for humans to love all the animals and the nature see the fears of our world to dissipate with the scarcity a natural effect that will and return with the abundance.

This creation of abundance, that hippies talk about is the fundamental next step in human happiness and freedom from poverty.

In a very wild sense we have plenty of abundance now in the wild and plenty of intellect to use it.

This story hopes to inspire animal freedom as well as diverse

horticulture and both inspirations in harmony and guidance with natures examples and not the creations of modern tech who "know better." What story are you apart of?

A focusing on and love of nature is what will bring this all back together.

True love is....

My ultimate chicken food creation was simple. Extremely diverse food and plants waste, left in bucket cycles for flies to hit with larvae and grubs to form. I waited weeks, until the whole bucket would be consumed and large grubs would be crawling over the other. This was my chicken food, and it was free. Chicken egg production went up 3x and I never saw my chickens so happy.

In hindsight is the love element vibration, or whatever.

The meat of free-range happy chicken is much tougher and has much more flavor. It forced creativity and longer cooking times in the kitchen. We used papaya leaves once to help break down the meat overnight.

I gave my chickens children, peace and great life and full life, and I thanked them and the great spirit when I would harvest the chicken for food. We are each servant to the cycle of life on this biological plane whether or not we embrace that fact.

If I harvested a chicken that was in old age, I would take her away from the rest, say a prayer and a thanks, and it would hurt my heart a little. I however learned that the blood spilled in this thankful manner, seemed to work as the most potent fertilizer ever experienced by my lime tree. Within weeks the tree was covered in limes. I would not know this without self-experimentation. But this is described in Steiner's Biodynamic Agriculture lectures.

In hindsight I feel this result was ultimately a product of the love element. We did good with these chickens and I have tried the big company blood and it does not compare.

Eating our chicken versus the big company chicken are two completely different experiences and feelings and muscle supports.

This last year we updated our testing to take a hard at look at Dr. Steven Grundy's seed lectin discovery science.

In short, he has found lectins that protect seeds and argue that we should not be eating beans and nuts - seeds. Right away, we agreed that all seeds should be planted, and we also thought quickly after hearing of this, that bean plants usually have very good for us, edible leaves.

He said however if cooking in a pressure cooker, the lectins are destroyed. This is a good example of food state change. If we can plant the seed, we can avoid experiencing lectin lag.

Ultimately this result can be considered a product of the love element and there must be a dynamic to wanting and intention to help the plant reproduce. It could even produce a bean that is set for us to be the protector rather than the lectin? This is the level III plane of testing.

By the way all signs point to- this experimentation ends in more evolution and more advancement both physically and spiritually!

I choose to love the things I should hate. I choose to appreciate them, they have certainly sacrificed their souls to be the problems that good men can galvanize themselves with. They are the rocks that sharpen our blade, and I may call them names, and call them what they are but I love these problems and evils because they are what we use in the end to become strong. It is is beautiful in fact that we all get to decide what will be and I do from the bottom of my heart thank them for choosing the wrong, and testing my faith and goodness regularly. I love them and I love that I decided differently, and find myself in a different realm completely. I no longer feel sorry for those, who choose the wrong, I am hoping to see my little one choose the right, but through the decision to love without judgment but with understanding of the entire process I no longer have any hate in my heart, and to a degree I loose an edge that helps to cut through the toxic world. Love is King. I say this to my training guys as Character is King. It is. I choose love, I choose the road of intelligence and diplomacy, and I try to watch out for small-minded control-freaks as much as I can. I try not to build my castles with sand, but I love everything and everyone I am extremely grateful to be here, and to be part of this Great (God's) plan.

Physical Food States

Food states, of ripeness, of rottenness, of dryness, heated, nonheated, smoked, blasted, mashed, liquefied, cruciferous, fresh, hard, soft, chunks, powders, and fibrous have their places in a wellbalanced ND diet.

Food is a multifaceted system made up of several substances such water, fats, proteins, carbs, minerals, and vitamins. The organization of its parts, the mobility of its particles, and how it reacts to outside pressures can all be used to characterize the physical state of food and they are part of nutritional diversifist diet plan.

Solid state food are Vegetables, fruits, meats, and cheeses. Temperature, humidity, and particle size are a few examples of the variables that have an impact on the physical properties of solids.

Liquid state food are soups, milk, juices, and water. Viscosity, surface tension, and density are some examples of variables that affect the physical characteristics of liquids. Xxxvixxxvii

Gas state food are whipping cream, froth, and carbonated beverages are examples of gas foods. Gases' physical characteristics are affected by variables like pressure and temperature. Foods that are colloidal are in the middle between solids and liquids. Larger than molecules but smaller than visible particles, they are scattered particles. Foods like mayonnaise, cream, and cheese sauce are examples of colloidal foods. Particle size, surface charge, and viscosity are a few examples of the variables that affect the physical characteristics of colloids.xxxviii

Learning to feel in the gut and make sure there is proper construction of different food states to enable good movement, good brooming of the stomach and digestive line, healthy stimulation and feeding of the microbiome and promoting of a high spectrum of assimilated nutrition for the user, is a science in itself.

"Timing is everything," they say in so many fields of work and of play. Ripe applies to a time in the life of a fruit or plant, that usually means when it is at its most sweet or most edible state.

Different food colors, such as black, yellow, and green, impart pretty interesting qualities to them. For example, each color is linked to a different flavor and nutritional value.

I can feel in my body the difference between a green, yellow, and black plantain from hands, to mouth to stomach. Black plantains give me sweeter taste, a more alkaline, less acid form in my system, and I feel both calmed and energized by them. Green plantains rip up my mouth are hard and too hard to eat at all.

Here in Panama a traditional food is the 'patacone', which is a double pan fried in oil (not olive oil usually), smashed green plantain that can cause extreme constipation, and is locally reputed and joked about to be passed through the system 'next Thursday.' This way is admittedly edible and good! To simply use coconut oil improves taste and nutritional properties immensely from those fried in the black death that is vegetable or sunflower seed oil.

We must consider that the deep or double frying process is something to go extremely light with, for very special occasions almost never should this technique be employed.

Patacones are fried twice and they are a staple to Panamanian diet. Interestingly most everything traditional here today is fried, outside of beans and rice.

Panama has some of the worse general health numbers in Latin America.

The yellow state is of the plaintain or banana is a combination, a mid state of these two states, but it is sweet and quickly digested. Yellow with some black spots is most sweet and 'ripe,' before getting more black and turning to an even sweeter cream state.

Waiting until the plantain is completely black with even some mold spots on the outside, renders it a great sweet taste, optimal digestibility, and it also dehydrates, better than a fruit role up and keeps that way for a year or more. Black with a little mold on them is the best state for dehydration.

Following this state comes a state in which I myself would obviously not longer touch the material, and likely it will be ridden with other living creatures in or out of a nice storage by that time, and that is the completely rotten state. This state sends multiple signals in multiple forms out for other creatures to come in. It is time for the decomposition of the dead to begin returning it back into a food for other living things.

Although for other certain fruits this more decomposed state is desired. Like the Sir Plantain, Sir Breadfruit and Sir Jackfruit for example become taste sauces all on their own at this stage. Borojo. BidiBa. So green (more vegetable-like vitamin composition)

Leaves and fresh greens are always best picked right from the stem and consumed quickly.

Most red stuff is also best fresh as possible, but likely can sit in a fine, slow changing state for little bit.

Yellow and orange foods that start green, usually have these modes of ripeness, the best being at the softest state just before rot, or fermentation.

Certainly a few spots of heavy decomposition of the material is indication that the fruit is ready for optimal taste and digestion on a natural fruit, and at times, maybe half of something is to be tossed back to the compost.

The truth is we must be weary of the pretty perfect plasticity stuff from the grocer, real food comes with holes, bad parts and some rough edges. This is the real fresh stuff. This is where the experience, the flavor, the soul is when it comes to natural selections I myself don't mind scars. Anything to "Well balanced" is likely the closest to perfect we can ask for in this life.

Food states are important modes of throttling and cleaning the digestive track. The five times protein plant fiber ratio rule, is largely effective for performance because of the way it runs everything out of system exposing new surface for gut garden growth

Just as you may suspect this is exactly the food state pattern we are going for. Two altitudes two sets of steady produce we can do our selves, and one high staple diversity we can refine and work on over time.

Living in nature for a while removes the need to understand certain science, and fractions of plant values such as words like chlorophyll. None of those words are actually in nature but the same things are still communicated there, even more clearly.

Just to have a nameless direct relationship with the plants, is functionally the better relation. We must be very careful with titles and names, they are a means to whereas we remain afraid of actual relation, stuck in the comforts of thinking we know better for the title — as obviously off as that sounds it is the current cultural modality.

The fresh ripe state is clearly the biologically intended state of foods preferred in the interest of natural uncooked nutrition, and nitrification by most primates and mammals.

The fresh state means unprocessed, from organic nature, grown among a diversity of thousands of other things in biological dependency known as the circle of life.

Ideally the fresh state is eaten within a few seconds of harvesting or natural fall so that nitrogen, chlorophyll and other essences needed for a happy healthy existence, are still at high level for your Nutritional Diversity intake.

Even so small parasites can enter fruit in the trees, although that potential goes up significantly for fruits on the ground for a time.

One thing important and known by the Native American's was parasitic control. Moccasins for feet, and anti-parasitic foods on the regular, plus a good cleaning of leaves and flesh of potential larvae and harmful bacteria. Skin creams and colors were used to fight ringworm prevent mosquito bite and ward off other parasite and pestilence.

Likely on a very robust Nutritional Diversity diet, the sort of things we see on modern people living with no information (after it was destroyed by Spanish conquest) in more rural settings today is many times a product of that lack of information and certain domestication and toxification of the people over generations.

A culture strongly in opposition to daily alcohol consumption does exist in New Mexico or Philadelphia but marijuana was most popular among the poor, and the ingenuousness alcoholism is the most destructive force in each community besides casinos.

Interestingly the first things you will see on signs is about liquor stores and casinos as one enters any reservation, after tax-less tobacco.

The United States Navy and in the Republic of Panama, are cultures where most everyone drinks.

New Mexico gang culture and Rastafarian culture are the two main cultures I have found that have a cultural interest in one another's soberness.

This fresh picked mandate can instantly effect depression, happiness, focus, flexibility and a range of disorders and ailments positively. This is how "fruitarianism" recruits its extremists.

Interestingly several diets including the traditional Panamanian diets include very little if at all fresh vegetables and fruits. Never when in a grocer or restaurant will you get a freshly harvested item.

But in the small encampment on the farm or homestead itself you will.

This COVID-19 that we experience today is very much something that could be due to our encroachment on nature and living outside the natural specifications. But in this case that not what happened. The narcissistic construct known as U.S. Health Care, is now more less at the ripe state of weaponized. This happens in small narcissistic constructions known as Parental Alienation, which is fueled by the U.S. "Social Health Services" agencies also.

I know it may be egocentrically difficult but we can look to most any other mammal for examples of optimal immune system protocols here.

After years in practice I have now narrowed a 5-day programs regimen whereas I can show someone this 'extreme' personal performance effect to another person, who can start to realize the benefits in just five days.

In Nutritional Diversity studies here in the forests and jungles, mountains and beaches of the tropics we have eaten thousands of different leaves and plants out in the jungle. We spend much more time with each plant than likely needed because it is important, and nature teaches one lesson many need today.

Humility, and observation that this is not a game are strong messages for such a tranquil state. Appreciation and almost instantaneous healing, quickly become normalcy and easily creates a risky attitude at times- a product of the polar positive mindset that comes from taking nature in.

Nature if connected correctly will put you on your knees and decide to take you or save you far beyond your imagination that today's world has allowed you to cultivate, can conceive. Another benefit of this high diversity eating is that the imagination starts to cross this boundary and leave it far behind, imagination too is helped by a highly diverse nutrient spread. The spread itself came become strategic, and interestingly to me; something you can bet on. It really is an over-the top sensation for those who dive in and many times there is chapter of life that follows, that is a bit carried away.

Bio-dynamic farming, paganism and many other "weird" ways start to make perfect sense and mind-blowing also is how this access is right there for everyone however no one plugs in.

I incorporated wild foods. I made the jump one specie at a time. I have so much ahead of me in this journey into natures vast dynamic depth of resources it almost seems that it all could consume me and it very well maybe that within the greater schematic of things we are patiently waited for to reverse our overall body's trajectory of selfish pig narcissist destroyers to land enhancers and transformers.

We took the time to do it right, and educate ourselves about how to approach this safely. Allergy testing, field edibility testing procedures of a safe and scientific protocol. We have made ourselves

tremendously sick at times, and we have risked the worst a few times too many, but we are today, all tremendously healthier than we have ever been.

The fact that there are no wise-men today to teach us the human foods in a more advanced way is curious. We should have extensive knowledge of this over all other things no?

What we do have is slave story after slave story to hear about and these stories are what I believe to be the underlying reason for narrow diet and information/trend culture intending to produce a weak man. Something wants to keep us in the stable, keep us docile, controlled, ear tagged and purposeful to whatever that control-freak is.

Body Count's song Manslaughter, and Pop Bubble and Get shot, and Sick of it All's Death to Tyrants Album, and Suicidal Tendencies song Pepsi, as well as most youth trending music from mid-80's till now is reflective of a negative, dying, killing, throwing it all away, weakness in society that is rooted in institutional-level deception and false information or an intentional lack of information.

We have a narrow spectrum of education. Nature is no part of that accept separated item dissection. This knowledge is for the chemical/pharmaceutical and machine/manufacturing industries.

I don't want too many college degrees on my team. They are too

Prone to Hurting and Dumb stuff (PHD in biology), and too many of them have zero ability in the field. It's a highly convoluted knowledge base that comes from academia. They are all in the

'direction of dissection anyways,' that's not what we are doing. No discredit to this direction in science that has surely realized mountains of useful knowledge.

This Nutritional diversity way of eating is original to our time, but was surely the evolution to spear and fire using diet that has somehow been lost for ages. I think so know, we have an idea that the King's feast was always quite diverse. We know from the food tour (chapter of this book) that Queen Victoria paid gross amounts of money for exotic foods.

There was certainly a time of balance when we were not overdomesticated and without modern agriculture which would have circumstantially forced us to have more knowledge and eat more diversely. During this time the benefits of large spectrum diversity would have become clear, and several historic athletic cultures have been rumored in legend to highly outperform any of today's cultures.

The recognizance that even in the grocery store, all items are best left on their shelves is astounding and heavy to our society now.

The Incan empire had the "Chasquis" who ran up to 240 km, and possibly much more than this, a day while pioneering an advanced communications relay system delivering messages from Southern Chile to Northern Peru in the course of a week some believe was tide and star information. The Aztecs had the "Titlantil" who were trained from childhood until they could run over 100 miles in a day, and from Canada to the Carolinas the Iroquois trail network featured runners like "Sharp Shins," a native who wowed observers by covering 90 miles in a day.

Ultra-Walking was a thing of the 1700's in Western culture. In 1928 the Great sports promoter named Charles C. "Cash & Carry" Pyle envisioned a groundbreaking footrace across America, and organized the "Bunion Derby" which had nearly 300 participants attempting to run 3455 miles for a $25,000 first place prize.

According to the Real Endurance 2018 Ultra Marathon Summary there are over 2000 races today that are considered Ultra's mostly 50 to 250 miles (example the MOAB 240) but there are some for more and one for 1000 miles, the "Western States Endurance Run.

Chlorophyll is believed to be by many, the divine exchange between plant and animal. This essence alone could be the guide of positive mood and in turn, in more positive relations with nature that unlock more benefits. There is a game in nature where certain mental states are affected by certain food states, and through these states certain doors open for certain new ideas and influences.

Officially I recommend at this time, Nutritional Diversifists eat 10 to 30% of things in a fresh state just before eating them in a cooked state.

From the moment a food is harvested, and no longer biologically active in its living state it starts to lose important nutritional value. It starts to receive a different nutritional value, and certain changed values. When heated it goes through more of this. It can be very helpful to the throttling of performance, recovery and managing the lag of digestion to understand a few concepts concerning cooked foods.

Fresh, ripe fruits also can take on great new tastes, and combined with spices other ingredients can take on brand new elements in the pan or other cookware.

Cooked is the primary state of food consumed in today's human culture. Cooking is good. Fresh can also be good. When fresh food needs to be cooked in order to be consumed you will know from previous teachings passed down or through onsite inspection. That is, it. There is no tech that will tell what needs cooking and what doesn't.

The popularity of other softer packaged foods we have conditioned ourselves weaker mouths and stomachs and the adjustment back to raw meats and raw vegetables could be jolting. However difficult at first this pursuit is among the healthiest of pursuits.

Wild game in a bio-diverse nature, according to legend anyway, can be eaten raw, bloody and has been by humans for thousands of years. Sushi today is a popular raw food, concoction famous for being a healthy food.

Heated food, one would think, loses life in essence and depending on how long it is heated it goes more and more towards a simple carbon state. Heating and cooking food are not bad, for humans, interestingly we benefit greatly from cooking things and it is arguable how much of that has to do with our evolution in good ways and in bad. None the less, today for humans heating breaks down toxins, heating is how we can clean up water, and soften food for our delicate jaws. It would appear that just like for the leaf cutter ant, humans are into a bit of preparation and changing the food state before consumption.

Certain soups and heated preparations can be effective, also for healing.

The gradual balance of fresh versus cooked, can fluctuate and fluctuate intelligently as the Nutritional Diversifist learn themselves more and remembering that more cooked food can be assimilated; reform their   rest-play-breath-meditate-workout-create-

stretcheatfresh-eatcooked-*othergutmycology-microbiome*
algorithms.

Chlorophyll, most important substance highest in green leaves, and even higher in green grasses, helps humans with mood, depression and fitness performance. It is a vital ingredient to human and primate life, performance and happiness. Chlorophyll is not present or use-able from cooked states. This is big discussion today also in anti-aging interests. So essentially, when feeling down, you can simply up the fresh uncooked green foods intake and level out with gains of new perspective and good mood, which is always a better place to decide for your life from.

Popular cooked foods are often root foods. These foods have great history of strength in humans, they are the foundations of their respective plants, most of which produce very healthy edible green tops. There are largely thought of having to be cooked by the modern man, and they do change into great flavorful cooked states. Many of them do have to be cooked to be edible at all. They are said by some to be high on the alkaline binding, and I feel them feeding my muscles on heavy performance days.

Cooking bones for long periods of times some recommends say 15 hours, is said to release use-able bone marrow, and through experimentation with this, I have found myself that it helps build a stronger joint, and keeps bones dense enough lots of heavy lifting. Remember it is heavy lifting that will program nutrients to be used for heavy lifting.

There surely could be harmful out comes to cooking, we know that certain things cooked together sometimes produces an awkward, unexpected result. We also know that certain things cooked together can digest easier together and athlete can use this to take some digestive work out for his system, and apply that energy to training. Diet science today as unreliable as it has pointed out certain understandings of changes in food that don't seem so cool when cooking it.

Acrylamide is a chemical that can be used in the manufacturing of paper and plastic, and is often found in products like caulk and food packaging. Studies on animals have demonstrated that exposure to acrylamide can result in cancers in a number of organs, including the thyroid, mammary gland, and adrenal gland.xxix

Alarmingly, acrylamide is also found in certain foods that have been prepared at a very high temperature — i.e. food that was fried, grilled or broiled. It's found more in starchy products like bread and potatoes. How come? An amino acid called asparagine found in these foods forms acrylamide when heated at a very high temperature.

The American Food and Drug Administration (FDA) has not established any limitations for the amount of acrylamide that may be included in food products, but it is aware of the possible health hazards and urges people to adopt healthy eating practices to lower their exposure to acrylamide.xl

Cooked foods are soft, you need to be sure that you mix in hard foods, 5x plant fiber ratio for the cooked foods is a good rule of thumb also. If your trying to cook more to eat more, and to save the energy for digestion but get the fiber, and the jaw strength, go more strong fiber foods, like broccoli, asparagus, red torch ginger flower, avocado leaf, piffa or peggi baji palm nut.

Another concern is the HCAs (heterocyclic amines) that form on chicken and meat when grilled over a high flame. HCAs have also been linked to cancer in animals, though research in humans is still limited. Funny thing is there is also a school of thought that heterocyclic amines are very helpful to athletes.

Interestingly and not often considered or thought of is soaking, which interestingly brings chick peas and root foods alike into soft states, as if cooked, but never were. The soaked state is simply the opposite of the dried state where the food is introduced to more water. This is used often with beans such as garbanzos to soften them. There is an essence from plants that can come from soaking especially when in the sun. The water is nutritious and the material could be more ready for cooking, steaming, etc.

My good friend Dr. Daniels is cooking up cow brains into fudge pops two ounces a day with a carbohydrate snack. She says her brain performance has never been better.

Drying foods has been practiced for ages, and certain valuable changes take place in food that is dried. Dried foods are like super vitamins, highly condensed nutrition. Eating dried state foods, means drinking twice the water to digest them.

I myself am a huge fan of this state, you can front load a portion of your food supply, get greater tasting stuff much of the time, and solar methods of dehydration are easy for me, on my farm which has lots of sun regularly.

Food dehydration is easy and there are many ways of dehydrating food. Dehydrated foods can be stored for long amounts of time without going bad or changing in form too much at all.

Powdered states follow dried states, and have been formed by humans for thousands of years. It's a great way to store different types of nutrition. Powders are also quickly and easily assimilated or passed through the system.

When using powders in a drink, living fresh vegetable or fruit should be eaten at the same time, so that the powder can bind with the living plant matter and digest easier. Digestive helpful foods should be considered such as papaya or avocado.

For now Nutritional Diversity science excludes extracts outside of oil extracts.

Hydrogenated vegetable oil, should be labeled "Black Death." This is the cheapest stuff used by nearly every restaurant and household today. It's terrible stuff that really binds to the lining of the digestive track and does not want to come off. The process of hydrogenating oils is not natural, and therefore dangerous. Most will agree that the trans-fat product of this process said to give the product more shelf life is unhealthy, but still don't realize that with an oil made this strong, the residue stays in the system. Keeping things on a steady movement towards exit is keystone to human health, any hold ups and stay behinds outside of our natural microbiome in the digestive track can lead to all sorts of problems.

Here in Panama, finding good oil is going to the newer richer stores, you won't find it in the neighborhood and at all smaller markets.

I recommend a table spoon a day of coconut oil to everyone, six weeks on, six weeks off to repair any serious gut scratching, and also to cut bad grease in the gut from fried foods.

We get into oils again in the food tour.

Hard states are good, they sweep out the bowls and promote regularity and to keep teeth and gums strong and healthy. For every gram of soft food should really be 5 grams of hard stuff. This is a guarantee for no soft food build on the walls of the digestion or get stuck anywhere on their journey to supply different nutrients to different parts of the body.

"All biology grows against resistance." IF its too strong a resistance biology will grow around it. This number one core value to Nutritional Diversity doctrine is important here, we want to build strong stomachs, strong digestive engines and we can train our stomachs just like we can train the rest of ourselves. Our stomachs and dental health had been documented in various ways in various times throughout history as being much more useful, less sensitive and healthy. Condensed pharmaceutical pills and injections have had a lot to do with this and these too should be left in their boxes on the shelves of their stores. Eating harder foods, and spicy foods are some ways to improve dental health, and form a stronger, more robust digestive engine. Interestingly an herbal rule of thumb is that sour, bitter foods often are the most medicinal.

Tree leaves cooked with high fiber ground shrubs, even some Yuca cassava leaves a few berries and fruits, some really crunchy shoots, and some fresh katuk, garlic vine leaf, cranberry hibiscus with the Mexican

yellow flowered energy plant, with a lemon juice, elder flower dressing appetizer is an example of one of my favorite quick to make farm plates. Notice everything cooked and a few fresh items have harder foods qualities?

Imaginatively, the hunter-gatherer's gatherings would likely have been shoots, nuts, fruits, softer shrubs as much smaller amounts, compared to tree leaves, mushrooms and small herbs in meadow clearings. What I am identifying here in other words is that tree leaves, such as that make up the howler monkeys' complete diet and some of the stronger leaves such as dandelions or common hibiscus are almost the perfect hard food in our diets. Some of this should certainly be cooked at first, for those starting out, but moving to the point where the fresh leaf burrito contains a few tree leaves is a good direction.

The Core Principles

The Nutritional Diversity considers the modifications that must be made due to the modern diet culture. The following are the main tenets of the nutritional diversity food diet:

1.   All biology grows around or against resistance. This is the primary principle to keep in mind at all times concerning your cultivation, training and nutrition. To outperform normal nature simply take the path of most resistance and become stronger.

2.   Everything received is nutrition. Nutrition is all things practiced and received by the body, the mind and the spirit. It is then processed by the body and the soul into who you are, physically, emotionally, and spiritually. Information is brain-food and it is important. Half of our physical nutrition is food and water. The other half is exercise and productive physical output. They are equally vital for optimal health and performance. The choice to seek the genuine, the most true, and most quality is the most important choice.

3. Intense exercise is mandatory, it is the programming function used to tell the body what to do with nutrients it has consumed. Food and exercise, go hand in hand for the health and this is really recognized when one really steps it up in the ND diet.

4. Rhythm and cycles are a vital art. To be an optimal human, you must sync yourself with the rhythms and cycles of the nature in which you come from and depend on. The worst thing, to happen to humans, is the deception that they are smarter and know better, and can disconnect from nature and be better.

5.   The more species the better, a starting minimum of 30 for the weaker older stomach, and 60 for the younger healthy stomach. Incorporation of kombuchas, food states and ferments can be used when digestion is slow. The plant diversity should be between 30-60 species for beginners and after 12-week time, more of a diversity of species can be ingested. Our team has leveled off mostly at 90 to 120 in experimentation thus far, going as far rarely as 200. Unbelievable

athletic and farm work performance, brain performance has been recorded every time, for every case. We have yet to find stomach and digestive problems as a result of even wild food eating.

6.   The vegetable food group should make up the volume of 5x the amount of protein called for in the diet plan. We focus on protein first, high protein leaf species. There are several ways to help digestion outlined in the Complete Nutritional Diversity Diet text.

7.   Keep your people circle small, and require

absolute honesty from everyone in it. Today one of the biggest threats to human health is social, emotional and spiritual disease. Psychologists refer to these modern societal sicknesses as pathogens just the same as military Chemical, Biological & Radiological warfare defense specialists refer to biological weaponry.

The dose decides remedy or poison. There is a point of overload and overkill. Paracelsus theorized that everything was both toxin and remedy and that the dose is what decided which. Any diversity in excess of 100 species should be stacked with digestive aids like avocado, and kombucha. African tribes learned that any group of people in excess of 180 people should break in half and go a certain distance away or to a new river, which could have saved much of the world's problems and populations should we have kept through today. Imagine if U.S. Populations did this. Extremism should be noticed and avoided. Coffee, alcohol and hot liquid, extracts should make up, combined, less than 2% or nothing at all of diet. Overkilling, and overloading should be avoided.

8.   Sodium and salt minerals should be in the range of 3 to 10 grams per day, oils should be in the range of 1 liter per week
depending on size and output. This one place we are highly under maintained. We need this oil, we need this salination. Most people

today ingest fluoridated table salts in quantities of one gram or less
per day.

CHARACTER. We should be grateful for food and
water.
Dynamics at its best. The best of nutritional dynamics. before the
harvest, during the preparation, and afterward. The water and the
plant flesh that holds the water both have a dynamic quality that
responds to an attitude of thankfulness. Plants (references above)
telepathically preserve honesty and integrity, therefore keep in mind
that your moral character comes first in everything. "Character is
King" with me. I look at character first when I look at people. I get
sick of people, and go hang out with my plants because they never
lie.
Fresh, raw food should constitute 10-30 percent of diet and the rest
of the food consumed should be cooked. A diet of leaf and tuber, no
seeds (nuts or beans), in the diversity described above is best. I do
eat meat, and lots of different kinds and parts of the animal, it is a
mission to get parts like the brain, and turns out the best brain-food
is well worth it. The fresh portion here if at all
possible should come directly from the plant to your plate
and consumed within a five minute time period. This is "living food
or electric food."
Hydrational Diversity should be a totally dedicated process. I
have so much water treatment that I do. Leaving water out 24 hours
with good insect covering, in a glass container is a good, and
costeffective treatment. I use carbon-activated charcoal
filters, and distilled water also.
Share what you can spare and always share what is fair. GIVE
PEOPLE WHAT THEY DESERVE. If this varies give more not
less. Dynamics again, let's see what you can do. Decide what you
don't need, and then privately give it to someone who does need it.
A selfless act today is of the most noble, and spiritually healthy

practice one can engage. Those who give the most in life receive the most in life, that they can keep the most in life. Share with others this helpful information.

"It is the mark of a great fighter when he has character plus skill. Because a fighter with character and skill will often rise and beat a better fighter because of this. Character is that quality upon which you can depend under pressure and other conditions. Character makes the fighter predictable. Character helps him win." – Cus

D'Amato

Recently in a two and a half month stay in Panama City, following a month in Boquette, and expensive ex-pat mountain town that claims to have the best coffee in the world, I re-learned the Anglo-Saxon dominated city culture. I also visited the wealthy "Spanish Social Club," where those who also have the Spanish passport (there are many who have the Panama and the Spanish passport -the Spanish never gave up their strong hold and remain some of the most luxurious property owners in the country), sat in luxury dining hall, like in a fancy hotel, fit to seat a few hundred people with an Olympic pool just out of the window, presenting a mighty attitude of being the Elite echelon.

In their positive credit this would be a very capable group and it seemed each one owned several pieces of real estate. Collectively this very civilized and mannered community is no doubt likely one of the most powerful houses in the Country. The most powerful house however in the big city is the Jewish community who also has a very fancy Social Club and one I would not be permitted to visit I am told.

The parking lots of these two places however give a reflection of the group, as also the richest car collections in the 'pais (Spanish name for country).'

To complete the full story on some of the basic components of the classes here; the "Nugle" tribe are always the grunt work horse of the slave class both in the city, and on the farms, the darker the skin, the lower in class naturally attributed, this is of course changeable by family wealth.

The lighter skinned Latino is usually the preferred class for politics and the

"ballroom" level of this society. Black populations stay relatively to the Caribbean side and the areas where they were imported, such as Colon, Almirante, and the Northern Caribbean Islands here in Panama.

Very interesting tribe here known as the "Kuna, or Kuna-Yala," pronounced "Gun-Yala" with incredibly interesting, highly preserved culture, vibrant dress and well-organized ranks, are said to be the only un-conquered tribe in Central America. A success attributed to being once nomadic, they did a brilliant job of claiming for their own, a sum of the most beautiful islands in the world, and a top five tourist destination here; the San Blas Islands. There tapestries are most distinctive and recognized style of "Panama art."

The albino gene is very popular in the Kuna and those who have it are seen as blessed and spiritual powerful.

I often looked to the sky and thanked God for my poverty in youth. I don't like a proud person and so I would not want to be one. I realized how weakened a strong man can become by city sickness.

Furthermore how brainwashed we were by a negative street culture — which took time, because of most of my life I saw Albuquerque people as a smarter and tougher version of most of the other people I met nationally and internationally.

Of-course my own weakening of late was a compilation of more so other factors granted from an incredible force of negativity no descent person would wish on someone, or severely damage a child to evoke (parental alienation). This in my case and in and in many; It's basically one of these Satanic rituals we hear about celebrities performing to get rich, but in this case the Government facilitates and incentivize these kidnappings and brainwashing of kids to gain a monetary income.

You have to lie, in every direction and pile skeletons and secrets in the closet to win, but if you are willing to trespass against your own child this way and use them as the missile that destroys an ex, well you will make a minimum 20k a year doing so.

The truth in this matter is that every "Yancy" that follows this doctrine of health, soldiering for God, and supporting our ecology, should come up with a good mark and punishment for any piece of shit doing this to a kid, or supporting it being done to a kid. Although now my "good document" promotes violence. I too am working on myself, and the day is near when I can thank such lowly lives for being the fire that I galvanized my edge with. I can't wait for the maintenance mode I must admit, where galvanization is no longer the word. But the real truth is I must thank these scum of people for sacrificing their own souls to be the problems that others find solutions to, and overcome

Now, I quote to you a recent Mark Twain Award recipient, Dave Chappell's quote of the evening, a special phrase from his mother (he had a good one, most do), " Sometimes you have to be a Lion, to be the Lamb you really are." I am so grateful I grew up tough, I am so grateful to be strong, and I am so blessed by my persecutions, that I am today a Lion no one wants any quarrel with a sort of King of the

Jungle, certainly in a small population. I never thought I would be saying that or in this situation. I will say that what I am most proud of is inside I am truly a Lamb. I am truly dedicated to God, goodness, good people, good food, and good actions. Today, I love being the guy strong enough to pull other tough guys through more than any other thing except my honesty, my good taste in music (because I get to listen to good...) and my babies; my plants.

The day before the ugliest of voodoo rituals commenced (parental alienation) I was a pretty tough guy most everyone respected, to the point of following, even for other really tough guys older than I, several times over. I was what they call a solid cat. I lack the terminology to really explain this, and I don't like a braggy person so I don't want to be that, but I do want to give the context in this story.

When CONTACT DENIAL began, and my child was kidnapped

and the Voodoo commenced, in one blink; I wanted to kill everyone, could not sleep, could not eat, I could not say nothing but read and I went to the hills. Had I been in the States I would have suffered the fate of ten million other fathers, in a cell. I likely would have killed every person involved with the kidnapping and brainwashing of my Princess who I no longer know, have not seen in 8 years and have only a general idea where she is. As I type this

now my hands shake, the red comes back, the knot in my back the size of a water melon returns, and the Nutritional Diversity diet is the real medicine that can keep me straight. [this section was not updated since last version, and the more to this story in the final chapter]

This time, after years in the hills and various farms obsessed with plants, the honest love of nature that saved me, still a bit dazed and confused; I was swayed by the ultra-rich, when I thought I landed a few times an actual genuine rich person. Out of three hopefuls, I did find one. The other two where hopefuls until it was discovered they were liars, otherwise known as bullshitters, full of false promises offered only if what they want is given, and even then, they would likely not deliver any kind of fair trade. These people live in the world where they walk across a thousand backs every minute. They have the best real estate, the best machines, and they realize this in deeper layers than their immediate first consciousness. This walk of backs was seemingly learned like they learned to walk on the earth, you   never think about "moving your legs," or give a thought command, you just move them.

Many of us must fight with our own nature to become our best selves.

A true person who is in search of truth and true meaning in his life, who is able to obtain STRENGTH, and who has ONLY the intention to be honest and fair with others will be in constant disappointment with other men around him in this life. However a TRUE man in this nature will continue in this nature, even when he knows it won't be reciprocated by his surroundings. - yours truly

Whoever [has] will be given more, and they will have an abundance. Whoever [does not have], even what they have will be taken from them. Mathew 13:12

What is it that you must have?

A Nutritional Diversifist's Basic Guide to Knowing Plants & Other Nutritional Elements?;   - or may I offer the real answer?

GRATITUDE

Author, artist and craftsman, Jesse Cornplanter (September 16, 1889 - 1957) commented on the Iroquois philosophy of Muskrat Root also Known as Water Hemlock,

"The old people say that Muskrat Root is like any other herbal medicine you want. When you want it, it stands up where it grows calling to you. That is why it is easy to find a medicine you seek."

In this case, interestingly it is those who want to die that is being referred to here, as this plant is highly toxic and just little bits will kill. It is recognized by the tribe as a plant with this aim only, and for this particularly species they may argue with the idea that all things are both healing and toxic, and that this difference is keyed by the dose. This teaching, that comes from many of life's experiences, contains the message that intention is very important.

Really knowing plants, and food items is to clear your stomach on a one day fast. Go ahead and clear the mind while you are at it. Stand with the plant, talk to the plant, treat the plant(s) as if it is a member of your family. Bring it water, play music for it, talk with it, and protect it from the bad guys. This plant likes you so much it will let you pee on it, do that urea is a main ingredient in commercial and home fertilizers and many medications for us, nitrogen. A breathing mantra practice for yourself there in front of it wouldn't hurt. Remember this biology in front of you in your bio-dependence, it's like you breathing with it. I know this all sounds a little hippy dippy but stay with me, it's pretty scientific actually. The love and appreciation of plants can be earned, and if so the plant will communicate a new level of truths to a body able to receive them.

The Nutritional Diversity diet concept is focused mostly on edible plants largely, although arguably, all plants are edible considering a proper dose is known for it. On your clear stomach, now having spent time clearing that stomach with the plant, or Nutritional Diversity of plants; eat one plant by itself at a time over the next course of days so that your body and mind can meet each plant in your

Nutritional Diversity individually and so your body has a chance to get to know, recognize and appreciate that plant on a one on one basis.

Keep in the back of your mind throughout this getting to know your ND process that certain plants and food items have both helping and inhibiting elements to them. As Nutritional Diversifists we are looking to come to know what plants work well together and what

plants cancel each other's essences out of play. As a Nutritional

Diversity community, we cannot at this time answer the question, "Do they consume well as a group if they grow well together? In the case of the most functional and well covered attack team of specie, turmeric root and black pepper, for this to be true there would need to be a third and maybe even more plants to the equation being that, the black pepper vine, would rather grow on another structure type than the small hedge green leaf of the turmeric root, or even its cousin ginger.

Through this very practice most users begin to develop an appreciation with nature in general and loose the hard heart it takes to throw seeds in garbage bags while preparing their food. They may find themselves picking up trash when they see it in nature, they may have done this before but now it is with a new attitude. To see proposals to cut down thousands of trees for whatever purpose may come up on the job, and the once well acclaimed pro now has emotional problems making the big new road. He may latter on become one of the "funny," or "crazy men" we see running around picking leaves and having long beards, no longer at all invested in their outer appearance.

Prepare yourself. To get to know nature, in a deep personal way, according to my suggestions, is an extreme thing. Any of us familiar with Sean Penn's movie "Into the Wild," based on the book, and story of Christopher McCandless early 1990's adventures into the wild eventually dying on his last a deepest trip from starvation and toxic plant consumption of a look-a-like to something in one of his books.

If he had used a different method of plant identification and better planning, he could have met different ends. Also, if he had

been consuming a full range Nutritional Diversity Diet, he likely would have been just fine consuming the toxic plant. xli

To really know a plant, is to grow a plant, so get out there and do that.

Without the 25 million square miles of leaf, humans and livestock don't eat and don't breathe. If used correctly

it is plant essences at the base of all healing and providing for every need of the human. All life is brought "through the sweetness of photosynthesis," as so eloquently put by Peter Tompkins and Christopher Bird, in the book "The Secret Life of Plants."

Agriculture for most, and for most of time determined, the wealth of the nation or state. Uphof did a six hundred and some page "Dictionary of Economic Plants," that has remained a good reference on the subject of plant economics.

Carl von Linne, the grandfather of modern botany declared that plants only differentiate from other species in movement, or lack of. Charles Darwin smacked that down when he proved each tendril could move independently, later siting the observation that only when it is of great advantage to them, they will display the movement which is so slow that most will not notice.xlii

Cleve Backster a 1966 expert lie-detector examiner, and teacher to the world of polygraph examiners around the U.S., and the world, one day in sheer curiosity hooked the machine up, to small palm in the office chosen by his secretary, happening to be a very sacred, but popular house plant known as the Dracaena. The plant secrets a sap known to the homeopathic world as "dragon's blood," and many homeopaths claim it is a miracle. The red sap with medicinal properties goes for about eight dollars for half an ounce worth. Long story short, Backster discovered that the plant knew when he was a threat to it, and knew when he was faking threat to it. Under real intention of damaging the plant just before actually doing it, he was able to create electronic surges in his machine concluding the plant knew he was going to attack it and released a response. This is now a term in botany called the "Backster Effect" and it refers to the

recognition that plants have a very perceptive intelligence, and the likely communicate with these very electric pulses to other plants.

2013 research from the University of California, Davis showed that couples in love did not only skip a beat when seeing each other, but their hearts and respiration cycles would also synchronize with one another.

Lew Childre, Jr., did some interesting research like this which he called 'tapping into coherence,' which he described as a sort of personal fluency or attention to being calm and happy at all costs, an inner peace of mind in which people are able to synchronize themselves and their heart rhythms with a worldwide happy, healthy frequency. Today his Heart Math Institute has focused on stress management techniques and identified life stressors and the permitted effectiveness on us that they have to be a leading cause of illness both physical and mental.

Backster continued his research, living out his day with various plants connected to the galvanometer, when the making of his breakfast started triggering a response in one of the plants, as he cracked his eggs open; accidentally finding out that an unhatched egg, which he eventually hooked up to his galvanometer had a faint impulse at 160 to 180 beats per minute, matching the heart rhythm of a one to four days old chick.

New Jersey cytologist Dr. Miller concluded that some sort of "cellular consciousness" must be common to all life.

Backster eventually found that across all living things there is a

reaction to dying tissue, and murder of a living thing, as small as mixing a jam preservative into a yogurt that was killing some of the micro-bacteria in the yogurt.

Marcel Vogel, an expert in luminescence picked up the study and in interesting possibility of quantum physics, determined that one plant reacted to the pain of another plant more so when Vogel was paying attention to it. Little did he know at that time, that his journey would eventually theorize that plants were able to read minds; not just intentions, but attentions which increased the response level.

Vogel also an expert in Native American knowledge and culture, said that the American Indians knew very well about these facilities and would go into nature, putting their back against the pine trees to rejuvenate themselves with their power. Finally, Vogel demonstrated to the producers of a TV show called "You Asked for It," The plants abilities to read his and their minds and emotions before demonstrating how they might re-establish a connection with nature.

xliii

Further-more Vogel felt that there was realm of essence we could not detect, with our organs or with our science, that held an instant form of intelligent communication all its own. Some may imagine this as the innate and perception of certain dogs, who can tune into a person's intentions, character, spiritual consistency or fears. He was

able to determine this, by exhalation strongly, from first one foot away to later one hundred feet away, achieving the same response in the plant. At 100 feet away from it became very clear that there was some other force of energy or communication with the plant that doubles with reparation. Vogel theorizes that possibly with a concentrated thought made while holding the breath in, could make the communication more specific and complete.

After tons of experiments Backster went on to form elaborated theories such as that plants and maybe certain animals, wish to be eaten, and assimilated into life forms but only under a communicative relation like that of a kosher ceremony or something similar to the Christian rite of Communion.

He observed that the plants would give a calm if not no response when this type of communication happened between Backster, others and the plants hooked up to the meters. He continued to favor the Dragon plant for many tests, and realized that mindless brutal slaughter of living specie did provoke a very emotional reaction from her, a reaction unseen when a self-made ritual of thanks and honor would be performed.

Another plant ability of perception, can be easily tested by any Gardner and that is plant a vine, near a pole and observer the vine crawl ever so slowly towards the pole, then just before the vine reaches the pole, move the pole and notice the vine also changes its direction to the new place of the pole.

I pose the question that it could even be plants can speak to birds and birds can deliver their seed to a certain nearby or worldwide location(s) that would make for a nice home for these children. A stork delivering the baby metaphor? Further along on the trail of Native belief is the idea that before or after certain human life, comes bird life depending on which polar direction we grow in.

Human beings are the only things that live outside of nature at this time. I mean as to take pills, develop chemicals, take those, and to build cities and structures where most biology dies. Could we really be devastatingly somehow separated from a nature right in front of our eyes?

Certain studies in permaculture have well illustrated that if we live in harmony with nature we can support, many billions more humans, animals, fish and trees. It almost seems as though right now the earth is in communication to try and rebuild itself and utilizing well the few resources we have left her with.

From me, now having read this information if you believe you can know your plants better, that's a fun experience. One that I myself am most thankful for.

Transactions between pollen producing plants and pollen moving animals, make up a significant portion of what biological scientist are now calling bio-diversity.

Gary Paul Nabhan

We could say that the whole result of the psychedelic experience is the understanding that nature wants to communicate with us.

Terence McKenna

The complex chemistry present in non-monocrop natural systems automatically limit the emergence of disease and insect epidemics and resistance.

The larger number of plants with diverse chemistries that occupy the largest number of ecosystem functional categories, the more vital and healthier the ecosystem.

Stephan Harrod Buhner

There are many men charged with duty of examining the construction of the plants, animals and soils which are the instruments of the great orchestra. These men are called professors. Each selects one instrument and spends his life taking it apart and describing its strings and sounding boards. This process of dismemberment is called research. The place for this research is called a University.

A professor may pluck the strings of his own instrument, but never that of another, and if he listens for music he may never admit it to his fellows or students. For all are restrained by an iron bound taboo which decrees that the construction of instruments is the domain of science, while the detection of harmony is the domain of poets.

Professors serve science and science serves progress. It serves progress so well that many of the more intricate instruments are stepped upon and broken in the rush to spread progress to all backward lands. One by one the parts are thus stricken from the song of songs. If the professor is able to classify each instrument before it is broken, he is satisfied.

Aldo Leopold

In the absence of complete understanding, this apparent species redundancy is best regarded as a system adaptation against a highly variable and unpredictable environment. In many cases it is likely to be an essential component of, and in fact may well be used as a measure of, the system's ability to continue functioning when stressed or disturbed.

B.H. Walker

Any given environment usually contains several plants with widely different attributes, showing that there is seldom a unique solution to a given set of environmental changes. This is consistent with the finding that complex, non-linear, highly linked systems (such as plant metabolism) have multiple stable states.

R.J. Scholes

The Food Tour

As we tour several plantations and discover the science behind their development, come along on an immersive food tour. From the permaculture of hot pepper and guanabana to the fields of mango and banana, this section will offer you a complete understanding of how crops are cultivated and raised.

A quick food tour to identify some of the plants and edibles on that specific farm is one of the first things volunteers and students undertake when they arrive at a permaculture farm. Typically, they are not as thorough as they could be. We gain a particular set of values through an understanding of other civilizations' relationships with the crop or plant. Knowing some of the scientific breakdown of the plant can help us better understand how to utilize it and with whom.

So much can be said for this fast-growing food! We grew lots of bananas and plantains at the Original Nutritional Diversity &

Permaculture farm in Panama. They are strong fast growers and along

with papayas a great starting canopy for shrubs and other smaller sized plants. Perennials, and productive at that, these are the largest herbaceous flowering plants.

AVOCADO

The avocado, also known as aguacate, is an extremely beneficial meal for human enhancement! The best avocados are currently produced by numerous farms, and avocado is simple to obtain. Avocado trees are simple to grow in Central America and   at Nutritional Diversity & Permaculture Learning Centers.

The recommendation is to consume one avocado fruit every day in addition to the items listed in the Nutritional Variety diet plan. It's also advised to consume three leaves throughout the day by chewing and swallowing them or adding them to smoothies. The roughage found in avocado leaves is excellent for encouraging regular bowel motions.

Alligator pear, also known as the avocado," in Spanish called the "aguacate" from the tree Persea Americana of Mexico,

the Lauraceae family, refers to the large berry with a single, large, quickly and easily starting seed – one of the largest basal angiosperm families with over 50 genera.

High in healthy fats, the avocado is a unique fruit of roughly 4.5 grams of fat, 3 grams of carbohydrate, and 2 grams of dietary fiber. Many diverse studies show it to be a significant and broad source of human health benefits. Most people on the modern diets as we know them now don't get enough potassium, which avocados are a great

source   of (14%   FDA   daily   recommend)   even
      more

than bananas (10% FDA daily recommend). A Nutritional Diversity diet plan is a helpful, natural food digestion and optimal, nuclear like uptake. Nutritional Diversity diet recommends an avocado or two a day in small spread out servings. This is also because of its high, healthy oil content also – Nutritional Diversity athletes need to stay well oiled!

Best Avocado is a nutrient uptake aid for other nutrients in the stomach because it is high in soluble fat. This fat prolongs the existence of the local microbiome or gut culture. According to a recent study, adding avocado or avocado oil to salad or salsa can boost the body's ability to absorb antioxidants by 2.6 to 15 times. A daily avocado can help with glaucoma, eye health, brain support, and prevention of stomach, colon, and altimeters diseases. It also contains vitamin B, which is good for the brain.

For improving carotenoid absorption from carotenoid-rich foods, researchers have experimented with the addition of avocado to meal options including salads, sides of leafy greens, and small servings of carrots, or tomato sauce. Traditional use indicates this benefit also.

The amount of avocado added has varied from study to study but averages approximately 1 cup or 1 small/medium avocado providing 20-25 grams of total fat. As expected, this added avocado has been shown in the study to increase absorption from all of the foods listed above. Anywhere from two to six times as much absorption was found to occur with the added avocado! These results are both in favor of eating high nutritional biodiversity of species and eating avocados, every day.

The best avocado "superfood" presents a myriad, or odyssey of benefits, the Persea Americana fruit, tree, and leaf has been severely important to Americans for ages. xliv

The diverse species found to have 100 accessions comprised of the three racial types, Guatemalan, Mexican, and West Indian and today plenty of diversity across many cultivars are available.   xlv   The avocado oils can be an essential part of life, skin health, and digestive promoter. xlvi

Avocado (Persea Americana) belongs to the family Lauraceae, one of the largest basal angiosperm families with over 50 genera. Basal angiosperms are the first and oldest families of flowering plants that originated well over 100 million years ago and are represented by only a few hundred species compared with hundreds of thousands of species of monocot and eudicot angiosperms. Indications suggest avocado oil may be as valuable as olive oil and coconut oil.xlvii

Side effects and toxicity has been evaluated to occur in cases where too much of the plant is ingested.   Despite tons of articles recommending seed and skin use, the toxin "persin" that is in those two materials causes heart damage and brain damage in small animals.

They are quite toxic to horses.xlviii

Whereas s there could be homeopathic applications, they should be controlled and few with far between time. Generally, Nutritional Diversity Diet Sciences subscribers do not use seeds and seed foods in our diet.

Nutritional Diversity science recommends healing teas, soups, and heated preparations are cooled before ingested and be taken only for healing purposes, teas should not be taken regularly, because of the way they inherently offset the body's PH.

Avocados are incredibly nutrient-dense on their own, and they also significantly boost the nutritional content of other plant meals like aguacate tree leaves. Avocados help to lubricate the digestive culture and intestinal inner skin due of their rich lipids and because they are so full of fiber. According to Nutritional Diversity Science, one to two avocados per day should be consumed in areas with high nutritional diversification.

AMBROSIA

We have been fortunate to have wonderful colleagues who have recognized this herb as one of the most beneficial additions to a Nutritional Diversity plan. It is even possible that the ancient Greeks used this plant to make a beverage that they referred to as an "Immortal Herb of the Gods." The best "Ambrosia" is one of the miracle plants.

A seriously effective anti-cancer ingredient that is a whole food and possibly an extract is probably now within readers' reach. We've merely spent so much time travelling by trains and airlines, which is understandable, but there are probably dozens to hundreds of truly anti-cancer compounds right outside the door. For those who want to learn about true strength, though, keep researching the best ambrosia.

The fact that in English this particular strain of "Ambrosia" is known as "Ambrosia Perruvianna" is another intriguing linguistic feature of this plant. "Ambrosia" is a name that refers to a drink or herb of immortality that was frequently drunk by the Gods. The Spanish word for the precise species depicted above is Artemis, which is also the name of Zeus' daughter and diet, "Goddess of the Hunt

Artemis." Do two languages pin this plant with two different words that refer to Greek mythologies of Gods necessarily mean that it is a miracle substance? Certainly not, although it makes what I am about to say that much more interesting.

There is arguably another mistake in this theory that Ambrosia Peruvianna was the plant they were talking about in Greece. Lots of information, disinformation possibly out there claiming this particular strain even though named 'Peruvian,' originates from the American continent. The plant is world-wide as my collegue has pointed out several times to me, it get's renamed a lot and may have sharper leaves in colder regions its essentially the same plant. To theorize one origin maybe off, especially considering it's function in nature is to come in to land decimated and restore it. It is a powerful technology that attacks mono-cultures, and you will see "ragweed" at the top of the herbicides list of things to kill.

Combined with new algae injections being studied in Texas (and, or other new discoveries) this specie could be used to help restore the most severely damaged lands in good time.

The herb has a wide range and could have existed where it does today, including Greece and the Americas. A name is typically accompanied by some picture, and oddly enough, there are various pieces of art that appear to depict a leaf and branch structure that is very similar to, almost exactly like this herb.

Ambrosia Peruvianna is one of many plants listed, examined for having mechanisms that could treat HIV.xlix Other various family members have been used, A. confertiflora and A. ambrosioides showed the best anti-mycobacterial activity in vitro. The activity of Guaiacum coulteri is consistent with the traditional use by Sonoran ethnic groups as an anti-tuberculosis agent. For these reasons, it is important to investigate a broader spectrum of medicinal plants in order to find compounds active against Mycobacterium tuberculosis.

It is important to highlight that several plant-derived products (compounds, essential oils) from Artemisia plants have shown high inhibitory potential against Leishmania spp., such as artemisinin and its derivatives.li Ambrosia cumanenesis has long time use in the Caribbean more specifically Trinidad for menstrual pains. liiThe whole plant as food cleans up neurotoxicity in patients.liii The Global Invasive Species Database says this plant is to blame for the most allergic response during her season.

The permaculture expert explained that he thought with cancer patients, consuming iron on an empty stomach with an iron pill should form a direct line from the stomach to cancer. The concoction which would make for quick direct uptake of the healing essences to cancer affected part of the body was incredibly simple to make and was ingenious, I thought. The milk and the oil, he theorized would help the dried leaves (or for fresh ones) get through the stomach walls quickly and be absorbed well into the process of healing

The process with dried Ambrosia Peruviana will be like take an iron supplement tablet at least two hours before the first dose. Place ½ liquid ounce volume of the powdered product, packed firmly, in 1 cup of WHOLE milk, mix, and drink quickly, as it has an unpleasant taste. Repeat [not the iron] 4 times at 4-hour intervals. If the results seem slow, repeat in 8 days.

Ambrosia Peruvianna is now grown and propagated at the Nutritional Diversity & Permaculture Study Panama & Costa Rica sites as well, as a few urban gardens among group members. The

plant wants to grow, it is a strong grower, birds and bees and other plants that are on my terraces here in Panama anyways seem to appreciate its inclusion somewhat drastically. My thoughts are to work with it more as it seems purposed, to help new babies come in.

ASHWAGANDHA

The best ashwagandha is one the most famous and central of Ayurvedic herbs, 'Ayurveda' roughly translated into "Knowledge of life", in which the magic herb is royalty in therapeutic measures to boost physical, mental, social and spiritual harmony in order to improve the total quality of life.liv

The nightshade family includes the tomato. peppers and cucumbers as well. ND typically avoids nightshades entirely, and because of the lectins they contain, peeling and de-seeding are crucial. These lectins are proteins that act as splinters to sugar molecules, releasing poisons that impair function and hasten the ageing process. The *could be avoided by eating solely leaves.

The greatest ashwagandha has been used in Ayurveda treatment for over 3000–4000 years, according to the teachings of revered rishi Punarvasu Atriya. The Charaka and Sushruta Samhitas, two of the oldest and most revered sacred writings of Ayurveda, both discuss it. As an "adaptogen," ashwagandha is also used to lower blood pressure, boost immunity, and help the body deal with daily stress.

There are so many advantages of ashwagandha that it is difficult to list them all. The greatest hot peppers, other peppers, and black pepper are only a few examples of various plants that can be used to unleash these "together" effects. It can treat Alzheimer and other neurological conditions, effects of HIV. lv lvi A maximum stress relief agent,lvii and even sleep-inducing aid.lviii

Striking antioxidant properties are contained in the miracle herb. lix

Like the best gotu kola, the herb acts in many ways as a brain cell protector, displaying anti-cancer actions and compounds have neuroprotective against glutamate insult, a potential that may serve as a great supplement for brain health.lx lxi Also as a strong general anti-anxiety and oxidative stress reducer.lxii

Anti-cancer activity is a main study of the best ashwagandha herb, and has been known as a cancer medication for a long time. lxiii Key essence known as Withanone. The herb enhances sexual function, atop all these other things.lxivThe shrub has enhancing effects on the reproductive system overall.lxv

Also, like gotu kola, the best damiana and many medicinal shrubs of her type, ashwagandha can be helpful to insomnia and nonrestorative sleep (NRS) issues.lxvi

The Ayurveda staple even helps regulate correct body weight.lxvii

Important brain activity changes have been noticed and evaluated in a really interesting study whereas mice were dosed with Scopolamine, an alkaloid from the Datura flower I have a little experience with that of many things that cause amnesia. Withania somnifera, the hopefully memory restoration ingredient. lxviii

The blessing is anti-aging, and anti-free radical. lxix It is packed with serious vitality enhancing substances and steroidal compounds have been extracted from her seeds.lxx Cognitive functional improvements and reaction time improvements have been well known for the power herb.lxxi lxxii

The superfood has been the focus of regenerative health possibilities is an ongoing track of study. lxxiii

Glutamate neurotoxicity a cause of some stroke, head trauma, multiple sclerosis, and neurodegenerative disorders has pointed a search for herbal remedies. lxxiv

In the traditional system of medicine in India, the magic herb has been used to treat rheumatoid arthritis. This could surely be helped further by the addition of turmeric.lxxv The magic plant is traditioned in treating epilepsy, depression, arthritis, diabetes, and palliative effects such as analgesic, rejuvenating, regenerating, and growth-promoting effects.lxxvi

When doses are exceedingly high, clinical trials have noted headaches, drowsiness, and stomach trouble. Always start slowly when dealing with anything because uncommon allergic reactions are always a possibility.

In general, withania somnifera is thought to be very safe.lxxvii

Nutritional Diversity

The Withania somnifera, on which we have been focusing for the past five years, is particularly suitable to the ND food combinations and ratios. It blends in perfectly. We place it high on the list of people our customers, permaculturists, athletes, and general admirers want to see.

BASIL

The term "basil" (/baezl/, often pronounced in the US as

"bezl";Ocimum basilicum) refers to a vast family of nutritious herbs in the Lamiaceae family (mints).

The herb was extensively researched by Ancient Greek authors like Theophrastus, and it is also referred to as the "king of herbs" and the "royal herb." The word basil is derived from her Greek name. Basil is now grown in 160 different kinds, with more variations being added every. This excludes the numerous wild cultivars of this plant that may be easily found all over the globe.

Exceptional in flavour, potency, and nutritional value is The Strength of Basil, The King of Herbs.

Most commonly today in modern culture dried basil leaves are used as a seasoning spice.

Basil is available and easy to grow in home herb gardens, which is recommended. It's higher in protein than it is in carbs, for your bodybuilders and strength enthusiasts out there that want nothing but a lean machine.

It's high content of minerals, like magnesium, calcium, iron, and zinc and manganese. Choline and Thiamine, are important to a regular amount of also, and are sometimes unavailable in many of today's primary consumption foods, while important nutrients to many athletes, who would otherwise get these from vitamin supplements.

The unique spread of active constituents and flavonoids found in basil provide protection at the cellular level.

Orientin and vicenin are two water-soluble flavonoids that have been of particular interest in basil, and in studies on human white blood cells indicate the components of basil protect cell structures as well as chromosomes from radiation and oxygen-based damage.

Basil has also been shown to provide protection against unwanted bacterial growth.

Glucose lowering and antioxidant effects of O. basilicum was evident biochemically in this study. O. basilicum could protect the kidney against diabetes-induced nephropathy as revealed biochemically and histopathologically.lxxviii

The present data demonstrated that Ocimum basilicum potentiates sleeping behaviors without any cytotoxicity. lxxix

Antimicrobial and antibacterial power of basil oil is there, and if more is needed combinations with Lippia

multiflora Moldenke, Mentha x Piperita L. (peppermint) can be done to enhance the efficacy.lxxx

Basil could light the way on the road to breast cancer treatment and elimination. lxxxi The anti-obesity study explored phytochemicals, porcine pancreatic α-amylase (PPA), and lipase (PPL) inhibitory activities and antioxidant potential extracts of the leaves and flowers of Ocimum basilicum and the interaction between these enzymes and the major chemical constituents of the herb. lxxxii The best basil shows a heavy application for antifungal activity. lxxxiii Certain animal tests indicate the best basil could be employed to help improve memory in high doses. Lxxxiv

Essential oil antifungal armada including cinnamon should do any antifungal need several times over. Most of the oils were effective in inhibiting of mycelia morphological transformation. Our research revealed also that cell membrane seems to be the most important target of ingredients of investigated oils. Lxxxv

The present study examined the efficacy of Ocimum basilicum (basil) extract, a natural herb, with antioxidant properties, against testicular toxicity induced by cadmium (Cd), which is one of the most important toxic heavy metals which lead to infertility. lxxxvi Indicative of a mosquito repellent ingredient both as an agent in diet and topically.

One fascinating discovery demonstrated that O. basilicum essential oil has an important anti-hyperalgesic profile, suggesting that this oil, isolated or complexed with β-CD, can be an interesting alternative for the development of new therapeutic options for the treatment of chronic painful conditions, as fibromyalgia. Lxxxvii

The leaves of O. basilicum are a rich source of flavonoids that possess various biological properties related to antioxidant mechanisms. Caffeic acid is another component in the leaf of the O. basilicum that has antioxidant, anti-inflammatory, and cancer chemopreventive activities lxxxviii

The herb is safe in moderate doses. We say 15 grams would be a good limit for adults, especially if they are new to her. However, there has been testing to suggest high doses help with memory loss and other serious conditions.

As with any substance go slow to assess tolerance.

We have wild basil that grows naturally across the family farm, here in Panama and have witnessed its existence as a small but strong, multiplying, and determined plant, that possesses a dexterous growing method and whose potency is as depression medication and an overall system super-food.

BANANAS

The leaves are excellent for serving and wrapping other food items for steaming or baking, while the fruits are a staple source of carbohydrates for many tropical populations. Consume a banana to get vitamin B6, potassium, and other vitamins and minerals while working out and studying.

A fella can get going on the farm with a few bananas. I like them a lot since we can receive a lot of cover material or till-less bed topping from banana trees and because I am familiar with several practical methods for doubling output. The harvested banana plant's trunks are excellent for building terraces. The "banana circles" have recently gained popularity among permaculture designers, who claim that adopting this technique, productivity can increase by up to 8 times.

The most common circles are described as 4 to 10 meters, I have a few circles at different diameters even one about 25 feet across with a 7 feet high compost stack in the middle of it now. I fertilize our terraces often and the banana do very well there. They do well on regular hills also on flat grounds.

Chiquita bananas plantations are a 45 minute 5$ speed boat trip from the island I am now, and I have seen the ships load up with container after container countless times, in the Almirante, Panama port.

Another growing trick I like to do, is to chip away small sides from the base of the banana tree, which stimulates more baby rhizome shoots, for crop doubling, or now quadrupling. Remove and transplant these rhizomes and all seed planting, and other transplanting on new moon to first quarter moon. I plant at the top of a hill or terrace sequence first and work my way down to speed production of the overall crop.

Another thing I really like about bananas is there quick use of liquid nutrients, which is a large amount of our homemade fertilizer production is very liquid. I fertilize all the time with an 80% water, 20% plant material, compost sun tea in large 20-gallon clear plastic tanks. We through everything in these things, scorpions, cucarachas, fruit peels and tops, egg shells, dog poo and quarter pitchers of Nutritional Diversity Batidos!

"Good design depends on a free and harmonious relationship to nature and people, in which careful observation and thoughtful interaction provide the design inspiration, repertoire and patterns." Permaculture 'co-originator' David Holmgren

I find the best growths with bananas generally, is on a 1- inch raise, on a well-draining slope with the banana circle form or terrace form, with ginger root planted around the base in a dedicated two foot covered and tended zone. The way I treat this zone, is by adding various fertilization elements after my base chipping procedure. I will dump a bag of beach sand, rake a pile of postured and sunned cut grass around, dig away a piece of earth from its base and throw in a shovel of super black sledge from an irrigation channel nearby. I will shove small twigs in around, and place rotting wood branches as Lincoln Logs in a square.

Of-course, if you take your time and dig large holes in your terraces, and fill those holes with chop and food scrap and old wood pieces, and form large composts there, and then plant your bananas, the results are astounding.

Another permaculture uses of the banana tree I imagined for an area is to hold large wood pieces for ground leveling, and at the same time path lining. I am using a row of banana trees who have grown well and in sync together I notice, to hold large logs from branches we cut away from the house. I will then fill in behind the logs, and once level plant peanut grass to take over and hold it clear of other growths. Then we will cut back the jungle a bit more on the other side of the bath and again line it with bananas, but this time in between each tree we will add cassava, red torch ginger, turmeric, backed by coconut trees to make a firm wall against jungle growth.

The 8-meter banana circle with the cut leaves piled in the middle, are said to produce up to 8x as many fruits as those planted otherwise. I would say on flat land this is my go to technique if I am going to through some plantains or bananas in.

Because of its sweetness and flavor, the banana is considered one of the three "royal fruits" in Tamil Nadu, along with mango and jackfruit. These three fruits are collectively known as ma-palavazhai. For my "Royal & Angelic" tropical Nutritional Variety this training season, I have chosen these Royal Fruits, a Royal Herb, and "Angels Fruit," to mention a few.

We are employing the North American Hopi three sister's permaculture method, sowing pumpkin, squash and bean plantains instead of corn.

An unfortunate history, brought forth and unfortunate change in the banana I am sad to say. The banana we eat, has no seeds that actually grow, and are pretty much a genetically modified banana, the plantain has undergone the same kinds of changes. They are effectively sterile mutant species. Every banana eaten is an exact clone of the last, and we spread them by rhizome transplanting only. The original species had many more seeds, perfectly round little black BB gun pellet looking things that could crack a modernday human tooth.

None the less, the processes involved back then were almost bioacceptable and chemicals were not used, and so also the nutrition is effective.

Until the 1960's a different banana was the choice, until monoculture cropping allowed for the infestation of what we now call the Panama Disease. The near extinct by the pathogen species that died largely at that time was the Gros Michel. The new banana is known as the Cavendish. Permaculture farming models can grow either or both specie with little problems

BITTER MELON

Bitter Melon also is known as Bitter Gourd or Korela (in the Hindu language), technically referenced as Momordica Charantia has been the focus of many studies concerning the treatment of cancer and other serious pathologies such as AIDS patients, and diabetes.

In 1982 a study of the effects of bitter melon on the herpes simplex virus-1, MAP30 inhibited the reproduction of the virus, as well as reducing its capability to form plaques. According to certified nutritional consultant Phyllis Balch, Momordica charantia extracts were more effective than the drug acyclovir, which is the leading herpes inflammation treatment in the form of a pharmaceutical pill.

If you follow the ND standard (A) of consuming 5 times as much protein in plant matter, then I advise eating roughly 10% of your daily green food consumption fresh and cooking the remaining 90%. The bitter, melon-like nutrients are always going to be more potent when consumed fresh. In our case, it was all fresh as an addition to the typical modern diet that is still served in every restaurant today.

The Asian Pacific Journal of Tropical Disease and others find antidiabetic properties and noteworthy overall medical potency lxxxix xc. Published moreover are the fasting and plasma effects to prediabetics, and obesity patients.xci Extensive trials showed modest hypoglycemic effect and significantly reduced fructose levels from baseline among patients with type 2 diabetes who received 2000 mg/day. For diabetics, the common diabetic foot ulcer is a terrible side effect of diabetes lowering the quality of life for most patients.

the best bitter melon has been used to reduce this effect and improve the overall quality of life for diabetics.xcii

Studies indicate the properties of bitter melon to combat cancer, recently throat cancer.xciii

In vitro research has also demonstrated reduced rates of T lymphocyte infections with HIV-1 and reduced viral replication in infected cells xciv

Animal testing showed the successful conversion of bad cholesterol to good ones pinning one potential benefit as a balancer for cholesterol levels. The candle wax-looking zucchini balances cholesterol, reducing LDL, and increasing HDL. Xcv

Momordica Charantia has been known to have a slue of side effects. Eat the bitter gourd in small servings, one day a week. Too much of the good stuff can cause artery hardening. This could likely be eased by coconut oil consumption, but each of these points is just in theory.

Asian cultures and cooking have thoroughly tested out the best bitter melon; which out-performs pharmaceutical hypoglycemic inhibitors, and this may reduce blood sugar levels or glucose concentrations.xcvi

Pregnant women should consult with a professional or simply avoid searching out this hard to find vegetables at all.

The bitter gourd is a strong growing vegetable, on a nice vine with pretty leaves and yellow flowers. It looks good on a fence and can protect small roofing applications also.

The attractive vine belongs to the Cucurbitaceae family. Other ailments like colitis, constipation, intestinal worms, kidney stones, fever, psoriasis, and more have allegedly been treated with the best bitter melon.

CHICKEN

In the past, I've always recommended chicken as a starter protein source for diets. That may seem a little traditional, but it is what it is. They have small nutritional diversity diets of their own as I raise them. Chickens are devoted; if I let them out, they follow me around like they're on guard. That meat's quality appeals to me.

They will get it on too. As much as I don't agree with it, or abusive, tragic chain gang chicken farming; they fight chickens here. They scrap. Here on my farm, they have several big areas, I move them from one to another every fifteen days. No animal should be on its own feces any more than that. If someone forgets to give them their special feed, they will fight out of the pen no doubt about it. I like this fight, and this escape quality in my meat too. You are what you eat.

To me, chicken is a "food of the Gods," and I know that this year on NutritionalDiversity.com, we have talked a little bit about foods of the Gods. When it comes to livestock, chickens are the fastest and most productive asset on my farm because they can be produced quickly and easily. Chickens are courageous creatures with a fighting spirit who will engage in animal combat in order to defend their food.

Like anything else, chicken production can be highly efficient, and you can give chickens the best life they've ever known! Around the world chickens have become a standard option meat variety, that makes up a very large portion of overall global protein-focused consumption. This is because (1) chickens are fun and easy to raise. Chickens produce super-food eggs also (2). Cooked chicken meat is a super-food (3). Between chickens and their eggs, a human can build muscle and strength, in ways that are very hard to do without a meat source like it.

Chicken is a valuable food because of its variable but moderate energy content, highly digestible proteins of good nutritional quality (with low collagen levels), unsaturated lipids (primarily found in the skin   and easily removed), B-group vitamins (primarily thiamin, vitamin B6, and pantothenic acid), and minerals (like iron, zinc, and copper).xcvii

One research project examined the nutritional content of chicken meat from broilers (chickens reared for meat) and spent hens, which was published in the Journal of Food Composition and Analysis in 2019. (older chickens that are no longer suitable for egg production). The study discovered that while wasted hen meat had higher amounts of several nutrients, such as iron and zinc, grill meat had higher quantities of protein and lower levels of fat.

The findings imply that supplementing with organic selenium can enhance the nutritional value and quality of grill chicken meat.xcviii

Chickens are one of the most popular sources of protein across most diet's in the world currently. They are a good source of vitamins and minerals and cholesterol. Not all cholesterol is bad, in fact, much of it is good – it all works very well within the balance of Nutritional Diversity. The balance of the chicken is perfect in helping to quickly process and uptake proteins, and deliver minerals to the blood.

It's not just muscle food but brain and hormone food also.

Chicken is rich in several minerals like phosphorus and calcium, which helps keeps bones remain in mint condition. The recommended amount of daily protein requirements for an office worker, is 1 gram per 1 kg of body weight, or 0.4 g of protein per pound of body weight. Remember these numbers are for normal

people. For athletes, the daily requirement of protein is about 0.6 g to

2.0 g per pound, depending on goals and daily output.

Chicken is not only a very good source of protein, but it is a very good source of vitamins and minerals. The vitamins and minerals found in it are very useful in numerous activities in our body. Vitamin B12 and vitamin B6 are very important to brain function and hormone production. Vitamin D supports calcium absorption and bone strength. Vitamin A helps in building up eyesight and minerals such as iron are helpful in hemoglobin formation, muscle activity, also eliminating anemia. Potassium and sodium are important electrolytes (organic), and phosphorous plays another important role in tackling weakness, bone health, brain function, dental care, and metabolic issues.

Medicinal levels from chickens' vitamin banks in B vitamins are useful in preventing cataracts and skin disorders, boosting immunity, eliminating weakness, regulating digestion, and improving the nervous system, as well as preventing migraine, heart disorders, grey hair, high cholesterol, and diabetes.

Chicken has two nutrients that are great for reducing stress, tryptophan and Vitamin B5. These guys have a calming effect on your body and this makes chicken an excellent option after a stressful day, or a heavy workout. Chicken is high in magnesium making it supportive of testosterone production (chicken is also high in zinc) but also means it can work towards regulating intolerable PMS symptoms. In today's age, I always recommend stacking up stressreducing foods.

Eggs are a high protein superfood that the low-budget Nutritional Diversifist cannot afford to pass up because they are inexpensive, therefore eat them every day if you are raising chickens. I regularly consume chicken and its eggs and include them in my starting diets for people new to nutritional diversity. Eggs, contain the zygote that hatches into a baby chicken – the eggs contain everything needed for the chicken to become live.

The largest egg recorded so far was from a whale shark, and was 30 cm × 14 cm × 9 cm (11.8 in × 5.5 in × 3.5 in) in size. I wonder what kind of workout you could get after consuming that?

Eat them with papaya, or avocado, to get the most out of this great spectrum of nutrients. Eggs, especially the hard-boiled form, is great to pack in the Nutritional Diversity organizer, stick in the gym bag, backpack or briefcase, and eat correctly with your other nutritional plan ingredients (like a kick-butt hot sauce) throughout the day.

While tons of chicken can be eaten in a day with no problem, egg consumption should be in the 3 to 6 a day range. Exceeding ten eggs could be asking for some acid related, and possibly other problems. Eat a few raw for sure to make sure there is good material balance in the system at the end, I myself eat some shell even – toss a few whole raw eggs into a smoothie.

Do one quick search and find out about 'battery caged' chickens and worse, and you will see why any chicken raised on a small farm today is a lucky chicken. Do yourself and the world a favor and raise your own chickens and love them and they will give you every day their golden value nutrition -eggs.

COFFEE

You're about to read the most contentious yet finest information you've ever read on coffee.

Hopefully. At least, it won't be a sales pitch. Many coffee enthusiasts will despise me for one aspect of it, love me for another aspect of it, and be grateful to me for two aspects, I believe. But because coffee lovers have much more energy than I do, I am going to say up front, that this has been written with a certain degree of cynical humor -just for fun.

Coffee is the black strong drink derived from, dead and dried, roasted then ground beans from the genus Coffee, native to tropical Africa, specifically having its origin in Ethiopia and Sudan and Madagascar, Comoros, and Mauritius in the Indian Ocean. Xcix

Two primary strains are Coffee canephora (predominantly a form known as 'robusta') and C. arabica. More rare species include C. liberica, C. stenophylla, C. mauritiana, and C. racemosa. All coffee plants are classified in the large family Rubiaceae, evergreen shrubs or trees that can grow to 5m / 15 ft tall, with green to red-when-ripe berries.

The first coffee shop opened in Paris in 1672. Later the city's most famous coffee shop, el Café Procope, opened 15 years later. This coffee cultivation of the first social realm was arguably the birthplace of the encyclopedia, and an important meeting place during the "French Enlightenment," which is also the main reason she still operates today. Interestingly, coffee wasn't popular at first with everyone in Europe. Many warned it was the "bitter invention of Satan." Rumor has it, Clergymen in Venice condemned it. Later Pope Clement VIII gave coffee Papal approval.

I personally do not endorse or recommend coffee in my diet plans and ask my athletes to refrain from more than a cup a day. I recommend none at all.

The benefits claimed by the coffee houses for their black, leather tanning liquid consumed hot, can be achieved through several other food sources. Do you take sugar with your coffee? What about cream? Me recommends are, that these two substances be taken in very small percentages of one's overall consumption, if at all. Anyways, you can read all about the right way to eat in this introduction, later.

Coffee is one of the most consumed beverages worldwide. cAmerica however is the largest consumer of coffee at an estimated 1.6 billion cups a day, according to Food Industry News.

There are certain categories such as "one of the world's largest and most important economical crops," which are actually reasons for sales and deception in the interest of pockets, that also grow and the information behind this type of large industry, I myself become more skeptical of. The overwhelming push and door-opening (such as no import tax) from every direction for this enormous industry also has me skeptical.

I am also someone who has seen the countless error-ridden study and a completely flawed set of standards regarding how studies are produced.

Roasted coffee is a mixture of over 1000 bioactive compounds, with potentially therapeutic antioxidant, anti-inflammatory, anti-fibrotic, and anticancer effects, lower risk of cardiovascular disease, and premature mortality. Studies have been conducted that show coffee to be beneficial to type II diabetes, liver conditions, and more.ci

According to the study funding source Institute for Scientific Information on Coffee (ISIC), and other "Epic" studies; coffee is excellent for you in every way! It will make you live longer and everything! cii ciii

Certain studies indicate that daily coffee drinkers reduced their risk of dying prematurely compared with non-drinkers by 7–12%. civ There could be biofuel possibilities in coffee, and sugarcane, and corn, crops that speak to some of the largest cultivation in the world today.

I found this study a bit less conflicted, and this dive found a weak enemy to colon cancer cells. It was thought that the resistance could have been the caffeine boost to the other agents of the immune system. cv

Coffee side effects can be increased heart rate, trouble sleeping, the shakes, irritability, acid reflux, and trouble concentrating. In terms of the microbiome, the inside central energy producer of the human organism who takes in fuel and pumps out energy that is an actual organic micro-garden-culture; dumping hot black strongly acidic liquid made from the roasted seed, over things may not be so good.

That being said, several ancient cultures have had hot drinks, the reasons for which are unknown, but our current culture is not the first time. The effect that the acidic substance has on the heart rate is generally concerning to a nutritionist, and my general feeling is that if used, use a few times a week. The trade-off with a pre-workout supplement for caffeine or another stimulant boost, and also trade-off with no caffeine at all.

The idea that day to day performance is enhanced by coffee is something I am definitely not convinced of, regardless of how many studies say it will make you live longer. By the way, there is a lot you can do to make yourself live longer.

People with hypertension, children, adolescents, and the elderly, may be more vulnerable to the adverse effects of caffeine. In addition, currently available evidence suggests that it may be prudent for pregnant women to limit coffee consumption to 3 cups/d providing no more than 300 mg/d of caffeine to exclude any increased probability of spontaneous abortion or impaired fetal growth. cvi These limits seem a bit high to me for someone pregnant.

The liquid-like alcohol is too extreme to be consumed on a regular basis, a great tool from a sacred plant should be used within a large diversity and make up no more .02% of the overall intake. The microbiome will need time to heal from this so daily consumption is not recommended!

CHOCOLATE

Shrub-like trees, 12 to 26 feet in height known as the Theobroma cacao, produces a hard-shelled outer casing to protect the precious and sacred bean. A tree produces the cacao seed or bean, that is used to make chocolate, cocoa butter, and several other foods and healthrelated products.

The cacao tree is native to Central and South America, and it is one of the stronger trees I have observed, able to withstand and live in harmony with several plant species in close proximity. When Christopher Columbus, first discovered the Americas in 1502 he shared a cacao beverage with Montezuma, who reportedly drank a lot of the chocolate drink.

Wild cacao today still grows in the foothills of the Andes, in the Amazon, and Orinoco basins of South America, and in Colombia and Venezuela. Evidence suggests that cacao had been consumed largely by every civilization in those regions from Aztecs to Mayans to Incas and all the way back to the Olmec civilization.

Cacao trees grow in a limited geographical zone, of about 20° to the north and south of the Equator. Nearly 70% of the world crop today is grown in West Africa. The cacao plant was first given its botanical name by Swedish natural scientist Carl Linnaeus in his original classification of the plant kingdom, where he called it Theobroma ("food of the gods") cacao. Cvii

The word for Chocolate. The word 'chocolate' is said to come from the Mayan word 'xocolatl' which means 'bitter water.'

Not far from where I write this to you nowhere in Panama, a Harvard University study found, that the Kuna Yalla people living on the islands suffered fewer cancers, or heart disease cases than those not living on the San Blas islands and taking a cocoa-based drink regularly.

Theobromine and caffeine are the stimulant chemicals in cacao. The beans contain between 0.1% and 0.7% caffeine, whereas dry coffee beans are about 1.2% caffeine. Generally, cocoa is considered to be a rich source of antioxidants such as procyanidins and flavonoids, which may impart anti-aging and anti-cancer properties.cviii

Chocolate and cacao are so important to my diet I must have the absolute best chocolate.

Strong species, of super fruit, the tree's and the nutrients are robust and powerful. Many revere the cacao fruit to be a superfood. The highs in magnesium, calcium, zinc, and iron make it a perfect strong man's food. Cix

Chocolate helps the consumer digest other foods, and this is a key benefit to those adhering to principles of the Nutritional Diversity diet cx

The prevalence of hypertension among the San Blas islander's population is a very low 2.2% and blood pressure does not increase with age there. The population there also experiences lower rates of diabetes mellitus, myocardial infarction, stroke, and cancer than mainland Panamanians. cxi

Improves heart health; researchers globally who studied cocoa flavanols mechanistic pathways have agreed that cocoa flavonoids — in vitro and through animal models—upregulate enzymes that act as a vasodilator of the coronary arteries.cxii

Chocolate proves to be a healthy medium for probiotic bacteria.cxiii

A special study with elite football players determined that diets strategically containing cocoa phenols could relieve oxidative stress and muscle injury. The antioxidative effects induced by cocoaderived polyphenols were also confirmed on skeletal muscle cells in vitro.cxiv The Theobroma cacao tree, or cocoa, has recently garnered increasing attention and become the subject of research due to its antioxidant properties, which are related to potential anti-cancer effects. cxv

Too much, or too late in the day and you could up for a while. You could experience nausea, and headache, dizziness, and an intense buzz. This being said many, especially in this region, partake of the chocolate cleanse ceremony, an experience where mass chocolate consumption is meant to help away from the unneeded and become purer.

It is total muscle food. I can feel it opening up my flow channels inside the muscle, a small pump can come just from eating chocolate. I eat chocolate throughout the first half of my day on a regular, as it has a kick and has caffeine and so if you eat it too late in the day it can make it hard to sleep. I like to sleep early so I can get up early – this is the main power move of my nutritional arsenal, and all action is nutrition, so is the sunrise.

CINNAMON

Cinnamon, most commonly refers to the inner bark, in powdered form from the Cinnamomum tree. It has a long history as a soughtafter spice and medicinal herb in many sources including the Bible. It's recorded as a heavy import into Egypt around 2000 B.C. It goes good as a topping for lots fruit salads and many other things.

The phoenix supposedly builds its nest from cinnamon and cassia or kasia. Herodotus mentions other writers who believed the source of cassia was the home of Dionysus, located somewhere east or south of Greece. Today cinnamon is thought to come from India Burma, and Bangladesh regions.

The Greeks used kásia or malabathron to flavour wine, together with absinth wormwood (Artemisia absinthium). While Theophrastus gives a good account of the plants, he describes a curious method for harvesting: worms eat away the wood and leave the bark behind. Kasia and cinnamon were also the two herbs recommended by Moses for the making of anointing oils.

According to a study that was published in the European Journal of Clinical Nutrition in 2021, type 2 diabetic individuals' blood lipid levels were improved by taking cinnamon supplements. Cinnamon was discovered by the researchers to lower the levels of triglycerides, LDL cholesterol, and total cholesterol in the study subjects.cxvi

Cinnamon is also high in antioxidants, even more so than garlic or oregano. It has anti-inflammatory powers, and reduces heart disease, and treats and prevents diabetes. It cuts down on mucus in the body, and according to Professor Arnold Ehret's Mucussless Diet System (1922),cxvii this is the most important goal in human health.

Cinnamon has been shown to lead to various improvements for Alzheimer's disease and Parkinson's disease. It has also been significantly studied for anti-cancer properties, in both animal and human cell studies.

Cinnamon can be used for athlete's foot, indigestion, to improve brain function, and to help lower blood glucose levels, among many other benefits.

Ancient references seem to point out the significance of the oils in cinnamon. This oil has so far been shown to effectively treat respiratory tract infections caused by fungi. Cinnamon is further noticed for its ability to help stop the growth of bacteria as well as fungi, including the commonly problematic yeast Candida. Cinnamaldehyde, the main active component of cinnamon, may help fight various kinds of infection. In food storage situations a small amount of cinnamon oils can prevent harmful bacteria from forming such as salmonella.

According to a 2022 study that appeared in the Journal of Food

Science, cinnamon extract can help obese mice with their insulin sensitivity and glucose metabolism. Also, the extract was discovered by the researchers to lessen oxidative stress and inflammation in the animals. Cxviii

A laboratory study looking at HIV infected cells found that cinnamon was the most effective treatment of the 69 medicinal plants studied.

This is tree bark, filed into a powder, and I think it makes an argument for the edibility of solid woods, at least as powder. It also makes point for aromatic plants, in that they have potent medicines as well as aromas.

CULANTRO

Culantro eryngium foetidum of the family Apiaceae (includes carrots, celery, parsley, and parsnip) is a tropical perennial native to South and Central America, grows strongly, regularly around areas inhabited by humans and other animals, and in grassy, open areas. Culantro, which gets its name from its potent aroma, has been used for centuries to cure various conditions, such as burns, earaches, fevers, hypertension, constipation, fits, asthma, stomachaches, worms, problems with infertility, snake bites, diarrhoea, and malaria.

Since it has long been used to treat epilepsy or fits and to quiet the spirit, it is also known as spirit weed and fitweed in addition to being the stronger version of cilantro (and a distant cousin). Eryngium foetidum, the herb's scientific name, is also known as E. antihystericum; the latter name has a clear connection to the therapeutic management of epilepsy. Regular use of culantro has been proven to aid with and resolve asthma, other tension issues, excessive blood sugar, and high blood pressure. Rich in minerals and calcium for the bones, as well as A, B, and C vitamins, all of which are potent

antioxidants and support vitality and immunity. The genus Eryngium contains more than 250 flowering species worldwidecxixGenus Eryngium is the largest and most complex genus in the Apiaceae family.cxx Remembering always that the number one optimization and fitness killer is stress, I am quick to find out about the calming and balancing stuff.

Culantro is also a plant that you cannot stop from growing in and around your settlement here in Panama, which is not only convenient but indicative of her intelligence, connectivity, and strength. The herbs than come in for us when we clear a small bit of land and decide to live there, are part of complete health intelligence, that duplicates itself anytime land is cleared. It pairs well with chicken, onion, tomato, and avocado.

It pairs well with recipes that use potatoes, spice, or basil. I advise taking at least one gram of culantro per day because the balancing benefits become fully apparent within the first few weeks.

Coriander or cilantro is the long away cousin of culantro and a sure boast would be to have them both mixed in the guacamole. I love this best culantro out here because it grows like a weed, has a hard rigid tough-looking plant structure, tough smelling odor, insects barely touch it, and mixes great with chocolate, and vegetable mixes alike.

Traditionally employed in the treatment of diabetes, rheumatism, several anti-inflammatory, respiratory (cold, asthma, cough, sinusitis), and stomach disorders, the essential oil also portrays high antioxidant ability even to prevent the oxidative degeneration of other foods. cxxi

Cxxii

Studies showed evidence that methanol extract of Eryngium

foetidum could be a rich source of metabolites with antimicrobial activity to fight Helicobacter pylori (a certain family of digestive tract infections).cxxiiiIn fact, some genus Eryngium species are used as spices and are cultivated throughout the world and other species are used for the treatment of hypertension, gastrointestinal problems, asthma, burns, fevers, diarrhea, malaria, etc. Phytochemical analysis has shown that genus Eryngium species are a rich source of flavonoids, tannins, saponins, and triterpenoids.

Traditional medicine shows several uses for several genera. At least seven North American tribes specifically mention the use of Eryngium (typically roots) as an anti-snake venom therapy. A recent study concluded that the extract was indeed a functional snake bite medicine.cxxiv Among other anti-parasitic functions, the best culantro showed effective against leishmaniasis a common skin parasite infection in the neo-tropical region where it natively grows.cxxv

The anticonvulsant properties of an aqueous extract of the Spirit Weed, have been thoroughly examined and tested, in routine treatments for epilepsy. cxxvi A fraction of the essential oil rich in eryngium is the subject of a US patent application for its effectiveness against parasitic trypanosomes, nematodes, fungi and bacteria in humans and other mammals. These findings suggest the need for further research into this herb and its products. cxxvii

A diverse amount of wild edible plants is known for the treatment of reproductive errors in Trinidad one of which is our beloved culantro. cxxviiiA 24-week intensive high dose culantro study was done in animal testing finding very little side effects or harm caused by high doses of the plant. Kidney lesions could form if culantro only was consumed for a long period of time. cxxix

This specie is hugely popular in the Latin kitchen and to Latin health tradition. The best culantro is totally regarded as a healing substance. Calm energy is good energy as an athlete this is what you want, and wit the best culantro this is what you get. Culantro is heavy in iron, riboflavin, calcium, and carotene. It also is an excellent source of vitamin A, B2, B1 and C, powerful antioxidants that support vitality and immunity, including phosphorous for strong bones.

In ancient traditional practice, the leaves and roots are boiled for fevers, chills, vomiting, diarrhea, colds and convulsions, and the water is taken for pneumonia, flu, diabetes, constipation, and malaria fever. The herb is an anti-inflammatory and contains large amounts of plant sterols, so it can aid asthma, arthritis, and swelling. It also contains trimethyl-benzaldehyde, a powerful pain reliever. A tea can soothe earaches, stomachaches and headaches. In some regions, culantro is also known as 'fit-weed' because it is said to help prevent or aid epileptic fits.

CORDYCEPS MUSHROOMS

Best cordyceps mushrooms are a genus of parasitic fungi that grows on the larvae of insects that have been mentioned since the days of old Ancient Chinese herbal literature and used over Centuries as the cure to 21 different ailments in total.cxxx They work as fungi that attack their insect host body and as the larvae grow the slender stems that grow inside and outside the being taking control of the caterpillar or other host and guiding the creature into a dark damp place where it can go into a spore production cycle fulfilling the final biological destiny of procreation.

Here at our study center in Panama, we call it "Zombie Powder," and only effective stuff earns nicknames around this place. It is a Zombie stamina increase too; the substance will definitely help keep you going, in our experience.

Since we started include these fungi in our routine, we have obviously added an output multiplier because various performance indicators for testers, particularly stamina for non-endurance athletes, have significantly improved. This is based on our own study and testing, and it is the only method to truly develop precise consumption recommendations.

If you want to put it out, you have to put it in.

The remains of the insect and fungi are then hand-collected, dried, and used to treat fatigue, sickness, kidney disease, and low sex drive.

The entire idea at Nutritional Biodiversity Diet Model is to form minimum 60 specie, highly diverse, strategicly designed nutrition plans derived from nonmonoculture cropping systems, and measure up dramatic increases in performance

Lab tests and Centuries of use suggest the best cordyceps promote anti-aging and sustained youthfulness, exercise performance enhancements, and heart health. Several great athletic tests have gone on with this fungi species and the clear result of performance enhancement is there. It's great also because we get to see a model for our own athletic nutrition testing of the ND diet.

Best cordyceps athletic test findings support the belief held in China that Cs-4 could improve oxygen uptake or aerobic capacity and ventilation function and resistance to fatigue of elderly people in exercise.cxxxi

Cordyceps have effects on both innate body immunity and adaptive immunity, furthermore, cordyceps also feature a modulatory effect on the stomach's overall immune system, which may further influence systemic immune function. These same scientific examinations and studies show cordyceps fungi types to be antitumor acting medicine, as well as protective effects to the kidneys and anti-hypoglycemic effects.cxxxii Swimming tests confirm fatigue resistance.cxxxiii

There is a wealth of testimony out there now to the great effects that these best cordyceps are having on people. There are not too many side effects reported and the amount of existing

documentation for studying use is immense.cxxxiv You may not want to take the best cordyceps if you have a myelogenous type of cancer such as AML or CML. Cordyceps mushrooms have been shown to increase the proliferation of red blood precursor cells, who arise from the same lineage as the cells that cause myelogenous cancers. Or, if you are taking insulin or other blood-glucose-lowering medications as cordyceps may have an additive hypoglycemic effect and so blood glucose should be monitored. If a drug is taken that has a "blood-thinning" activity, cordyceps may further increase the risk of heavy bleeding. Cxxxv

Likely recognized initially for the appearance of animal transformation into a plant, this fungi-insect relationship as a food has been thoroughly investigated and used in ancient Asian cultures. Learning and memory improvements were dynamically shown

through supplementation animal testing.cxxxvi Drink more water while taking a cordyceps supplement.

It must be a combination of intelligently pursuing new colonies of caterpillars with the zombie caterpillar body and perhaps even intelligent flight of the spore to the new larvae, according to my abstract thinking about how the next generation of spores would discover new caterpillars. It's difficult to think of a kind of fungus that can endure in this manner. These two great species undoubtedly possess such wonderful medicinal marvels when working together.

CASSAVA MANIOC

A significant piece of our study on healing, health, and performance focuses on the Strong species, which empowers our team and the greater community by illuminating some of the manioc's potent traits outside of her robust development. Manioc is a member of the spurge family, a plant genus native to South America Euphorbiaceae.

One of the more potent carbohydrate diets utilized to support the strenuous labor in the oppressive heat on the tropical farm, the "cancer cure" root tuber offers many advantages. According to Dr. Cynthia Jayasuriya when a cancer patient consumes the cooked best cassava; Vitamin B17 combines in the normal human cell with an enzyme called Rhodanese, which breaks down the B17 into three sugars.

The cancer cell, which is an immature cell, has a different enzyme, beta-glucosidase, which breaks the B17 into glucose, benzaldehyde, and hydrocyanic acid. The hydrocyanic acid acts like an LTTE cyanide capsule, killing the cancer cell. To date, the doctor's claims have been proven true, time and time again

A study indicated that cassava flour has a low glycemic index and can help control blood sugar levels. It was published in the Journal of the Science of Food and Agriculture in 2021. Researchers discovered that healthy people who consumed cassava flour had lower postprandial blood glucose levels.cxxxvii

According to the United Nations Food Security & Nutrition leg (FAO), the woody shrub is also known as manioc, yuca, tapioca, and mandioca is the third most important crop to many of the developing worlds evaluated by food and welfare agencies.

On our farm we will surely never starve simply because of our stock in this one crop, we rarely touch the tubers. I grow it usually with a few other things, like basil, patchouli, or damiana. It is relatively unmolested by bugs usually just by itself. The in vitro cytotoxic assays showed linamarin extracted from cassava plants inhibited the growth and killed various cancer cells such as ovarian cancer, breast cancer, Prostate cancer and leukemia.

Their leaves have a strong antioxidant, and antiradical property, in this reactive oxidant species (ROS) is able to combat harmful infectious substances in the body. The leaves also present high nitrogen availability. The activity in digestion inhibits signaling associated with conditions such as stomach fibrosis and   Crohn's disease. The effects of these polyphenols will be explored, such as their role in preventing degenerative disorders like cancers, diabetes, osteoporosis, and cardiovascular and neurological diseases.

Lamb's health and performance were significantly improved by cassava foliage (leaves). Animal tests revealed that leaf extracts were effective at treating diarrhea. Do not ingest any ginger or ginger related goods, such as ginger beer or ginger-nut cookies, if you have been eating the best cassava. The dangerous hazards of pairing ginger with manioc are well known to the cultures who use it a lot.

The cyanogenic glycosides found in cassava, like linamarin and lotaustralin, have the potential to cause serious toxic consequences as well as various neurological problems, such as motor dysfunction, cognitive decline, and signs of tropical ataxic neuropathy and spastic epidemic paraparesis (Konzo). Both humans and laboratory animals have seen these changes that are linked to consuming cassava or its derivatives. This is reportedly reversed by Ginkgo Biloba extract our general take on toxic effects is that they become nullified by appropriate special diversity.

Cassava leaves have been shown to be a rich source of protein, dietary fiber, and important minerals like iron and zinc, according to a study that was published in the journal Food Science & Nutrition in 2020. Consuming cassava leaves, the researchers discovered, can assist in achieving the daily recommended consumption of these

minerals.cxxxviii

COCONUT OIL

Some claim that the coconut, "A Unique Miracle Ketone from the Tree of Life," is one of the most potent fruits in the tropics. They claim that the Caribbean coconut is the richest of all of them, and it is unquestionably the greatest coconut oil I have yet to taste. A coconut can be thrown, floated across the sea or down a river, and it can grow to large communities in almost any tropical or subtropical environment. The coconut tree, or Cocos nucifera, is a member of the Arecaceae (palm family) and thrives anywhere in the sand, swamp, dry terrain, salty beach, and up on a hill if you bring it there.

The oil found in coconut meat and water is arguably crucial to living in the tropics, and at ND we only want the best nutrition, which includes the best coconut oil, for our team as well as our friends and clients.

A systematic review and meta-analysis on "The impact of coconut oil in lowering cardiovascular disease risk factors" was published in the 2020 issue of Nutrition Reviews. According to this study, ingesting coconut oil may help lower numerous risk factors for cardiovascular disease, such as triglycerides, LDL cholesterol, and total cholesterol.cxxxix

Investigator Ancel Keys' 1950's unique findings of heart disease relations to hydrated vegetable oils, marketers switched gears with a crafty twist and sold the public on the demoralization of all saturated fats. Another completely unnecessary break-it-down "direction   of dissection" and tinker inside or cut something out because the Ph.D. knows better than nature – ridiculous mistake.

Coconut water is incredibly vital and sustainable for human beings, containing important electrolytes and vitamins, and can be a more than viable cultivar for this purpose. Phytochemical studies of the best coconut fiber (mesocarp) ethanolic extract revealed that the presence of phenols, tannins, leucoanthocyanidins, flavonoids, triterpenes, steroids, and alkaloids, while a butanol extract recovered triterpenes, saponins, and condensed tannins. The best coconut balances cholesterol levels.

Coconut material, from inside to out is valuable stuff. the husk functions as charcoal and several brushes are made for various purposes around the world from it. This husk material which makes up 40% of the overall material, in the form of powdered particles and long fibers is also inherently resistant to fungi.

The delicious waters at various stages of growth have been evaluated for the treatment of anemia and bleeding disorders, presenting affects hematological and coagulative.

Too much can cause heavy blocks, this is rich food. Vomiting and bowel issues can be a result of over-consuming. If eating the white meat, shredded or by the piece, I would say one coconut's worth, or

20 grams a day, throughout the day is an appropriate amount and consumption rate of this food. All nutrients or combinations of the mode of function for healing or toxin lies in the dose(s). There are no seen side effects from coconut oils, except for a change in stool composure.

A randomized, controlled, double-blind study titled "Virgin coconut oil supplementation attenuates acute chemotherapy-induced diarrhoea in colorectal cancer patients" will be released in the 2020 issue of the journal Supportive Care in Cancer. According to this study, adding virgin coconut oil to patients' diets helped lower the frequency and severity of diarrhoea brought on by chemotherapy.cxl

The best topical oil and skin treatment ever invented. It keeps

mosquitos off me all by itself, on a hot day, it may need to be reapplied a lot. To help with the flavor and improve the absorption of the   fish oil essences, I will recommend to take the best fish oil supplement everyday along with multivitamins.

CANNABIS

Hemp (Cannabis sativa) was probably the earliest plant cultivated for textile fibers. Archaeologists found a remnant of hemp cloth in ancient Mesopotamia (currently Iran and Iraq) which dates as far back as 8,000 BC.

This superfood herb is also believed to be the oldest example of the human industry. In the Lu Shi, a Chinese work of the Sung dynasty (500 AD), we find a reference to the Emperor Shen Nung (28th century BC) who taught his people to cultivate hemp for cloth.

It is believed that the power herb made it to Europe around 1,200 BC. From there, it spread throughout the ancient cultures of the world. This is just a speculator idea.

Controversial in so many ways the conversation is an interesting one no doubt.

Interesting because of the incredible botanical essence, growth, medicinal successes, and mystery that surrounds the hemp plant but also because of an-unmatchable, that once existed in history, home crop production model.

It can produce biofuel, paint, biodegradable plastics and is one of the most potent and nutritious shrubs for the herb garden.

Fantastically effective as a super-medicine-food the unique species has many uses that are easy to accomplish.

It's seed although we here at the cutting-edge diet team don't do seed foods, is touted as a super and perfect food.

The leaf is nice salad include, so is the flower. Cannabis, damiana, cranberry hibiscus, wandering Jew, gotu kola, Brazilian parsley, and garlic leaf vine and some type of mushroom was once the makings of one of the best salads I have ever had in Costa Rica. We have to learn to eat the wonderful diverse foods again urgently, for more reasons than we time for here.

The stems are roots that are delicious and delicate fried up in the stir fry or the cooked with the potatoes. Katuk goes well with this recipe.

The flower is beautiful smells great, and tastes good too. Smoking the herb like damiana produces a slight cognitive difference said to increase creativity, decrease productivity, help sleep and certain pain disorder, and affect both positively and negatively in different ways for different brains and conditions, the overall mental health state.

Bone fracture repair, dental and bone maintenance, and joint health is heavily supported with cannabis consumption according to the Washington Post and the Tel Aviv Bone Research Lab who also stated that cannabidiol, or CBD, enhances the maturation of collagen, the protein in connective tissue that "holds the body together. After being treated with CBD, the healed bone will be harder to break in the future," Dr. Gabet.cxli

The very controversial docuseries "W.E.E.D." where the CBD extract oil was issued to children with epilepsy was a striking argument for medical cannabis use in the treatment of seizures. cxlii

Muay Tai kickboxers in the extended family camp we know have already been taking CBD in high dose around sandbag shin conditioning.

New headlines and studies all around now indicate the substance may help with diabetes.cxliii

Other study shows it helps focus and with treating ADD/ADHD.

To know something first-hand can take a lifetime of personal investigation, depending on the thing. Open your heart and your mind get the best nutrition, and good rest and apply yourself to the study and you will find whatever truth. That is a guarantee.

Medellin Colombia has approved Medical Marijuana, has export goals, and a push for cultural change on drug standpoints globally.

"The most industrious herb." On the permaculture, the cannabis can be used as textiles, paper, biodegradable plastics for health and is one of the fastest biomass production crops known (fastest production crop)cxliv

Unlike cigarettes, the herb could be medicinal to the lungs when smoked. Marijuana smoke does not harm the lungs.cxlv

Stress management is very important in today's life, and medically this herb is recommended most for stress management. That being said, there are plenty of daily best cannabis smokers that never touch alcohol or other drugs. Most of them suffer anger or painrelated issues.

Now we covered all of that; all of these nutritional ingredients are meant to be used in balance, strategically and dynamically for certain times and applications. All this nutrition can be used as medicine as energy as focus, it is really beautiful and amazing. It is amazing this part of life is missed by so many.

DANDELIONS

Dandelion's are the most obvious first pick of semi-wild food to graduate athlete's, dieters and nutritional enthusiasts anywhere in the world into wild harvesting. That's because dandelions are all over the world, likely in walking distance from your front door right now.

The taraxacum genus from the asteraceae family is most often found in the temperate zone of the Northern hemisphere.

At the Nutritional Diversity Study Center's staff and students are consuming between 10% and 40% wild foods in the overall intake meal plans. That's right nearly all of our greens come select from the farm (10-20% domesticated species) stronger species or the jungle

Wild harvesting and greens are extremely important to the human experience and the human system. Watching monkeys and other primates here eat greens all day long, and not one to ten different ones, but next to all of them stripping down hard materials with their gums and teeth that never see the dentist.

In the wild realm, there are some things that will make you sick or kill you, so you need to know what you are doing, or know the best dandelion well, or know wild food testing well. You can eat the entire dandelion plant, they say some of the best eats from it are the flowers and roots. We eat them mostly in fresh in salads or smoothies, or vegetable burritos.

Dandelions are everywhere! That means they are strong, and they have what it takes to pump on through the day and the night across the globe and to all the islands even (we are one of those islands now). These guys have a happy look and feel and are a tough guy food. These guys have been tested out in all sorts of ways, to show the benefits from this bright, soft, magnificent flowering plant.

Dandelions are a great source of calcium, they contain more calcium then kail. Add two to three cups of dandelion to a smoothie with calcium-rich fruits like orange, kiwi, fig or papaya for steady bone support. Besides vitamin A as beta-carotene (186% RDA) and vitamin C (21% RDA), each cup of chopped dandelion greens are also good sources of vitamins B1 (9% RDA), B2 (11% RDA) and B6 (11% RDA), vitamin E (13% RDA) and especially abundant in vitamin K (357% RDA).

Nutritional Diversity

Several large tests have been conducted and covered in articles that promise dandelions combat cancer directly. Every part of the dandelion plant is rich in antioxidants that prevent free-radical damage to cells and DNA, slowing down the aging process in our cells. It is rich in vitamin C and vitamin A as beta-carotene and increases the liver's production of super-oxide dismutase that also protects all of the members of the digestive tract.

In 2011 the Journal of Ethnopharmacology quotes "selective induction of apoptosis through activation of caspase-8 in human leukemia cells (Jurkat) by dandelion root extract." Among many other keys looks at dandelions and cancer cells.

Dandelion increases bile and saliva production and reduces inflammation to help with gallbladder problems and blockages. It is available in several areas around the world. In many countries, it is used as food and in some countries as therapeutics for the control and treatment of T2D, and HIV.

The benefits are so stacked with the best dandelions, that the University of Windsor in Canada's chemistry department has recently launched the "Dandelion Project," to further investigate the awesome properties of the plant.

The root of the dandelion has traditionally been known to address gastro-intestinal issues, a diuretic, an insulin stimulant, and a digestive stimulant making it a select for the Nutritional Diversity diet.

The anti-diabetic properties of dandelion are attributed to bioactive chemical components; these include chicoric acid, taraxasterol (TS), chlorogenic acid, and sesquiterpene lactones. Dandelions are being used as food and treatment for Type II Diabetes around the world today.cxlvi cxlvii

It gets even better with dandelion as the plant has been seen to feature, diuretic, choleretic, anti-inflammatory, antioxidative, anti-carcinogenic, analgesic, anti-hyperglycemic, anti-coagulator and prebiotic effects cxlviii

Hepatocellular carcinoma (HCC) is one of the most common malignancies, which accounts for 90% of primary liver cancer. HCC usually presents with poor outcomes due to the high rates of tumor recurrence and widespread metastasis (Mao and Wang, 2015). Recent results pointed out that natural products, in particular those present in Taraxacum root extract, have great potential as non-toxic and effective alternatives to conventional modes of chemotherapy available today. Studies indicate strong liver support in the root extract, and possible treatment of HIV.

Overuse of this precious root could cause runny bowel, and other irritations or inflammations of the stomach.

Dandelions will grow wherever you stick them, clear an area recently, and beyond. I like to use dandelions along trails into the thick, as they take hold and help to improve the trail's life expectancy. Mixed with peanut grass transplants, you have a nice easy to groom carpet that keeps other stuff free of invading back into the trail clearing. As I mention in earlier about dandelions, they are a strong little plant, that has set its roots everywhere in the world. I don't know about you but that's nutrition to take advantage of if you ask me.

DAMIANA

The most common usage of this herb in Mexican culture has been as an aphrodisiac tea made from the blossoms. It is a highly powerful grower that invades heavily near clearings and people. It is endemic to New Mexico, Texas, Mexico, the Caribbean, Central America, and South America.

Damiana Turnera diffusa, Turnera aphrodisiaca of the Plant Family of Turneraceae is a small shrub with tiny yellow flowers, and bright or dark green leaves depending on the moment and geography. Either leaf shade fresh turn blended green drinks or juice cleanses glowing neon green.

Damiana has been used as a herbal treatment for a very long time. Native American societies had been utilizing it for generations as a nourishing herb and bladder-cleansing cure before the Spanish sailed across the Atlantic. According to several seasoned nature guides, the electric herb reduces coughing, enhances regularity, and significantly increases oxygen transport and connectedness.

Most people are unaware of its edibility and its smoke-ability. I have made a blend of this herb dried with many other herbs as an afternoon smoke; since seeing ambrosia Peruviana herb cure a friend's lifelong asthma. The plant has been studied for longevity because of its anti-aging activities and the specific inhibition of internal self-created biological essences associated with aging.

In 1875, La Damiana was introduced in the United States by way of a Baltimore resident doctor, J.J. Caldwell, who wrote in the Virginia Medical Monthly of extremely old Mexican men fathering dozens of children with the help of their daily Damiana tea.

"Damiana, beyond doubt," Caldwell added, "is the most reliable, useful, and permanent tonic to the genital organs of both sexes that we have thus far discovered."

This is something that after years of experience, want for my family, for my animals for my whole farm.

This is something easy to cultivate and looks good all at once, so I will strategically map her out all around.

This is permaculture, with placements inside a greater diversity of things grown together in the most self-maintaining way possible. Most people walk by this type of agriculture and see nothing.

Damiana offers a wealth of benefits to our diet plans it is pretty much a year-round staple for us here at the Biodynamic Nutrition Study in Panama. We have done a decent amount of performance testing on it specifically also in the ongoing tropical nutrition athletic study work.

Damiana really does have and emanate a truly free attitude. I'll probably use this as an opportunity to demonstrate why nutritional science and nutritional experts today are to blame for everyone's poor health and performance.

None of these scientists are anywhere near us in human health science. They are going in the wrong direction altogether. They think they know better than nature because of the degree they got from modern education. They pay no attention to nature.

Studies show that the Turnera did have inhibiting effects to phosphodiesterase-5 sets, an active mode used to treat erectile function showing, that very possibly this herb can treat erectile dysfunction.cxlix

Damiana contains certain potential anti-cancer properties, and essences that treat wounds on the skin. cl

Breast cancer studies are ongoing. Possible positive substitute to tobacco and cannabis, smoking this herb has slightly euphoric and better mood effects.cli

Various other traditional and potential benefits of this species include the treatment of anemia, anxiety, antibacterial/microbial, antidepressant, antidiabetic, antioxidant, stress reliever, anti-obesity, antispasmodic, antitumor, bronchitis, chronic cystitis, coughs, fever, frigidity, fungal infections, gastroprotective, hepatoprotective, laxative, to relieve pain, respiratory diseases, skin disorders, and to promote healthy menstruation.

Antidepressant confirmed for the electric herb that I got out of bed with, sent from above, in a recent central study.clii

Its Side effects can include morning erections, or in the case of taking too much, it could result in nausea.

As with everything take with sufficient diversity, and not more than 10 grams in a day without building up to it.

I can sum it up by saying that it relieves tension and gives you more energy.

a carefree mood booster. Sexual performance improvement and restoration. One of its many nicknames is "flor de Amor," or "the blossom of love." It's a big hit with the author. Excellent in salads with a zesty flavor, perhaps with some avocado and olive oil! Terrific in smoothies that turn electric green from her! Herb that fights cancer.

FADOGIA AGRESTIS

Historically, erectile dysfunction and other health issues have been treated with a shrubby plant called Fadogia Agrestis. It is common in sub-Saharan Africa and is widely seen in Nigeria. The performance of the sex organs is the main goal of using this as a supplement.

The aqueous extract of Fadogia agrestis stem increased the blood testosterone concentrations and this may be the mechanism responsible for its aphrodisiac effects and various masculine behaviors. It may be used to modify impaired sexual functions in animals, especially those arising from hypotestosteronemia.cliii

While the drug has traditionally been used as an aphrodisiac, it has recently acquired favor as a pure testosterone booster. While further research is obviously necessary, it does appear to be pretty intriguing in that regard. Long used as an herbal medicine, it is currently becoming more well-known as a result of the promotion from numerous fitness and health authorities.

Due to Fadogia Agrestis' capacity to control male hormones, sportsmen regularly use it to enhance performance. The medicinal components found in it, including saponins, anthraquinones, flavonoids, and glycosides, all contribute to this effect. There haven't been many researches on it, but those that have seemed to have great promise. In one study, levels in people who took Fadogia, which is the equivalent of 1000 mg daily, their hormone level began to rise after just a few days.

Fadogia is a powerful alternative for raising healthier testosterone levels, hence it is advised to use it in cycles to prevent the body from adjusting and lowering natural products. Three weeks on, one week off, or two months on, one month off are possible programme cycles. It is a natural product that aids in reducing excess body fat and speeds up metabolism, preventing the intake of more fat.

The astringent properties of Fadogia Agrestis are extremely potent. It has been used to decrease skin imperfections and excessive sebum production. By closing the pores around the eyes, this herb can also alleviate puffy eyes. In this medicinal plant, there are lots of antioxidants that protect against free radicals that could speed ageing. Antioxidants not only guard against cancer but also protect the skin from UV radiation harm.cliv

It contains chrysophanic acid, which helps anaemic people increase their red blood cell count and thereby improves their health. Salicylic acid, which is present in it aids in avoiding bacterial adherence to the uterine wall and the development of illnesses following childbirth. Yohimbine, a powerful alpha 2-adrenergic antagonist found in this shrubby plant, helps diabetics better control their blood sugar levels. Moreover, this astringent reduces the requirement for insulin in diabetic people.

It can help reduce high blood pressure because it has antihypertensive characteristics. Also, by preventing plaque from accumulating on artery walls and LDL cholesterol from oxidizing, it can reduce the chance of developing heart disease.

Fadogia agrestis, an African plant, can ultimately assist individuals in overcoming a variety of health issues and gaining a number of significant health advantages that translate into easier and healthier lives.clv

GINGER

Ginger (in Spanish: Jengibre) is a flowering plant, and most commonly used is it's the root or underground stem (rhizome) which can be consumed fresh, powdered, dried as a spice, in oil form or as juice.

Herbalist Stephen Harrod Buhner mentions in his outstanding book, "Herbal Anti-virals", that powdered ginger is useless against viral disease. You need to use fresh ginger. It can be in tea or food, but it must be fresh ginger.

Nutritional Diversity

Its scientific name is Zingiber officinale. Ginger is part of the Zingiberaceae family, alongside cardamom and turmeric, and is commonly produced in India, the Caribbean, Central America, South America, North America, Europe, Fiji, Indonesia, and Australia.

Ginger is thought to have originated in the Himalayan foothills of Northern India. It is easy to grow, in permacultures and home gardens, even in buckets – making it a Nutritional Diversity top pick.

The best ginger is a common ingredient in Asian and Indian cuisine also, ginger has been used for its medicinal properties for centuries among many cultures.

The root has an extensive history of use for relieving digestive problems such as nausea, loss of appetite, motion sickness and also has been used to treat several types of pain.

It is an herbaceous perennial which grows annual stems about two feet tall bearing narrow green leaves and yellow flowers (there are many strains of ginger with alternate flowers and stem lengths). Ginger is loaded with nutrients and bio-active compounds that have powerful benefits for your body and brain.

Ginger is easy to grow, it likes water, it likes to be wet, but not too wet, or waterlogged. It does well in pots and out in the garden or just on the side of the house in the tropical climate. It works well lined in front of hot pepper plants in the Nutritional Diversity & Tropical Permaculture Centers.

This stuff needs a good place where it has some shade, and will not be dug up during times of the year where it goes completely underground and invisible. I have seen it grow well in the sun too and depending on variety, some you can't stop growing anywhere. It can be used like patchouli, to ward off certain insects I have noticed.

You want ginger in your diet, and I would say as an all the time staple but as needed. I recommend about a quarter teaspoon-sized chunk in a blend daily. This can be upped for healing and medicinal purpose.

Ginger leaves almost never discussed make great addictions to stirfries, smoothies, and my famous fresh leaf burritos.

Ginger is high in copper an essential trace mineral for all living life, copper is important for the development, and maintenance of bone, connective tissue, brain, heart, and many other body organs. Copper is involved in the formation of red blood cells, the absorption and utilization of iron, the metabolism of cholesterol and glucose, and the synthesis and release of life-sustaining proteins and enzymes.

These enzymes, in turn, produce cellular energy and regulate nerve transmission, blood clotting, and oxygen transport. High in copper and iron makes ginger great blood food, for the thick blooded strong man, high in vitality.

The insulin sensitivity and glucose metabolism of diabetic rats were enhanced by ginger extract, according to a 2020 study published in the Journal of Ethnopharmacology.

The best ginger has an interestingly long history of use as seasickness and motion sickness remedy, and there is evidence that it may be as effective as prescription medication. Take a slice of ginger on your next long ride. It relieves morning sickness and other pregnancy-related stomach discomforts.

Ginger contains potent anti-inflammatory compounds known as gingerols. These substances are thought to explain why people with osteoarthritis or rheumatoid arthritis experience reductions in their pain levels and improvements in their mobility when they consume ginger on regular basis. A 2020 study that appeared in the Journal of Medicinal Food demonstrated that ginger extract decreased pain and inflammation in rheumatoid arthritis-affected rats.clvi

Ginger topical compresses are effective joint and muscle pain relief. Simply heat some water with ginger pieces in it, to have a ginger tea, then soak a cloth in that tea, and apply to the affected joint or muscle. Ginger contains chromium, magnesium, and zinc which can help to improve blood flow, as well as help prevent chills, fever, and excessive sweat.

According to a 2021 study that appeared in Food Chemistry, ginger extract has strong antioxidant properties and provided both in vitro and in vivo protection from oxidative stress.

It can help treat those suffering from yeast infections, gum inflammation, and even gingivitis. Colon cancer preventative, and also treatment is indicated by a study at the University of Minnesota which found that ginger may slow the growth of colorectal cancer cells.

Those suffering from common respiratory diseases such as a cough can find relief in ginger's ability to expand to the lungs, loosen phlegm, and acts as a natural expectorant that breaks down and removes mucus. Several observations of indigenous communities throughout the world have pointed to the effectiveness of this herb to help with congestion.

Ginger is through the roof on the mineral manganese, which is helpful to the body and necessary for most biological existence in the appropriate doses.

Chronic exposure to excessive manganese levels which are very high in the best ginger can lead to a variety of psychiatric and motor disturbances, termed manganism. Generally, these symptoms are recognized in exposure to ambient manganese air concentrations in excess of 5 micrograms, and not so much by ginger consumption. While the risk of experiencing this from ginger consumption is very low, I find it important to talk about these minerals in our foods and in our bodies. I think it is important to start recognizing certain key basic periodic elements, and vitamin levels, how they relate to certain conditions and how they can be used in a regulated manner from day today.

It also has positive effects on testosterone production, respiratory function, immune system, and joint function. It has the ability to suppress illness, to include sudden stomach ache. Consumption of ginger on its own has a way of energizing the system. Ginger stimulates saliva production also.

Use ginger heavily when you are leaning down, cutting weight, it's anti-inflammatory and mucus expellant abilities are powerful, go slow, too much ginger is not recommended for optimal health.

GOTU KOLA

Gotu Kola scientifically, Centella asiatica is the herb that comes to mind first for longevity. Centella asiatica, apiaceae or umbelliferae family of plants; mostly known are the aromatic flowering vegetables named after the type genus apium such as celery, carrot or parsley.

It would appear it also supports neurologic and cognitive function and treats Alzheimer's, Parkinson, and other neurological disorders.

Gotu kola also known as Penny Wart has been used as a strong antidepressant, antianxiety medication, seriously reducing stress and literal toxicity. The herb increased circulation and decreases swelling and inflammation, and relieves joint pain.

Gotu kola with botanical name as Centella asiatica helps insomnia, stretch marks, and the rapid healing of cuts and scrapes minimizing scarring.

It's easy to see why the best gotu kola herb has been a staple to Chinese, Ayurveda medicine, and many other cultural contexts throughout the ages. It likes tropical swampland but grows well also in covered soil areas, such as in a greenhouse.

Other well-known and economically important plant relatives of this family are ajwain, angelica, anise, asafoetida, caraway, chervil, coriander, cumin, dill, fennel, poison hemlock, lovage, parsnip, and sea holly, as well as silphium, a plant whose identity is currently unclear to botanists, a specie who may now be extinct.

Centella asiatica is a perennial herb, considered an invasive species, which to a Nutritional Diversifist's ear automatically translates into "strong grower" and "I want it."

Active compounds including pentacyclic triterpenes, mainly asiaticoside, madecassoside, asiatic and madecassic acids, make gotu kola a proactive wound coagulant, even for infected, more compromising wounds.

The ingredients combat scarring and prove cosmetically very beneficial. clvii clviii

The magic herb has been shown in vivo testing to regenerate nerve and brain tissue cells, and combat systemic brain diseases. Correlation between mice and general cognitive and memory function improvement from the herb was also demonstrated, clix as well as antibacterial activity.clx clxi Alzheimer improvements clxii clxiii clxiv clxv Even the treatment of dementia.clxvi

The superfood has also demonstrated faster vascular cognitive repair after stroke. Circulatory improvements are observed in most of the vast testing that this particular herb has undergone. clxvii

Can it do no more? On top of it all, the beautiful ground cover improves mood, though it's complex modes of neurological treatments.clxviii

The herb is so beneficial that it has scientifically been studied as a

"cure-all." clxix effects. It has impressively shown to protect life. clxx It can even attenuate spine loss! clxxi

No wonder it has been used for such a long time and continues to be so popular with medical science.clxxii

If it couldn't better, it is very safe! Start small and work your way up to assess tolerance.

I am a huge proponent of the best Gotu kola! I use this stuff all the time. It is easy to grow and a small bed can keep me and a friend upon supply. Once you bring it around it will also nicely add itself around. It has been an all-around happy experience cultivating and consuming the mood-boosting brain stimulator.

Jackfruit, damiana, ashwagandha, basil, licorice and zornia, ambrosia peruvianna, maybe some mango would be great longevity stacking smoothie companions. This shake would get the training started I tell you that.

GARLIC VINE

Garlic vine, garlic leaf vine, or fake garlic, (Mansoa hymenaea, Mansoa alliacea) is not related at all to real garlic although it has almot identical taste. It is native to South America and is quite delicious, and useful. The vine begins well and quickly develops into a robust, heavy wood.

These are some of the top statistical characteristics I seek in a specie, naturally for nutritional diversity sciences. It is semi-tropical, USDA

Recommended Zones are 8B 9, 10, 11 and that cold protection will secure the longest life and earliest bloom.clxxiii

Although it is incredibly tasty and it is claimed that the plant master says it improves the quality of the medicine, there hasn't been much research done on this particular species. In general, cardioprotective power study of leaves as nutrition, a great list for the heart concerned herbalist mentioned this strain in their examinations. Residents of Brazil and Peru's cities and jungles alike turn to this herb for relief from headaches, arthritic, rheumatic, cold, flu, and fever.

In a very slow but natural building model, the direction of a vine like this one can be watched and directed to tie together bamboo connections. The vine, which is highly lush and healthy, can be used for roofing, fence for chickens or other animals, crossing into another vertically, or covering the growing environment for other vines like chayote or pumpkin. clxxiv

HONEY

Nature's best remedy is The Best Honey. According to some, honey helps arthritis, levels blood cholesterol, prevents cancer, gives quick energy, and can be applied to wounds and burns to speed up healing. The initial field test of foods and oils is simple application to the skin, which reveals clear vitalizing characteristics.

The majority of honey offered in supermarkets is phony to some extent, and even in beehives where it is produced, there are widespread abusive techniques such "sugaring" that result in subpar products.

Bees are some of our earth's principal pollinators, and without them, our very existence would not be possible. Their products are extremely valuable and extremely rare commodities. It is theorized by many scientists that hominids, evolved their brains searching out the energy-rich substance. Humans have been consuming honey for thousands of years. One of the oldest human paintings, is of a bee man, holding mushrooms – another theorized food of the evolved mind.

In Paraguay, the Native Ache people believe honey to be their second most important food following game meat. Honey may be used to provide an Ache with up to or even more than 1,100 calories per day. Honey was reported to provide upwards of 80% of caloric intake in the pygmy people of the Congo. The Tanzanians were noted to consume of their caloric intake from the sweet syrup.

Here in Panama there are Melipona bees whereas much of their honey's use is documented of, in the Peruvian and Colombian Amazon traditional folk medicine, where it is mixed with plant extracts and alcohol. Many here buzz about the medicinal properties that come from this Melipona bee. In total there are around 20,000 different species of bee-s in the world.

We can now more accurately estimate how many bees are lost annually as a result of more than ten years of COLOSS group study, but the figures are not as attractive as the insects or their products.clxxv Bees are under major threat from modern agriculture chemicals and cattle intentioned land clearing.

Finding a good beekeeper, that has a completely non-fraudulent and quality product turns out to be quite the task. Finding one that takes the importance of their impact on the surrounding ecology would be a divine find, as honey bee importation to foreign areas disrupts other natural pollinators.clxxvi

Honey helps the digestive system digest other foods better, and so do papayas, which are great with honey, and a dash of cinnamon makes for an ancient healing remedy and nice dessert tasting snack that will energize. Honey inherently saves the body from having to make enzymes, a process that depletes energy. Honey and papaya together could allow athletes to digest more nutrients more effectively and efficiently. Add in some avocado and mushrooms, a diversity of selected other ingredients, and you're really off to the races. Basil and turmeric are other favorite honey soaks.

Honey is packed with vitamins and minerals in already highly soluble forms such as vitamin B6, thiamin, niacin, riboflavin, pantothenic acid, and certain amino acids. The minerals found in honey include calcium, copper, iron, magnesium, manganese, phosphorus, potassium, sodium, and zinc.

The golden blood-blood builder honey is also one of the most potent cell protection and anti-aging compounds on the planet. Certain studies indicate cellular regeneration resulting from honey, it has also been clinically evaluated as a cancer cure.clxxvii

Traditionally, honey is used in the treatment of eye diseases, bronchial asthma, throat infections, tuberculosis, thirst, hiccups, fatigue, dizziness, hepatitis, constipation, worm infestation, piles, eczema, healing of ulcers, leishmaniasis, atherosclerosis antibacterial, anti-inflammatory, antifungal, antiviral, and antidiabetic effects. It also reports immunomodulatory, estrogenic regulatory, anti-mutagenic properties.clxxviii

Loved by all and especially the little ones (over the age of 8) pure honey promotes optimal sleep, and great physiological recovery at night for better immunity and energy.

Honey even contains an enzyme that produces the disinfectant hydrogen peroxide when it touches a damp surface like a wound. Honey is highly cytotoxic against tumor or cancer cells while it is non-cytotoxic to normal cells. The data indicate that honey can inhibit carcinogenesis by modulating the molecular processes of initiation, promotion, and progression stages. Clxxix

Honey healing and honey harm are often in the dose and too much honey would not be a good thing and could lead to nausea, headaches, bowel problems, and other abnormalities.

In my experience, a slight head buzz is the lifetime indicator that too much is being consumed. Topical use makes up most of my intake just at my own preference, but I would say two tablespoons within a four-hour period is around about a good limit.

Unfortunately, at this point in the food tour it is crucial to highlight several severe risks and frauds involving honey products and modern food production in general. Understanding these concerns is essential if we are to develop fresh, improved solutions and food sources free from them.

HOT PEPPERS

icante, or spicy hot peppers are the fruit of plants from the genus Capsicum, members of the nightshade family, Solanaceae. The name comes from the Aztec language, Nahuati. not as popular here in Panama, as they are in my home town of Albuquerque, New Mexico.

Hot peppers have been used, cultivated and cherished since man existed. Mostly for a good purpose, sometimes for bad. Ideas of hot foods making hot heads in history are all theoretical. Mostly the thought was spicy food love started during specific cultures who practiced developing intentional pain tolerance.

Recently, phytoliths of garlic mustard seed (Alliaria petiolata) were found in carbonized food deposits on prehistoric pottery from the western Baltic dating from 6,1 k.a to 5,7 k.a cal BP (Ertebölle Complex).

This archaeological evidence suggests much greater antiquity to the spicing of foods than previously thought within a hunter-gatherer or ancient premise.

The tale of Braun's adventures in the Chinese Communist revolution is packed with enough twists and turns for a big-screen thriller. In the clutch of culinary history, one quote from Braun's autobiography recalls his first impressions of Mao Zedong, the man who would soon go on to become China's Emperor.

"The food of the true revolutionary is the red pepper," declared Mao. "And he who cannot endure red peppers is also unable to fight."

The concept of self-medication now generally accepted in primates but also in other vertebrates was first proposed by D.H Janzen (1978), an ecologist at the University of Pennsylvania.

On our own we know that eating spicy foods activates an expulsion of mucus from the system, namely in the sinuses. These sinuses are bone lined hollow cavities, located throughout the body and perform varying functions. Sinuses are typically associated with the cavities within the skull.

This is important cleaning, and many health theories such as Arnold Ehret, a Godfather to vegetable healing have been logically formed around mucus-lessness as the real code to staying healthy.

Electrophysiological records in both peripheral and central nervous systems show that the primate sensory taste system is basically organized around two major clusters of fibers and their cortical projections. Co-variations between the neural responses to various compounds were observed for sugars, on the one hand, and for tannic acids and alkaloids. Our human taste perception system is not different from other primates as far as discrimination of noxious v/s beneficial substances through taste; clearly in the case of hot peppers not so much, nor in garlic, black pepper ginger or turmeric.

Liken to the spice, bitterness is normally suggested to represent a reliable signal of toxicity for animals and humans but a number of secondary compounds are bitter tasting (Saponins, Alkaloids, and some Sesquiterpenoids, Terpenoids and Steroid Glycosides) and many of these substances possess important pharmacological activity. clxxx

"Acceptance of food depends not only on taste, but also on olfactory, tactile and visual signals, as well as memories of previous, similar experiences and social expectations. Food palatability and hedonic value therefore play central roles in nutrient intake. As a result, ancestral humans who liked spicy food—and therefore gained from its health benefits—might well have had longer, healthier lives and more offspring" (Nilius & Giovanni 2011)

In addition to its ability to reduce pain when applied topically, capsaicin may also have analgesic benefits when taken orally. According to studies, it can lessen the discomfort brought on by ailments including cluster headaches and neuropathy.clxxxi

They also help in Reduction of Blood pressure and cholesterol level. Hot peppers also have vasodilating effect means they widen the blood vessels and help better blood flow. Nutritional Diversity diet.

Studies showed that eating spicy foods was the factor behind a 14% decrease in overall mortality, compared to folks who can't take the heat. They also greatly help in weight loss.clxxxii

Anti-inflammatory characteristics that could aid in reducing inflammation all over the body. Those who suffer from diseases like arthritis and other inflammatory ailments may find this to be very helpful. The presence of antioxidants in hot peppers can aid in preventing the body from being harmed by free radicals. These antioxidants might aid in lowering the chance of developing chronic illnesses including cancer and heart disease.clxxxiii

Apart from giving many benefits, consuming hot peppers can make some people experience gastrointestinal distress. This may involve signs like diarrhea, vomiting, and nausea. They can cause allergic reactions in some people, especially those who are sensitive to specific proteins in the peppers. Itching, hives, and breathing difficulties are all possible allergy symptoms.

Capsaicin, when it comes into touch with the skin, can irritate the skin. Itching, burning, and redness are a few signs that may be present. Make sure to wash your hands when handling the fire fruits. To some and depending on the current diet they can cause over-acidity.

JACKFRUITS

The fig, mulberry, durian, and breadfruit family's (Moraceae) highthiamine and vitamin B6-containing jackfruit is the largest treeborne fruit, with individual fruits weighing up to 35 kg (80 lb.), measuring 90 cm (35 in), and being 50 cm (20 in) in diameter. The jackfruit tree, whose wood is preferred for producing musical instruments, has the ability to yield 500 kilos of fruit annually, or up to 200 fruits, each year.

Artocarpus heterophyllu Jackfruit is a sweet delicious mango, pineapple, apple, flavor and dehydrated or frozen it is the best candy ever, much better than a fruit roll-up or ice-pop.

In Tamil Nadu, the jack fruit is referred to as one of the three 'royal fruits,' along with banana and mango, for their sweetness and flavor. This triad of fruits is referred to as ma-pala-vazhai.

The Jack fruit seed, is also a great food boiled or powdered into a

flour, and also boiled and sliced as a salad topping or stir fry ingredient. It is one of the rare fruits that is rich in B-complex group of vitamins. It contains very good amounts of vitamin B-6 (pyridoxine), niacin, riboflavin, and folic acid. The core and stringy materials of the jack fruit, can be fried or boiled and chopped down into a natural epoxy glue. Jackfruits can be dried, fried, roasted, added to soups, used in jams, juices, ice cream and we are lucky to have so many of them close to us in Bocas del Toro, Panama

The Jack fruit tree is thought to have originated in Asia (Southeast) or India, and is the national fruit of Bangladesh. Jackfruit is a powerful food that replenishes energy and revitalizes the body instantly, and has possibly had a positive joint tissue effect.

Sting-less bees like the Tetragonula iridipennis here in Central America are the jackfruit pollinators, and as such, play an important role in the super fruit's cultivation – you will see them hovering around the ripe jackfruit. The tree once established for five to seven years, is a very low maintenance high production tree that is fun to climb. After seven years it can live in the jungle for a very long time.

Nutritional Diversity doctrine places a strong preference on plants from the tropical jungle as the most potent nutritional sources, also to plants that may not be from the jungle but can hang in the jungle. Many popular foods today simply won't survive long at all in the jungle, outside of a handpicked one like my friends'.

The jackfruit tree although cultivated for over 6000 years, is easy to grow and very productive with valuable to wood to boot; is oddly passed up by the modern agriculturists of today. Jackfruit tree wood, is a high quality, rot resistant, beautiful timber, the softer of which is also used for boat making.

Nutritional Diversity

Jackfruit is rich in dietary fiber, which makes it a good bulk laxative.

The fiber content helps protect the colon mucous membrane by binding to and eliminating cancer-causing chemicals from the colon. Certain studies show that heavy Jackfruit consumption could treat colon issues.

Jackfruit is a big part of my miracle cleanse and human optimization trip to Panama or Costa Rica that I done a few rounds of now with friends, and those very interested in human optimization.

The fresh fruit is a good source of potassium, magnesium, manganese, and iron. It is also another great natural food to help regulate a healthy and optimal cardiovascular state. With about 95 calories in about a half a cup, they aren't quite as high carb or caloric as staples like rice or corn.

Around 300 B.C., the Greek philosopher Theophrastus wrote: "There is also another tree which is very large and has wonderfully sweet and large fruit; it is used for food by the sages of India who wear no clothes."

Jackfruit has a lot in it to support natural testosterone production, and regulate a healthy blood flow making it another athlete's choice. Vitamin B6 and thiamine concentrate, great for keeping steady testosterone production supportive nutrients in the system. The tree represents power and productivity in many ways, and has been named in many studies and ideas relative to hunger crisis help and nutritional solutions to help pull up poor communities.

This green jackfruit has been historically also harvested green and boiled into a nice edible state. In Indonesia, young jackfruit is cooked with coconut milk as Gudeg. In many cultures, the young fruit is boiled and used in curries as a staple food. In northern Thailand, the boiled young jackfruit is used in the Thai salad called tam kanun.

Rich in digestible starch, protein and minerals jackfruit seeds are a handy ingredient to a good Nutritional Diversity. The seeds can be dried for storage, and can be roasted also for include into a nice trail mix, I am experimenting with a honey, sesame seed roast topping. Jack fruit seeds can be boiled or soaked and made into a nice mash potato like puree.

Consumption of jack fruit regularly is also very healthy for the skin. I have always thought that a great skin cream for boxers could be made from the pulp, as the latex properties in jack fruit help very much with skin durability also when applied topically. Consumers of jack fruit will notice that much of the fruit consumed goes directly to the skin, without the need for topical application, and that there is also a slight change in the body's aroma after consuming large amounts of jackfruit.

Dehydrated jackfruit, is a great way to keep it over time and tastes better than fruit roll ups by like thousand times. The mineral and carbohydrate content of the seed is significant, and powdered seed flour and dehydrated fruits are easily mixed into Nutritional Diversity organizer containers.

Jackfruit is a muscle building, small tendon supportive, miracle food. I was taking a few things at once trying to repair an elbow injury my first year eating this regularly but it was one the fastest repairs and it did seem to be in large part due to the jackfruit consumption. It is having a direct muscle supportive effect also on the muscle build. I am studying these effects using the incremental isolated food testing techniques, and staying with its use over time.

The skin organ, is the large very important covering of the body. Jackfruit is great for the skin. One thing to consider about skin health, is that with chemicals in soaps, shampoos, conditioners, many skin creams and sun blocks, city water supplies, etc. the skin is likely fighting to maintain optimum health creating a drag on human optimization and athletic processes. Relieving this drag is important, and Jackfruit is well consumed and applied topically in addition to avocado, and coconut oil, among many other things.clxxxiv

KATUK

Nutritional Diversity

Certain tropical areas of Asia and Central America grow the leafy shrub Sauropus androgynus, often known as katuk, "star gooseberry," or "sweet leaf," which belongs to the Euphorbiaceae family.

The peanut buttery leaf blitz is packed with phytonutrients, micronutrients, vitamins, and minerals to help you get through the day. The seed pods of the Katuk plant really outperform croutons in taste and texture. The tiny flower-shaped seeds are straight out of a gingerbread house.

It grows well, strong and procreative, and quickly abundant on the Permaculture farm (tropical). Be Careful; chickens, leaf cutters, and goats love this stuff!

Significantly increases the production of breast milk to promote healthy child growth. The leaves of the best katuk plant have been traditionally used to treat certain diseases and for weight loss. It has also been used for exquisite vegetable dishes. These leaves contain an adequate bulk of macronutrients and having most of the micronutrients.

The micronutrients are phenolic compounds such as carotenoids, antioxidant vitamins, and minerals as the greenest leafy matters are usually. The leaves also have most of the essential minerals, including rich sodium, potassium, calcium, phosphorus, iron, magnesium, copper, zinc, manganese, and cobalt that are required for adequate daily system optimal fitness performance clxxxv.

The plant literally has the nickname of the multivitamin leaf, and this high vitamin content and high protein content is necessary to move through the farm all day in and all day out in the tropical sun – trust me! clxxxvi Remember that ultimately you want to maintain a balanced high diversity of whole foods.

The traditional medicine to relieve fever, treat urinary problems, and increase breast milk production consumed as a salad or prepared as curry, or stir-fried has exactly 17.4% protein out of 100g of leaves which is helpful information to diet strategists.

Compared to other dark greens like spinach has 2.0g, mint 4.8g, and cabbage about 1.8g, of protein katuk reports to be a much more valuable plantclxxxvii .

Thought to have anti-diabetic properties that in reality, all green

nontoxic plant vegetables like this possess; the unnatural condition comes verifiably from unnatural foods and refined sugars in extremely high doses coupled with a narrow spectrum insufficient diet plan. Clxxxviiiclxxxix

It should be used to make a nutritional diversity diet for chickens. A study in fact clearly demonstrated that 5% Sauropus androgynus leaf powder has real effects of increasing the body weight performance, hematological profile protection, support, and protection of the cellular and humoral immune responses in the chickens.

The supplementation also resulted in reductions of certain cytotoxic residues in the organs. Furthermore, the Katuk in the diet provided increased protection of liver, kidney, spleen, and BF histopathology, and small increases in the supplementation also showed in small increases of immune expression. cxc

Animal testing has shown that the high levels of chlorophyll contained in the best Katuk are curative to colon and rectal disorders as well as general oxidative stress. For this full chemical benefit, consumers must go "plant to mouth."

Despite its use as a medicinal and food product, several studies have reported severe pulmonary dysfunction as a side effect of consuming the dark green goodie. As with all things, in moderation, and within a wide diversity of food.cxci

It is great to grow, beautiful at my favorite teachers' place it took off like a weed! The particular spot is a testament that if you do a great canopy layer and you can have her as shrub cover for miles!

With a salad, the seed bulbs are preferable to croutons. Take your time with that until you have a lot happening; if done well, it can take over.

MANGO

The mango tree produces a tropical fruit, loved by most, worshiped by some and it has very delicious and nutritious reasons for that!

A juicy drupe belonging to the genus Mangifera, a genus of flowering plants in the cashew family, Anacardiaceae, contains approximately 69 species, with the best-known being the Common Mango (Mangifera indica).

This fruit is native to South Asia and is the national fruit of India, Pakistan, and the Philippines, and the national tree of Bangladesh – whose national fruit is the Jackfruit.

Mangoes have been shown to have significant quantities of dietary fiber, vitamins, and minerals, according to a 2020 study that was published in the Journal of Nutrition and Food Science. Mango consumption can assist in achieving the daily requirements for dietary fiber, vitamin C, and potassium, according to the study's findings.cxciiFiber is such a huge focus for the Nutritional Diversity diet, and mango really is a best source.

According to a 2021 study that appeared in the Journal of Agriculture and Food Chemistry, eating mango pulp can enhance gut health by boosting the number of good bacteria there. The researchers discovered that the levels of Bifidobacterium and Lactobacillus, which are linked to better gut health, increased when mango pulp was consumed.cxciii

Galla hormone production in the brain is supported by mango, it is a brain fruit, and this is why I have chosen it as a Nutritional Diversity original 30 – the first 30 plant species written about on

NutritionalDiversity.com. Other reasons for this priority selection are it's alkaline and anti-cancer properties (cancer is one of today's leading health afflictions), effectively and well-studied against several of the most common cancers.

Mango leaves and trees are great members of the farm, providing great cover, aroma, and we use the baby leaves in our green smoothies, often.

Mango peel extract contains anti-inflammatory and antioxidant characteristics, according to a subsequent study that was published in the Journal of Food Science and Technology in 2021. The extract, according to the study's findings, decreased oxidative stress and inflammation in cells.

Mango contains enzymes that help in breaking down protein, to include high levels of glutamine acids. The fibrous nature of mango helps in digestion and elimination. It is rich in pre-biotic dietary fiber, vitamins, minerals, and good sugars for blood building and nutrient uptake.

I really like mango's a lot, a few times in the week, because they are brain food, they really activate the senses especially while in the

meditative or training-meditative zone. It is even said that mangoes stimulate or strengthen the effects of other neurologically activating foods. So those of you advanced in Nutritional Diversity Science who are starting to narrow more effective shakes and come up with more dynamic combinations, remember mango's and brain stimulating fruits. Take mango with other certain herbal supplements, and while you study, and want to hone your focus.

Some say a mango a day keeps the doctor away. I say a mango, plus an avocado, and a variety of 60 more foods species a.k.a., a Nutritional Diversity, each day to keep the doctor very far away, and in an optimal human state – human optimization.

Like oranges mango's go great as a mid-gym snack, or half at mid workout and the other half after to help healthy vitamin uptake from other foods and supplements and to give the system a nice vitamin-C boost.

Mango studies have found that the fruit is rich in tartaric acid, malic acid and traces of citric acid that primarily help in maintaining the alkali reserve of the body.

Professor Ehret died in 1922, his popular lecture on a Mucusless Diet System of Eating Your Way Back to Health, which was published decades later, focuses on acids that convert to alkaline in the body and maintaining a sufficient level of alkalinity as the reining factor over human health and against human illness.

I myself, do not agree, with Ehret's entire published work under this title. How-ever on the main point, I do agree with alkalinity being a king factor over the human health.

Mango's and their leaves are incredible stomach nutrition, too good to pass up, also because its real good help to pass on; all the other foods you eat in your Nutritional Diversity. Mango's and their leaves aid the health of the stomach track in so many ways, preventing cancer's alkalizing the system, and providing the right ingredients to keep steady bowel flow, a key to human health.

In India they say that 'Aam ke patte' (Hindi) can bid adieu to many sicknesses. This is a reference to mango leaves dried and crushed into powder. The leaves of the Mango tree should not be ignored.

Mango leaves contain tannin, alkaloids, glycoside, steroids, triterpenoids, saponins, mangiferin, phenolic and flavonoid components. In addition, mango leaves have antimicrobial properties that can be used as a functional food. Mango leaves also can inhibit the growth of harmful bacteria. Anthocyanin content in mango leaves are expressed as a character in red, purple and blue.

The passage in the bible, about knowing if a tree is good by it's fruits, is very true for the mango tree, as it's fruits are delicious, and the entire tree is a powerful health benefit to humans and permacultures everywhere.

Antioxidants present in mango protect the body against cancers of the colon, prostate, breast, and even against leukemia.

Vitamin B-6 or pyridoxine is required for GABA hormone production within the brain. It also controls homocysteine levels within the blood, which may otherwise be harmful to blood vessels resulting in coronary artery disease (CAD), and stroke. Mango has a

low glycemic index (41-60) so going a little overboard will not increase your sugar levels.

So many recommend a tea made with the leaves, and while the flavor is great of this tea I do not recommend tea making, and if tea making is practiced possibly not drinking the liquid while it is hot should be employed.

I say take some green and the red baby mango leaves for 5% of a nice salad, and some more baby leaves and one adult, or portion of one adult leaf for 5% of a nice smoothie.

This mango and mango leaf, soak or tea is said to treat a wide variety of ailments, many related to blood sugars.

Mango tree leaves contain tannins and anthocyanins, which help to treat diabetes early. Mango leaves tea, or two-day soak, or blended up raw (best), is very good for helping to treat diabetic angiopathy and diabetic retinopathy. It also helps to treat hyperglycemia. The leaves contain a compound called taraxerol-3beta, and the ethyl acetate extract that has a synergy with insulin and stimulates the synthesis of glycogen, balancing out and optimizing the blood.

Mango leaves have been very proven as a home remedy for nervousness, even treating small veins, varicose veins, and the vascular system and related dysfunctions that can underline these issues. For other reasons too, in the mango brain stimulus, it has been considered a mood booster and even and aphrodisiac.

I use the reddish, new softer leaves mostly, which can be used raw. When cooking also I use the young leaf, but I have noticed a greater tea-like flavor can be gained through the thicker twig and leaf.

Give skin a vita-topical-boost while also naturally cleaning the pores of dirt's that cause acne. Better than any store-bought stuff with 20 cancer causing chemicals in it, Mango is all you need to balance out the skin, but this with jackfruit, coconut, and avocado rubbed on regularly and you should have the skin of Gods. Considering that the skin is a large organ and bleach and fluoridated water showers or hard water showers do their very visible damage

Mango Trees can be very productive if fertilized, loved and placed in the right spot. Mango trees grow to 35– 40 m (115–131 ft) tall, with a crown radius of 10 m (33 ft). The trees are long-lived, with some specimens that still fruit after 300 years. Maybe we get a longer life from partaking of the mango?

MANGOSTEEN

The tropical evergreen tree Garcinia mangostana, widely known as the mangosteen or the purple "Queen of Fruits," is assumed to be native to the Southeast Asian Islands. The small purple fruit with a green top that resembles a charm in a video game was offered 100 pieces of silver by Queen Victoria, according to fruit explorer David Fairchild. It's possible that this is where the moniker originated; any way, it appears that she was aware of its true worth.

It now grows mainly in Southeast Asia, Southwest India, and other tropical areas such as Panama, Costa Rica, Colombia, and Puerto Rico, where the tree has been since included. In these areas, and historically the fruit is touted as some of the best-tasting fruit around.

The exact origins of the purple globe are unknown due to its widespread cultivation since ancient times, but it is believed to have been somewhere between the Sunda Islands and the Moluccas cxciv. More recently there has been over 200 million dollars in recorded drinks sales that contain the mangosteen cxcv

On our farm, we use the whole thing. The shells are great fertilizer and contained compost additives and when in their respective season we do a few applications with them.

There is value in the shell as a drying or vitamin-rich chalk agent through processing. For this reason, it is the base of a successful and expensive new acne skincare product by Skin Owl.

The fruits are delicious and we pretty much each them fresh, maybe in a smoothie. The nice little ball-sized casing is great for snack

transport. This "exocarp" layer protective case preserves the life of the fruit inside very well. Be advised once you crack it the purple juices can stain clothing.

Anti-Cancer properties verified in follow up research concluding that "anti-metastatic potential of mangosteen xanthones (a highly bioactive compound) was shown to be mediated by the inhibition of matrix metalloproteinase (MMP) activities which is expected to result in less adhesion, invasion, and migration of cancer cells treated. Antiinflammatory. cxcvi

Farms, harvesters, and possessors are finding endless use of the strategic crop, ranging from top livestock feed to fertilizer. High in folate, something harder for teen girls 14 -18 as well as women in adult ages, to get enough of and something the U.S. Department of Health finds modern diet insufficient of, stating that most folate for people comes from supplements and vitamins.

Of course, this is something the Nutritional Diversity diet concept can help fulfill, especially a planned one with mangosteen and other strategically chosen species such as beef liver, darker leafy greens, oranges, or black-eyed peas. [AR,1]

The Queen has been found in the scientific study likely to treat colon cancer. cxcvii Tumorous cancer and another anti-cancer potential, also

as potent nanocarrier to anticancer drugs. Cxcviii

Encapsulation using Nano fibrillated cellulose effectively protected the encapsulated vitamins against environmental stresses which occur in industrial food production (such as pH changes, salt addition, and thermal processing). Moreover, Nano fibrillated cellulose extracted from mangosteen rind is a nature-derived emulsifier that is environmentally friendly.

Indications that the Queen of Fruits may help other living and dried essence efficiently process in the system and make her a key benefit as a Nutritional Diversity diet include.cxcix

Inhibiting effect to the Dengue virus and studies indicate a good antiviral treatment for the issue as well.cc The same type of effects was shown live against malaria. cci

As a topical the Queen has worked anti-acne activity, is studying at times combined with cream agents such as aloe. ccii Expect to see her on the beauty scene, the powerful health agent has worked well as pericarp bath scrub here in the nature farms.

She also showed potential in blocking the production in Staph (Staphylococcus pseudintermedi) infection as a crude extract. cciii

Results suggested that the use of γ-mangostin from the mangosteen pericarp against R. solanacearum may be used as a natural bacteriostatic agent in agriculture. These examinations mapped xanthones from the mangosteen pericarp that inhibit the growth of ralstonia

solanacearum, one of the most destructive bacteria in agriculture settings. cciv

These same xanthones help protect against kidney disease nutritionally. ccv

The xanthones also showed to significantly treat diabetes in animal studies. ccvi Further studies are called for regarding the heavy diabetes treatment potential of the species.ccvii

The present study showed that the combined effect of the fruit juice mixtures of Actinidia deliciosa (Kiwi fruit) and Garcinia mangostana was found to be a better treatment for postmenopausal osteoporosis when compared to the pericarp extract of Garcinia mangostana. ccviii

Here is a cool and interesting study on malaria that combines it with artimisin, which is of the oriental plant artimisen but we think

the ambrosia peruvianna as a whole is a better selection in treating heavy conditions such as cancers or malaria.ccix

A new prenylated xanthone, mangaxanthone B and a new

benzophenone, mangaphenone, were isolated along with two known xanthones (2014), mangostanin and mangostenol, from the stem bark of Garcinia mangostana. The biological evaluation of these compounds is underway. Ccx

Combined with cinnamon extracts supplementation is effective in increasing muscle strength, muscle size and, total lean mass, as well as endurance performance. After prolonged use such as 42 days, testosterone levels had improved in animal tests.ccxi

There is a need for new pharmacological treatments for people with schizophrenia that target alternate mechanisms of action to current treatment options.

There is evidence of anomalies in redox biology and inflammation in schizophrenia, including the presence of oxidative stress particularly implicating the glutathione system; changes in oxidative status with treatment; and evidence that other glutathione and redox-active agents have therapeutic value. Preclinical evidence suggests a range of compounds in mangosteen may directly address these anomalies and efficacy should be investigated in a well-powered trial.ccxii

In addition to treating schizophrenia, the wonderous purple ball purports to solve certain neurogenerative disorders and bipolar disorder. Taken together, the theoretical biological rationale of psychiatric disorders, bioactivity of mangosteen pericarp extract and the available preclinical data, support the therapeutic potential as an adjunctive psychiatric treatment. ccxiii

More closely over 24 weeks of either 1,000 mg mangosteen pericarp may have implications for improving treatment outcomes for those with bipolar disorder and may contribute to our understanding of the pathophysiology of bipolar depression.ccxiv

Contributing to the prevention of DNA damage-caused disease by neutralizing free radicals derived by either cellular metabolism or

external agents, mangosteen extract, or isolated active compounds thereof may thus hold promise for pharmaceutical or nutraceutical applications. ccxv

There could be some mitochondrial development stoppage, which is suggestive that mangosteen consumption could be very well aided with other combinations of plant life.

As with anything new, start with a small amount and go slowly towards larger servings.

One of these fruits is the mangosteen. I use this to explain that there is an essence that science cannot fully comprehend. In other words, there is an immeasurable spirit, if you will, of the species that is functional but not so much observable or measured in a modern scientific sense, and this makes it impossible to assess the value of the fruit solely by science or taste.

MACA ROOT

The Maca Root, which is scientifically chased by Lepidium meyenii, is a native root of Peru that can grow at altitudes up to 4,000 meters and -25 ° C in temperature, the studies show that we've seen cultivation for 2000 years Inca hairs. This root has many medicinal properties being used to increase vitality and libido, bringing great benefits to health.ccxvi

In addition to providing a lot of energy, as a result of maca and rich in fibers and essential fats that help to nourish the body. It can be consumed as root food, in capsules, or mixed with water, sugar, or vitamins.

In 2002 a study came out about the antioxidant action of maca root that fights some types of Oxygen-reactive species.

A root contains many proteins, lipids, carbohydrates, fibers, vitamins B3, C, B2, B1, and minerals such as potassium, sodium, magnesium, calcium, phosphorus, and iron, but as any excess is bad,

There is a maximum recommended dosage for the federal department of health of Canada to be consumed, being 3 grams per day. The same agency recommends that the maximum dosage for

people who have high pressure or use anticoagulants or antidepressants should be 0.6 grams per day.

The Maca Root is a healthy food that also prevents several diseases and is widely used in medicine to treat symptoms of PMS and menopause, reduce erectile dysfunction, prevent cancer, fight anxiety, depression, hormonal dysregulation, osteoporosis, and anemia, in addition to having several other benefits.ccxvii

There is evidence of aids to and improved memory and learning function in students and job professionals caused by the Peruvian root food. Best Maca Root is known to regulate the menstrual cycle for women and has a regulatory connotation of functionality in the system. ccxviii ccxix

Maca Root, is a strength builder, we call it "muscle mortar," and it is no surprise to our team that the scientists have found the substance to strengthen the immune system also. ccxx

The bodybuilding compound acts as a natural sun protectant when applied to the skin, this is likely a nutrient digestive-based support for the skin, and exploration with possibly coconut oil, neem oil, etc. should be conducted to find out more about topical digestion.ccxxi

The root may help with diabetes formulations and control and also likely helps with weight loss by increasing digestive activity and energy and through her regulatory nature.

Males of older ages, and with lower sperm counts, experienced an increased male fertility rate through supplementation with the best maca root.ccxxii Further testing shows, improvement in acne skin and increased libido results from the once South American and Peruvian cultural staple diet plan. ccxxiii

Improves mood and promotes increases in sports performance. An overall feeling of wellbeing is often noted through experience with this superfood. ccxxiv

Peruvian Maca proves to be quite safe if consumed in the right dosage, but it is not recommended for nursing mothers and people with thyroid problems because of substances that can interfere with the normal functioning of the thyroid gland.

As a precaution, people with problems in the uterus or ovaries, endometriosis, breast cancer, and pregnant women should consult a doctor before using the root. Ccxxv

Canada's Health and Sciences departments have indicated that they would patients interested in using more than 3grams per day of the superfood consult with their doctor. ccxxvi

For medical treatments, larger doses may be prescribed if necessary.

Root foods at times can conflict with bark foods such as cinnamon, and for this reason, our diet plans separate root foods from bark foods, and we also keep root foods separated from other root food consumption times (we never eat two different carbs together).

We find it mixes in well and digests well in protein and postworkout mixes. It also works very well with the best of preworkout mixes

Our team has used maca root regularly in a dynamic fashion over the last 6 years roughly. It has become a regular element around the camp, and in-house testing here has found it to be, a "muscle mortar," that helps build and maintain dexterous muscles and also joint tissue.

.

OLIVE OIL

Having the best olive oil is important for a few reasons, one is

cooking – against the popular belief that olive oil is not good for cooking. Other incredible uses of the divine substance include skin and hair, also joint functionality and heart health, gut health, and colon health is all in there too.

Having the best cooking oils is also very important because having the worst one is so dangerous. Don't forget where you sternly heard it, vegetable oil, palm oil, seed oils, and many of the less expensive cooking oils – are bound to give you health problems.ccxxvii

Human life without this important product is much less supported than life with a good amount of it. One of our first recommendations to new members of the flock is to get a good oil into their life, and get the bad oils out!

"Just remember: The purpose for food, is to get olive oil into your mouth." – Dr. Gundry

Starting now, readers should never again use the vegetable and seed oils, and you should use 1. Coconut Oil, 2. Olive Oil 3. Cow or Goat Butter (pure). There are plenty of great oils out there such as avocado oil,

Anti-cancer acete, with a protective role against the development of carotid atherosclerosis, and arthritis reducing joint edema and cartilage destruction in persons at high cardiovascular risk – miracle substance whose only possible foe is again pesticide contamination.

Ccxxviii

Colorectal cancer (CRC) is one of the most common malignancies in Western populations. Animal tests suggest the heavy use of olive oil, can prevent colon cancer and oxidative damage from the modern diet.ccxxix

A targeted look at mortality in connection with cardiovascular disease concluded that "greater consumption of total olive oil, was associated with reduced cardiovascular disease and mortality risk in an elderly

Mediterranean population at high cardiovascular risk.ccxxx

Our findings underscore olive oil consumption as one of the key components of the Med-Diet for cardiovascular disease prevention."

ccxxxi

Another study that showed that cooking with the oil in cultural "cuisine may improve the extractability of bioactive compounds such as polyphenols and carotenoids from the food matrix.

The migration of polyphenols, such as naringenin, ferulic acid, and quercetin, which are compounds not detected in olive oil, to the oil fraction during the sofrito preparation may enhance their bio accessibility and bioavailability. Ccxxxii

Like coconut oil, the olive essence even helps with neurological diseases such as Parkinson's and Alzheimer it is truly impressive. ccxxxiii ccxxxiv

Examinations key in on the assistive role to other nutrients played by the best olive oil and using a large list of different foods and herbs, the traditions of such practice and the effective function of infusing important nutrients in the oil medium.

These special effects have been confirmed in several studies, the best olive oil is well-covered thanks to the Mediterranean's better general health, then diet culture. ccxxxv

Age-related macular degeneration (AMD) is the leading cause of visual impairment among older adults in Europe and in the United States. This study reported a decreased risk of late AMD among olive oil users.ccxxxvi

Outside of rare allergic reaction olives and their oil are pretty safe. Topically and internally. With anything new, go sip, to half a cap full over two days and increase slowly to asses tolerance and possibly allergic reactions.

Recently, ordering a new oil source has become one of our favourite activities. Like with other nutrients, the greatest sources come from the widest variety of sources. Any bottle that genuinely stands out will be added to the list of the finest olive oils because the crew is always testing new ones.

PAPAYA

Christopher Columbus, who arrived on Island Colon in the Bocas del Toro province of what is now the Republic of Panama, described papaya as the "fruit of angels" and referred to it as such. Papayas are a tropical Americas fruit.

Carica papaya, one of the 22 recognised species in the family Caricaceae's genus Carica.

They were relegated to niche markets, such dehydrated forms in trail mix, because earlier generations thought of them as exotic plants. They are now frequently identified in global food inventories of common foods.

Botanist Lucas T.P. called his 914 work on the species "The Most Wonderful Tree in the World."

Papayas contain papain, an enzyme that helps digest and absorb proteins either in the stomach or directly on meat, for tenderizing. This behavior is like that of avocado, where the enzyme helps the breakdown of other foods. That is a key function for an aggressive athletic Nutritional Diversity plan.

Papayas are nutritious, and in the opinion of this author, delicious. As a crop, I have found they require a fairly intensive effort to deliver an excellent, unbothered yield.

They have been grown here for centuries and their use by ancient cultures is well known. The indigenous tribes in Colombia and Peru cultivate papaya today on primitive farms which can only be seen from the air.

I also choose them because of their digestive enzyme support. With more digestive enzymes, more nutrition can actually be used by the system, and in combination with an optimal level of exercise can deliver performance-enhancing results. The green un-ripe state is nutritious, but consumption is limited to the indigenous peoples whose digestion has evolved over time to process it. The ripe state of the papaya is orange, which is brought to richness under the intense tropical sun.

A medium-sized papaya's folate content is around 25% of the daily recommended amount. Lentils, and spinach, and kidney, pinto, and black beans are other common foods that contain high amounts of folate. Regular consumption is linked to increased resistance to the common cold, colon cancer, and liver disease, and in the tropic's resistance to parasites and mosquito-borne illnesses such as dengue fever.

Carica leaves have been used for traditional treatment of dengue fever and have been reported to exhibit an immunomodulatory activity by affecting the level of cytokine production in vitro and in vivo.[237] The leaf juice from the Angelic plant has also proved powerful in the liver for dengue infected animals in testing.[238] [239] [240] It also could be a good pharmaceutical source of natural nephroprotective medicines. [241]

Animal tests indicate antidiabetic activity in the compounds derived from the angel of plants leaf juice. Results suggest that the aqueous extract of C. papaya may improve the metabolic disruption produced by diabetes.ccxlii ccxliii

Seeds considered for tropical deworming programs in Africa.ccxliv In traditional medicine, Carica papaya leaf has been used for a wide range of therapeutic applications including skin diseases and cancer.

Ccxlv

The present study established that the mature leaf concentrate (MLCC) of Carica papaya Sri Lankan wild type cultivar is orally active, safe and effectively modulates nonfunctional and functional immunological parameters of several diseases that unequivocally corroborate the traditional medical claims.

The Angelic plant is a powerful herbal therapeutic agent for modulating the immune system in numerous diseases. Ccxlvi

Exhibits curative properties, such as improvements in hepatotoxicity and nephrotoxicity induced by drugs, antimicrobial, antimalarial, anti-parasitic, antitumor, anti-inflammatory actions and wound healing effects. ccxlvii

Like basil, the angel leaf could be a powerful employ in lowering overall overweigh rates and will be important for the development of novel natural products on the treatment and prevention of obesity and metabolic disturbances ccxlviii

During intermediate phases of papaya ripening, partial depolymerization of pectin to small size with decreased branching had enhanced pectin anti-cancer properties. In other words, at the middle stage ripeness, the Angel fruit has a cancer-curing range of production. ccxlixLeaf extracts help with gingivitis and related bleeding and are effective agents in natural toothpaste. ccl

Continually consume safe food. As with any new cuisine, start off slowly to gauge your tolerance and potential allergic reactions.

Papaya is an excellent topical applier, that tightens skin and reduces signs of aging in the skin. Papaya would go great mixed with avocado, and jackfruit, with some mango also, and these are some of the ingredients I am working with on my new product for the boxing/fighting community, called Fight Face, or War Paint.

A small volume of papaya seeds has been found to kill harmful bacteria like E. coli, staph, and salmonella. These seeds also help fight viral infections and cures dengue, typhoid, and numerous other diseases. In Nigeria, papaya seeds with milk is an excellent cure for typhoid fever.

The ancients may know this is a truly 'angelic' plant able to make its consumers invincible to the viruses, pathogens and preying parasites of the circle of life, very present in the jungle. Of course, this is only a researched speculation, I have no idea what the true ancient knowledge's concerning papaya are, but I would truly love to find out.

A new growing trend is papaya leaf juice which has acetogenin, with strong anti-malarial and the almost symptomatically equal; antidengue fever properties.

Papain and other papaya elements are believed to aid in hair growth, baldness prevention, skin health and hair cleanliness, a big ingredient for many shampoos.

Like the fruit, the leaf is rich in enzymes like papain and chymopapain, which aid digestion, prevents bloating and other digestive disorders. Apart from digestion, the strong alkaloid compounds like papain work effectively against fighting dandruff and balding. Papaya leaves also contain high amounts of vitamins A, C, E, K, and B and minerals like calcium, magnesium, sodium magnesium and iron.

Both in the fruit bowl and in the garden, they seem to get along fairly well with plantains and bananas, which is exactly how the majority of my terrace canopies are built. Currently, I have shrubs around young trees, basil, cassava, and ambrosia peruvianna on terraces.

PREBIOTIC SUPPLEMENTS

Nutritional Diversity

"Prebiotic Supplements" are usually non-digestible carbohydrate compounds that contain novel dietary fibers that have shown to increase nutrient absorption and digestive energy in the lower intestines of both preclinical and human models and well as invite other health benefits and aid in the prevention and treatment of chronic diseases.

Prebiotics are a category of fibers that contain ingredients like inulin, fructooligosaccharides (FOS), and galactooligosaccharides (GOS). Although prebiotic supplements have been linked to a number of health advantages, they also carry a risk of negative effects and may not be suitable for everyone.

Prebiotic pills have been found to enhance gut health by encouraging the development of good bacteria in the stomach. These microorganisms can strengthen the immune system, enhance digestion, and lower the risk of gastrointestinal disorders ccli. They can also increase the absorption of minerals like calcium and magnesium, which can boost nutrient absorption. For those who have problems with malabsorption or are at risk for osteoporosis, this may be especially helpful.cclii

Prebiotic materials can play healing and treating roles in ulcerous colitis cases. The best pre-biotic supplements could play a major hand in working with obesity. ccliii- Further investigations are promoted in the area of pre-biotic supplements and the link between gut microbiota and health. Prebiotic vitamins may also assist in reducing inflammation in the body. Many chronic diseases, including cancer, diabetes, and heart disease, have been related to chronic inflammation. Treating acne from the gut using the best pre-biotic supplements is right up to the front line of all skincare seeming to be potentially best treated like all other diseases through our innerecosystem.ccliv

Cinnamomum osmophloeum Kaneh (CO) and Taiwanofungus

camphoratus have been identified as an active and helpful pre-biotic combination formula. cclv Athletic application testing in mainstream science is largely undone.cclvi

Some persons who take prebiotic supplements may experience gastrointestinal distress. This may involve signs like gas, diarrhea, bloating and allergic reactions in some people, especially those who are sensitive to particular fibre types.cclvii An allergic response may cause hives, breathing problems, and itching. Prebiotic supplements may interfere with some medicines, especially those that have an impact on the gut microbiota for instance, can lessen the potency of some antibiotics. Chron's disease patients and patients with weakened immune system responses may experience side effects from supplements.

SERRAPEPTASE

Serrapeptase, also known as serratiopeptidase, is a substance created by silkworms. In many regions of the world, particularly Japan and Europe, this substance has been utilized as a medicine to treat various illnesses.

Serrapeptase is currently categorized as a nutritional supplement by nutritionists and food specialists, proving that this unusual worm is capable of producing not just fine clothing but also luxury food and medication.cclviii

As Si-Ling-Chi, a Chinese Empress, was merely strolling in her garden, she saw caterpillars and a "cocoon," one of which had fallen into her tea, on a mulberry tree. This is how the history of silkworms began in ancient China in 2640 B.C. When she picked it up, she noticed that the cocoon had started to unwind, creating a lovely string of what is now referred to as silk thread.

"Nature holds the key to our aesthetic, intellectual, cognitive and even spiritual satisfaction." -E.O. Wilson

Serratiopeptidase is a 'super enzyme' which has a huge list of health benefits. More than keeping sinuses clear there is a lot to say for helping performance here. Biofilm plaque is eliminated; an effect of the protease Esp. secreted by S. epidermidis acting as an anti-biofilm and anti-colonization agent against S. aureus cells living in the same ecological niche.cclix

Significantly lowered the attack strength of three of the four strains of Staph virus Increased clinical efficiency and healing in surgical molar removals. A silkworm wonder for the wound emerges. Successful encapsulation of serratiopeptidase, a sensitive proteolytic enzyme, was done into chitosan nanoparticles study. The ionic gelation method that was used in the procedure proved a simple, mild, and reproducible method for the fabrication of such nanoparticles. The high anti-inflammatory activity has been shown in animal tests.

Dentists favor employment after molar removal for pain and inflammation control. Modern research findings have revealed that inflammation plays a critical role in promoting cancer, in particular, the tumorigenesis, and a process of tumor formation.cclx In this respect, the agent can be considered and anticancer agent. Some anecdotal reports suggest it possess anti-atherosclerotic effects also, due to its fibrinolytic and caseinolytic properties. Despite being widely used there are few published studies regarding its efficacy. Thus, evidence regarding its clinical utility is needed.

Studies suggest gel products for topical delivery are possible and beneficial. Most recommend taking when needed or in a cyclic fashion, but taking regularly all year is also fine. I would recommend as always and, in this case, making sure to remember to get as many diverse sources of the enzyme as possible.

One user claimed that the high (SPU 120,000) dose was so successful in clearing his stomach of biofilm over time that he got sick from not having any! However, he did pass some items that didn't look good and thought the wonder worm stuff was performing well. He advised people to begin with a dose of 40k SPU or short cycles to allow the stomach biofilm, which is crucial for the health of the microbiota, to recover and regenerate.

10 mg to 60 mg nevertheless, measurements in this format should be used with caution, as this is not the metric for active enzymes (SPU is).

TURMERIC

Turmeric really is a staple herb to grow, and learn about partly because we know enough in scientific study to see food combination benefits. A point in support of the ideas of more diversity in diet, and increased health and performance potential in smarter herbal formulations

Turmeric was used and valued much more extensively by the natives of India than any people today. Turmeric was heavily valued by the ancient Indian-European people not only for its preservation properties but for its energetic and spiritual qualities as well. The 'Arya' culture was a group of people who worshiped the solar system and the sun as a deity.

The benefits of turmeric, at times, seem too long to list, and too incredible to be true, yet for thousands of years, thousands of people swear by the good tree neighboring shrub's root tuber.

This orange root wonder is used in cooking, as a dietary supplement with numerous health benefits, and even as a topical application for beautification. It is known to support longevity, and reduce all types of inflammations. cclxi

Be careful sourcing turmeric as a 2008 Consumer Review found many turmeric products were not the high-quality extracts advertised. Turmeric comprises a $70 million segment of the dietary supplement market and is one of the most commonly sold nutritional supplements in the US. cclxii

Turmeric supports digestion, boosts liver function and bolsters the immune system. It supports brain function and the nervous system, decreasing hypertension and joint inflammation.

It is also a powerful cellular antioxidant. Also, has been proven to be effective in the treatment of diabetes, multiple sclerosis, atherosclerosis, HIV/AIDS, and sexually transmitted diseases (hepatitis-C, genital herpes, gonorrhea).

Studies indicate the herb helps with irritable bowel syndrome, indigestion, acne, urinary tract infections, kidney infections, gallstones, anemia, hemorrhoids, and liver disease.

Nutritional Diversity

The superfood has also been employed in the treatment of leprosy, edema, bronchitis, common cold, headaches, conjunctivitis, food poisoning, parasites, fever, diarrhea, poor circulation, lower back, and abdominal pain also pain relief to sciatica.

It has been effective when used to cure external ulcers. It can also be used as a mosquito repellent, wound healer, and immediate cure for scorpion stings.

The cultivar does not exist in the wild and is rumored to have been a native of the Gardens of Babylon, one of the Seven Wonders of the Ancient World during the 8th century BC.

"The place that I'm from doesn't exist anymore." – Immortal Technique

I understand this line. This is a true statement for my own life.

One very interesting fact about Turmeric is that it is used to whiten teeth. This seems hard to chew on is that it is used as a bright golden dye but it has whitening power for teeth as well.

Different simple processes have been used to help enhance the benefits of turmeric such as ferments, sauces, and teas. The concoctions are believed to nurture the very health of the gut microbiota. Turmeric helps balance the female reproductive and lactation systems. It has been effective when used to cure external ulcers.

Due to its vast array of medicinal uses and versatility, turmeric is one of the most important herbs in the natural medicine cabinet.

Using turmeric has shown to have effects on slowing or preventing many forms of cancer. By slowing the spread of cancer cells through the elimination of them. Studies have produced evidence that turmeric can aid in preventing breast cancer from spreading to the lungs. It may help prevent colon cancer, and a study published in 2008 shows that it may aid in the prevention of pancreatic cancer.

"We have not found a single cancer on which curcumin does not work." Dr. Bharat Aggarwal, Jawaharlal Nehru Centre for Advanced Scientific Research, Bangalore, India.

Turmeric has been well studied, as a famous ancient medicine and it has been realized in several food combinations that when combined with turmeric, boost its healing capabilities.

All the depth in turmeric study has figured out the Nutritional Diversity diet applications and potentials a bit more than has been discovered with other herbs. Combined with organic black pepper uptake is increased and overall system effectiveness is enhanced by many times. When combined with cauliflower, turmeric may help prevent prostate cancer.

Onions may enhance the effects of turmeric on preventing colon cancer. Turmeric also helps prevent melanoma and stops the growth of new blood vessels developing in tumors, it is also thought to reduce the risk of childhood leukemia. In combination with neem and Amalaki, and just by itself turmeric helps to balance out blood sugar levels. Liver cancer has an adjudicative remedy in

Curcuma cclxiii cclxiv cclxv cclxvi

Combinations with hot peppers and mangosteen have also been shown to be effective chemical reactions and aid to several health factors in duckscclxvii

Turmeric prevents and slows the progression of Alzheimer's disease by removing 'plaque' from the brain. It keeps fibroid from gathering to form plaque that leads to complications of the brain. Curcumin is a powerful anti-inflammatory herb. It has been shown to be helpful in the treatment of Arthritis, Rheumatoid Arthritis, Osteoarthritis, injuries, trauma, and stiffness from both under activity and overactivity.

A study conducted in 1986 showed that a dosage of 1200 mg of curcumin a day was more effective in reducing post-surgical inflammation than either the placebo group or the antiinflammatory medication normally prescribed. Cclxviii

The essences affect the cartilage directly. A biological extract of turmeric reduced inflammatory responses of cartilage to LPS and contributes to the literary evidence for use of the spice to reduce articular inflammation and catabolism. The reason for the decline in calcein fluorescence in TURsim-exposed cartilage explants is not known but should be explored in further research. Cclxix

Turmeric also is known as Curcumin is also one of the most studied natural COX-2 inhibitors, which block an enzyme called cyclooxygenase-2. This is beneficial because the COX-2 enzyme helps make carcinogens more active in the body and allows cancerous cells to survive by growing new blood vessels.

Essentially, curcumin blocks the formation of cancer-causing enzymes, decreasing the likelihood of cancerous cell formation or growth. Other powerful antioxidant COX-2 inhibitors are red grapes, green tea, rosemary, and bee products.

The power herb root has shown powerful effects on stomach digestive disorders such as irritable bowel dysfunction.cclxx Protects the liver by enhancing antioxidation. cclxxi Effective in the treatment of ulcerous colitis.cclxxii Rosmarinus officinalis L., ginger and turmeric were all used in cervical cancer treatment studies. Oxygenated monoterpene compounds present in turmeric (C. longa) and ginger (Z. officinale) essential oils were possibly responsible for presenting better antitumor activity. cclxxiii

Exploration of fermented versions and enhanced treatments or alternative treatments have been initialed and signs point to possibility. cclxxiv Gun puffing of the wonder root enhanced its effectiveness and also purports to offer a new realm of that procession.cclxxv Measurable improvements to gut microbiota have been shown in vitro testing.cclxxvi

Root powder functions as an insecticide agriculturally for certain cabbage crops.cclxxvii The wonder root protects the longevity of neurological pathways over time. This information is supportive of the long-term use of the food.cclxxviii

Neuroprotectivity protects also against common neurological diseases. cclxxix In the brain department, excellent food also helps prevent the emergence of dementia.cclxxx Diverse cultivars now exist and a wealth of information from the scientific confirms all traditional lore surrounding the wonder food. cclxxxi

Too much of anything is never good. When it comes to this root and leaf, keep it around two to six leaves and one-quarter inch to three-quarters of the root, a day (when mixed with pepper).

Commercial products have been found to be of a lower quality than the actual small farm-produced herb. cclxxxii

Turmeric root and leaf are very regular important parts of our diets here and while subtle over time everyone around is converted concretely to Curcuma fan-hood. It is solid, healthy, physical, and mentally supportive food that we believe through our experiences relieves and prevents a plethora of ailments.

Fitness Training

The Cultural Practice of Health

I am a big honesty guy right, I need the truth from who I am around I only have the truth to give to those people.

You have to train. It is 100% mandatory. You will not be healthy if you don't.

Fitness Training is another ' it's everything.' Without it, you're simply not living the human experience. Strive to produce a measurable fitness, and circulation health result every day. Build on it, set further and higher goals each week, the results are the most amazing transformative results you can imagine.

This training is what programs your body about how to use the nutrition, where to put it, how to covert it, etc. It is everything to optimizing one's self.

You can eat great, but if you do not exercise you are not going to be in optimal shape or health, inside or out. There is no getting around it, there are no hacks, and we nutritional diversifists' don't cut corners.

Resistance is what tells you to be strong as a human physiological and mental being. All biology grows against resistance.

Nutritional Diversity

In essence an optimal human is one who can resist all forces that try and push it in another direction. The natural man, exercised all day, he had to in order to survive in the wild, and he had abilities and dexterity that we don't.

The Permaculture farmer today exercises in a mild manner, time frame and quantity, closest to the natural man as he is tending to the farm, although the Nutritional Diversifist is able to do so much more than this thanks to his intelligent nutritional component.

Fitness training is more or less the ultimate focus of Nutritional

Diversity Science as it is described in the final text, and in the final test. I mean physical performance is the measure of power in one's diet, Sure. It's a measure of plenty other things, to optimize is to push that peak of performance. To know if the nutritional spectrum is supporting peak performance is an ultimate pursuit – to our mind anyway.

Surely optimizing for fitness ability and performance strength, we optimize also against sickness and we have top notch immune systems. I take the same approach in growing plants, if we shower it with love, care, resistance and nutrition it will have no trouble surviving once adolescent and the treatment of life continues.

Once I study a plant enough and figure out what treatments it really likes, I become totally confident that it will be more productive and tougher than other plants of its kind.

Have a concept in this 'tough plant cultivation' that sounds crazy. I really see an endless sea of possibilities in creating new stronger ecology. Thus, in optimal human physiological performance.

Fitness is a depth-y technique to provide accurate feedback about one's food to the body, such as how the body should use it. To essentially program the body how to use the food, and in so much gain a deeper understanding about the particular food or food combination's impact and potential at those times.

Fitness really should be looked at as a programming function, telling your body how to use and what to make of the nutrition you have given it. Most gym-heads will tell you to eat great, and supplement awesomely without exercise, is exactly a one-way street to become out of shape. If you get real about it, and give it the inputs, your body will respond accordingly.

It bothers me when books, like the Four Hour Body become best sellers, with statements on the cover "hack your health" and statements in Tim Ferris the author's interviews like, "I put all that in there purely because market research data told me too," are exactly the things our culture does not need, it does not produce a genuine product and this is not going to really help anyone like a genuine things would. You simply have to put the time in, and cut the toxins out, and build a real discipline against what you don't like to do. I even recommend to people who want to toughen up quickly, to sleep on the floor. I explain to them that for those that practice, lower back discomfort will go away in a week or so and the bruises from the hips down, will return with a stronger and more resilient body. You may also use a rug, small yoga mat, or bamboo.

I myself am an athlete who is looking for fitness advantages. I am dedicated to an all -natural diet and health.

People often ask if I use synthetic health supplements, like the stuff in the bags and the tubs shown every other page in the muscle mags. The answer is 'yes'. Additionally, many of these supplements are not as synthetic as you might believe. The other thing is that I don't really take supplements at the farms; I only use them when I'm in the city. That's the extent of what I have or will use and I am very selective which products to try or use routinely. The supplement industry has actually done a pretty good job developing a functional array of stuff for us, and there are a lot of companies who really focus on health and natural derivatives and intelligent, safe approaches to their products, who have great reputations.

At the same time, I will offer a few disclaimers, before digging into the fitness regimen. I have never done steroids, or human growth hormones and I don't think I ever will so, this text won't discuss that. Just with this diet alone in a mass building plan, I start getting bigger than I intended to faster than intended too and with all natural there is zero risk!

I am studying the stem cell research in Panama. Panama is a place where alternative medicines are allowed to be practiced according to an alternative medicine allowance and law here protecting the indigenous and the alternative medicine practitioner. It is one of the only countries that features this kind of quality and it allows for this kind of specialized and less regulated research and testing.

This safe, logical science of stem cell injections is illegal in the states, although it's real ability to heal, slow down the aging process and help performance is clear now. Stem cells are human organic cells, that exist in everyone, and I am a big fan of the new stem cell testimonies coming out around the world, especially coming from the UFC Athletes.

Gene augmentation, and CRISPER technology is something to look at, although I am not there yet as a dedicated supporter to these technologies because I don't know enough about them yet, but I recognize the game changing potential there, and no chemicals are injected or ingested with these procedures, so they make for worthy mentions in a "Cutting Edge" text.

Ozone treatments, also are natural based elemental discoveries that have had incredible effects to athletes and medical patients. My formula is to be as strong as you can be for as light as you can be. I am not a bodybuilder, I want to be a functional athlete, I want ability and I don't care so much what that looks like.

I have found that adhering to the methods contained in the Nutritional Diversity Science as far as it has progressed today, and the things I am writing into the slowly forming, more "Complete Human Optimization Manual" enables me to out-perform those who do not follow this way of eating and organizing their nutrition.

An urban US population's dietary diversity (DD) was measured in a study to see if relationships between DD and 10-year atherosclerotic cardiovascular disease (ASCVD) risk were independent of dietary quality. No proof existed that evenness improved cardiovascular health. According to the research, diets rich in micronutrients and more varied dietary characteristics, as opposed to counting calories, are better for cardiovascular health.cclxxxiii

I have now been sharing with a fairly vast array of individuals this health miracle I call Nutritional Diversity over the past couple of years. I am currently setting up a few farms with new species here around the city, and throughout Central and South America, experimenting with a few small cooperative foods buying group. It's interesting. There are go-getters, and there are lazy people out there in the world, there are hammers and nails, leaders and followers. At this time the cards reveal common place in our time of, regurgitation and plagiarism rather than actual experimentation and experience. Although I've always thought it's ideal to reach the real root as close to it as feasible, it will still work at the telephone level. That's what we all need to actually want in this health crisis, at the end of the day.

Cross Training

"Cross training" describes the same rule of diversity; the more diverse the exercise movements and resistances the stronger, the more capable the athlete. So cross training became a popular phrase and most tennis shoe makers had cross training models through the 2000's.

Fitness breaks down into a fundamental start of stretching, natural and artificial resistance otherwise known as calisthenics, and cardiovascular / stamina exercises. The assorted tasks required when working on a permaculture farm target each of these areas pretty well, and this is done in a dedicated controlled, meditative practice that builds discipline and form, surely the way to hone these skills and abilities to their utmost potential.

Remember human optimization, certainly requires fitness programming to send the correct commands on how a particular practitioner wants to use his nutrition. One practitioner may want serious strength, another may want serious stamina, and the two different formation methods could call for some differences in consumption but mostly in the way the human system reacts to the physical training, and then adapts accordingly is seen as a most potent result. Everything goes down better with a plan. This moment right

now is the opportunity to pencil out a plant, focused on what ability, or better, a diversity of abilities that is desired.

A well-rounded, ideal athlete will without a doubt be able to accomplish it all, including extreme balance exercises, breathing techniques, yoga, grappling and wrestling techniques, and striking drills.

The most obvious consumption factor in training, is water. Also known elements of depletion are what's in the human water to include sodium and other minerals. Many sports drinks claim to address these factors. Covered in sweat and with fatigue setting in, we know lots of water is required, salt and oranges, the traditional youth sports sideline refreshers can help.

To be a fitness master, a good starting place of study is clearly in water, the conduit of life essence, the operational fluid that gets hard to keep at sufficient levels with more increased activity.

The next big consumption element of focus is protein. Protein consumption is a big task for many athletes, one that is hard to accomplish a sufficient level of in the modern diet, which makes a big market for protein supplements. The nutritional world definitely knows as solid as a rock that protein plus training, equals muscle gains and muscle recovery

Carbohydrates effect stamina and most studies show carbohydrate consumption has training benefits and allows the athlete to toggle their weight gain and loss torque. My nutritional computer (myself) tells me this common study conclusion is accurate.

Published in the European Journal of Sport Science in 2021. "Carbohydrate availability and exercise training adaptation: too much of a good thing?" According to this review paper, carbohydrate consumption is essential for enhancing training adaption in endurance athletes. According to the authors, having access to moderate to high amounts of carbohydrates while exercising may help with performance and training adaption.cclxxxiv

Fats and fibers and all the dissected nutritional elements listed across modern nutrition charts are the current focuses of most dieting fitness enthusiasts today. Who design out based on what they know or is recommended a diet and fitness routine of yesterday. Yesterday is a big mistake from agriculture to central distribution to genetic modification, to chemicals that kill our pollinators in waves which seriously threatens our planet. Today the wave we start to focus back on natural plants, and whole foods, and leave the zombie state one step at a time. The focus in consumption most important going forward, is getting 5x the proteins and carbs ingested, in plants, a diversity of at least 30.

Rhythm and routine are the next key for sure, and there are many ways Nutritional Diversity provides to expand on that rhythm and routine, for a more optimal self.

Plant fiber including non-digestible plant fiber are largely ignored necessities that are grossly under-consumed, which is a key consumption element poorly addressed overall in today's diet culture. A sufficient diversity is possibly the most grossly under-sought necessity, one that would be unconscionable to other primates and mammals.

Energies of motion or kinetic energies are always healthy. This goes for motion of your blood, heart, and bowels. Electrical stimuli in the body such as the brain and nervous systems should be able to operate at peak levels regularly. Humans who lived solely in nature would be this way as other primates who live solely in nature are today. A product of nature would strive to achieve mind-body coordination that is of another level than the modern city dweller. We have all heard if you do not use it, you lose it, and how many can still do their algebra?

Nutritional Diversity

Thinking and certain mind exercises also can open and stimulate connective pathways of an electrical type and chemical type just as physical movement activates chemical and electrical communications in the muscles, arteries and various other tissues. Certain natural

substances that effect the mind are a heavy focus point of scientific interest just recently. Mind to muscle concentration and connection can act as multiplier for physical results. Meditation, extreme focuses exercise, and certain mind games and techniques can be employed to build a complex and focused muscle and strength. To make a mind, muscle breathing pace to multiple motions and actions is what we are going for as an optimal performance state of functioning.

In contrast, stagnant non-moving things are usually decaying and dead or well on their way to being so.

Dedicated rest is important and that rest should be best done in dynamic accordance with the resting cycle of the world as in night and day to produce the most productive and creative energy.

In physical training we also have speed, breathing, resistance, time, balance and dexterity to consider. Temperature, heart rate, blood pressure, chemical balances, hormonal balances, mental state, stress, also play significant roles in physical performance, although focusing on a Nutritional Diversity diet diversity of foods is the best way to keep these things in good ratio.

Slow forms and slow-moving energies like plants and the sloths are healthy and particularly strong usually. Watching a sloth move is like watching a Chinese circus performer do his slow incredibly strong show of awesome strength and artistic ability in a fairly meditative state. Speaking of the slow-moving sloth, a unique study here in Panama is examining its waste products for its effects on specific cancers and other afflictions. One way to up the resistance in resistance training is to slow down the speed at which the repetition is executed. This can be especially help full to those who have limited access to a facility. Many of these disgusting corporate prisons, are perfect examples of places where people are unable to access gym and fitness anymore and what a crime all that is too. Kung Fu forms and other martial arts forms were very helpful and mandatory to practitioners, because of the mind to muscles connection s and also because of the practice slow to do very fast and accurate one day, is a great formula.

A boxer or UFC fighter, will likely train for explosive speed and sacrifice some power for the fast execution. A foot-ball player is also training for an explosive start, and the strength to grudge it out in short plays, some sessions are all running, some are all grudge and grill, some sessions mix it up and come game time, there is some good ability there in all the needed departments. If the football player is on the line, he is looking for short term strength and as much size as possible.

Limbs moving together and limbs moving on their own, new balancing techniques, flows of movement, are well covered across loads of texts predating this one. We train for a specific application usually, and most athletes want the benefits of cross training in many different and diverse schools and training environments. I have made Jujutsu and some form of striking mandatory focal points in my complete Tao doctrine for myself. These systems are so advanced there is no need to develop anything but only recommend the best wheelhouse for future human optimization hopefuls. I feel that some of those are Yoga with breathing focuses, Jujutsu, Muay Tai, Kung Fu, Jeet Kun do, Tai Chi, Chi Gong, and reading the Tibetan Book of the Dead.

A sedentary lifestyle is death to our health. Active is optimal. Sitting still, doing nothing, minimizing your productivity, being lazy etc., are all things that will remove quality from your life. Office jobs are now a known risk this way, human's pay a price for sitting in that chair all day in the artificial light.

When it comes to diet and fitness, I read everything I can get my hands on, but most important is when I find something excellent I incorporate it – I DO IT!

For the fitness training pages of this guide, I will cover the points that are not well covered by other sources, and important for all Nutritional Diversifists to know.

Nutritional Diversity

I like what Navy Seal, Army Ranger and 200-mile race runner, David Goggins says "embrace the suck, enjoy the pain."

Train for "an hour a day, do your "jog," is a thing of the past. We are optimizing now, this ND-dieting information is here. A big part of this is going to be expanding your fitness routine to cover across the whole day. Looking at other primates, and going into nature teaches you first thing, you are meant to be able to expel energy all day. A rhythm, is necessary to be optimal. Building a rhythm will be a large part of my fitness section.

The modern gym allows us to focus on muscles in a whole new way I totally say, take advantage of that. The tools in there are great for strength building, and the gym equipment industry has a lot of thought and know how invested in their machines and resistance tools.

In the gym it is important to understand some informational principles about today's mainstream printed and gym-lingo information. There is a lot of people who are not getting results simply because they are not getting things the right way or they are missing key elements. You need to know what you are doing, it should be a very disciplined physical practice and the risk is also great that you can hurt yourself.

In the gym following a good gym warm up routine, the human physiological possibilities are incredible. Not following a sufficient warm up, and rhythmic build up, possibilities will be slashed. There will be what we call gym killers in there that are doing things others can't. They will have different secrets to their game, and they may tell you them, they may not, I myself am always moving from city to city and I am always asking people to tell me the highlight secrets of their routine and diet. For me, it's been these tiny details and adjustments that have made a huge difference.

Most guys in the gym, are straight up get it done folks!

I always try to hire for my businesses out of the gym, boxing or the jujutsu club. You'll know the gym killer type because they walk always with their chin high, likely on their toes, ready for any challenge. They walk around like they own the place, like it is their domain. Maybe they use a lot of weight or can hang in there for hours, maybe they are just super cocky, maybe they have a fight record to go with their gym smashing abilities. Whatever it is they turn a few heads with the way the stomp around that place, and they know what they are doing so others watch them. Learn from those who actually have results is usually a good idea but beware of those who get those results in cheater ways. There are destructive modern chemicals I the gym too. Going with the allocated trainer from their gym when they haven't seen any results is a huge error that new people make, and   I constantly witness it.

Like anything else, if you are serious about getting results, you need to put in the work, take charge of your health and your training, and treat it with respect or it will harm you and possibly even you.

People like to talk, and to write. So many science and health documents are so wrong, just so far from beneficial, it's curious at times.

A million people will regurgitate everything I write and never be a formidable practitioner of it. A million regurgitate stuff that yields results minimally.

They will simply want to sound righter, or smarter, or ahead of others. Books like this '4 Hour Body' I am told is that large seller in diet. How can this become a best-seller, where how many people have seen a change in their life from employing the many "hacks?" It says it's a book of hacks to cheat doing it the right way no? I have not read the book, but If I read the cover right, I don't want to read that book.

There is no point in doing if you are not going to do it right. That learned working in nature, or in modern construction or most things with the hands, not including anything with the keyboard. Let's not hack, or haste to waste our time.

This is exactly what I mean, regurgitated material from a new source, is always a little less connected and less nutritious, especially those that claim to 'hack' you out of the old school get it done right- the best way.

There is a great error, in "knowing," without experiencing. Regurgitated material should be avoided. If a fat man starts telling you how to get skinny, and you listen to that, you are UN-experienced. Try to concentrate on gaining actual experience in your life. Start experimenting on your own using a diverse amount of information, and we have that in our pockets now.

Let's go into a few ground rule things on that avenue.

Gym wraps and belts are purchased by the thousands each day. There are a lot of products for working out. I do not recommend wrapping joints, and using belts. Do more joint building exercise and work your core more, do tons of sit-ups, push-ups, pull ups and light dead-lifts and leave the belts and wraps on the shelve. I can do more than the wrappers can. Interesting right. If you are wrapping something to use it, you either already injured it, or you are going to.

Exceptions are boxing or kickboxing wraps can be good to start with and for fight night but even than I highly recommend you build up a non-wrapped self-sustaining strike power and ready joints.

Knuckle push-ups and working into it slowly like anything else is the way. Take the gym away and keep putting your hour in and you will find out the muscle just knows tension and resistance and there are plenty of ways to create that.

Working out of the system of convenience is absolute priority for let's just call it a diversifist.

Instead of driving walk, or run, maybe it's far, park a good distance away and walk half. Work it out, start cutting down convenient things and making everything suck a little bit so get tougher.

Start looking for ways that you can build yourself out of convenience and off sugar completely. We have over domesticated not just our nutrition, but ourselves. It is to the point that we are evolving into a weaker species. In everything from plants to bee's human being issued domestication is a process of weakening for control and this intention bleed into everything good and contaminates it in dynamic multifaceted ways.

Next wake up early and try walking or jogging with a backpack of clean clothes to the local gym, workplace or wherever. These things and even sleeping on a harder surface or jogging in the rain (adults only, with cleats, on field), cause the body to switch into a more progressive, and functional physical performance state.

Everything is Possible. You can do it all on your own. You just need to study up and have a good head game and plan about it like with anything else. You can't hear "you can't" anymore, because you can't, is a lie to begin with. Whatever else, they told you in the modern health information world, could be just as fickle as that also.

The following sections and articles provide the finishing touches of the nutritional fitness concept. Let's get started with this now.

Nutritional Diversity Application

At First, we need 60 species from permaculturist's. We can order, we can go to them and have a personalized learning experience and meet the plants we plan to consume. I went through that whole rant just now in hopes you will select option two and go to the permaculturist's meet him, pay him more, and don't hesitate to ask him to grow what you desire from your research. '

I do not recommend this diet as a plant-based model at all, for those who will continue to get their produce from grocery stores. The agriculture chemical add-up will be more damaging than helpful. I can't really say I recommend any meat products from the store either.

Permaculture or some type of agriculture alternative that uses no chemicals is required for this diet.

It would be cool to design and select and read up on all the species and have a perfect list. You will see quickly we need work with what we have, inspire or support the alternative agriculture around us each step of the way and start learning and experimenting in a very

dedicated fashion if we are going to really get this most important science "our less evolved" ancestors had -or better.

I can't tell you how many people I have shown this too that never really get it, and equally I can't tell you quickly how many people I have worked with that tell me it has changed their life, saved this, saved that, and they love it!

I also adore this aspect of the diet. This response is shared by the best people. Usually, you can separate the two into different levels of intelligence and ways of thinking and doing. Clinically described as a

narcissist, someone who was on the higher road while being dishonest and prepared to lie. Let this be a quick side- lesson in clinical

terminology. It is always negative, and it always takes away from the potency of the real thing in which it describes. This is true for any terminology but most-so for clinical terminology in the English language.

Like most of the previous section of this text, some people are just not going to get it, let alone apply it.

Before we get into cooking and smoothie making that is highly diverse, lets break down the basic tools in the digestive tool kit we can use to throttle and toggle digestion and performance.

Increments

Eating increments, or food increment adjusting is a powerful tool, and can be more or less the human throttle to digestion, nitrification and efficient energy production.

Nitrogen is a vital component of life, and certain schools of thought believe that it is essential to preserving a youthful body and mind. That as much time as feasible should be spent on top training and readiness periods in order to maintain a correct nitrogen balance.

Ancient long-distance runners would take pinches of salt, and small amounts of green food every fourteen minutes to an hour as a constant nitrogen balancing installment.

Nitrogen comes into the body mostly through the fresh food that is eaten. It can come into the body topically, through the skin also.

"Hara Hachi Bu," is the regularly occurring Japanese phrase referring to, eating 1/4 of what your stomach can hold.

Americans generally eat until they are stuffed. Three times a day, everything cooked, a variety of foods ranging from three to eleven usually, including a few spices.

Many other world cultures besides the Japanese have similar traditional rules to the effects of not filling the gut completely for the purpose of health, longevity and performance efficiency. Japanese culture outside the Art of Sumo, is relatively free of the obesity plague.

The neighboring Chinese say you can eat until your 80% full.

Across Asia the regular diet variety is especially narrow, although the amount of species and agriculture methods that they are willing to use is much broader. While some may argue skinniness is a product of poorness, and in many cultures that is true, United States Citizens rank among the fattest of world cultures.

The 'Prophet' Mohammed said that a full stomach was one third air, one third food, and one third water.

The French language phrase for "it's time to eat," translates to "I have hunger," and when they are done the common thing said is, "I no longer have hunger."

Modern food culture is 100% void of sufficient diversity, and adequate nutritional guidance information.

Current social culture and agriculture are both operations to limit physical and mental health and performance.

Micheal Pollan, Author of the Botany of Desire, a writer whom I am a fan of, in a 2010 presentation strongly said " that the food industry is undermining our culture and is set to destroy it." cclxxxv

As a starting point, we can assume that eating can be beneficial, but we must keep in mind that times of vegetable and tuber collecting would naturally resemble what I have been describing thus far, and that a feast might be present following a hunt. What I'm trying to say is that while we can feast on meat, we may want to eat veggies separately due to how differently they digest, and when we should eat vegetables, it would naturally be in little between-meal increments that build up to a cooked finish. Feasts require that arrest time be taken before performance is resumed.

Nutritional Diversity

Breathing, eating and hydrating can be in different increments to support different performance needs.

The healthiest, strongest plan is going to be the consistent, cyclic, momentous, refueling with intelligent increments of the different food states designed around the goals of the Nutritional Diversifist.

Find out where your lines are the right way, and then you know your "range of motion" in digestive ability.

The traditional three large plates of mostly cooked four to ten items is a total human limitation, causing fatigue of digestion, ill combined constipation, and much of the nutrition is not converted into efficient energy but sends a rather different message to the body – not that of a performance machine.

According to a study done on obese and overweight adults, numerous little meals resulted in a higher decrease in body weight, body mass index (BMI), and waist circumference than did fewer, larger meals. Also, the frequent meal group showed improvements in insulin sensitivity and fasting glucose levels, indicating better blood sugar control with this eating pattern.cclxxxvi

Chewing time and materials, and the physical process of eating play an important role, in food assimilation of the increment and human health altogether.

We can program our bodies with our actions and even chewing behaviors will play their part on final performance.

By exercising daily in different ways, people are able send commands to the body about how to use the food we eat, and to convert it and send it to the muscles, organs, joints and bones that are being used.

By chewing our food longer and eating harder foods we can (1) strengthen our jaws as physical athletes (2) assimilate more of the

foods we swallow, or don't swallow, (3) improve the health and strength of teeth and gums.

Monkeys have no dentist, and are seen often to chew sticks, and chew many different leaves, and they chew for a minute or a few. Each are scientist and explorer and harvester. Each uses their God-given computer to know the potential different plants can give them.

Whether an on-site test is conducted or information about the forest is passed from one to the other, or both in the case of their food species, is largely speculative.

Laurels and cedars alike seem to receive similar care and love from the little fellas who naturally promote and nourish development in addition to pollinating, so it appears that they don't show much discrimination.

Although it's not as speculative as I made it seem, they are specialists in their environment. Ultimately, we are unsure. We must maintain an open mind because there are some things we will never understand and cannot change.

They are resilient enough to survive in nature, and the tribes they belong to have few illnesses. Like everything else in nature, the jungle does not have many sick people, and those who do tend to be affected by some nearby man-made installation.

Monkeys move from tree to tree, eating for a while from each one before resting for a short while before moving on to the next. They consume food continuously all day long. gaining access to the food by means we could only hope to achieve. They eat from the natural tree, living and from the tree.

I would like more input from a wide range of athletes and diet explorers on what they think about the incremental role of nutritional intake for certain times and functions.

When compared to eating bigger, less frequent meals, eating small, frequent meals resulted in a more maintained energy intake throughout the day and lower appetite, according to another study on healthy people. This implies that eating smaller meals can assist in controlling hunger and preventing overeating, which can lead to weight gain and other health problems.cclxxxvii

I have paid attention mostly to increments in relation to food states, making sure that for each increment of soft food there is an increment of hard food, a x5 increment of whole plant material, etc.

Nutritional Diversity

I have studied at some length, the ideas of constant nitration and the imaginative ancestral gatherer running here to there gathering and snacking.

Well-developed incremental eating systems could be a dynamic and calculated as the designer can imagine. Cooking up increments is as step by step as cooking up incremental ideas within a next level intelligent diet plan. Like with anything a little forethought and some planning is going to contribute to a better outcome.

Using completely direct and rational intelligence that incorporates evaluations made in the heart, the stomach, the body, not just the mind.

A cooking and preparations session would have not only speed up the current meal time in the process but jerky's and dried goods, as well as a good few waters and complete broths would go into the complete nutritional pack.

The "two-bites-until-very-hungry-again system" is the starting place to learning a paleolithic gatherer's probable increments of constant nitration, that opened the evolutionary door to spears and fire. I am alarmingly in better condition when I have constant "electric, living," food intake.

Incremental eating tells your body, you are on the go, you are a machine of performance. As you eat in smaller increments throughout the day you will surely notice your stomach becoming a furnace more so .

I do a two bites incremental process per half hour, per quarter hour or per hour depending on how fast we need to clean the gut, at the start with almost every client as a personal trainer I put them on this extremely simple incremental eating system.

The fire-maker quick start of the gut microflora; "the secret to human fruition is the addition of more diverse nutrition." In order to maintain a consistent, heavy work speed on the farm and fast deplete the system, I find that a tiny incremental eating procedure that leaves three-fourths of the gut empty and a half liter of water to go with each is very pleasant.

Try out the concept by eating little amounts of food throughout the day—just two bites every 30 minutes. Now if you're exclusively eating plants, which I highly advocate for some purposes, you can continue with a half or quarter plate every 30 minutes.

I personally recommend, especially when starting out with this experiment that you go all green, all living, all fresh.

Going to volunteer on a tropical farm is a great way to do this. On a tropical permaculture you can do this walking around while you work, and learn with nature. We call this the Agro-gym, and it really is the best gym.

I think one will start to notice as long as they have those little bites of food available on that exact timing they can figure an optimal running increment pretty quick. They will notice they can run at good steam, be a little more productive, alert and creative across the day.

If the minimum diversity exists in the body this is at the very least a sufficient performance model. It is arguable whether high activity sports should be conducted at all without it.

Assist this throttle with other dynamic factors for example: A person who jumps out of bed, gets a cold shower, gets right to work, on his daily selfcare and mandatory maintenance, is a person whose system has received the message that it needs to be a lean, ready at all times, working machine. A person who wakes before dawn and goes to be just after sunset, is going to perform better.

When I look to build something a business, a wrestling camp. I am looking for people on the track and in the gym around 5 am. I am looking for the guy who never missing Ju Jitsu class. I am looking for the hardest bag hitters in the boxing gym. After that I am looking for grateful attitudes, and total honesty.

To speed the readying for nutritional wonderment process further, run hungry for a bit, do some responsible fasting.

In addressing firstly, the general incremental modes of eating Nutritional Diversity doctrine, we should address briefly the value and use of incremental non-eating, otherwise known as 'fasting.'

Morning or "intermittent" fasting is fundamental in many successful dietary and health systems currently. Prof. Arnold Ehret, who passed away mysteriously in 1922, was sure of many important health factors and dynamics. A big fan of fasting, who professed even spinal corrections can come from fasting, this result would be from a

prolonged fasting. Professor Ehret was also the author of the "Mucusless Diet System, Method of Eating Your Way to Health," cclxxxviiiwhich concentrates on alkaline forming and acid forming processes of the body in relation to the foods of the modern age and resulting human health crisis. Nutritional Diversity has worked with, tested and agrees that engaging alkaline binding material is the right idea in human health and fitness. I do not agree with all of the Professor's quoted findings in this publishing.

I can go on and on about the benefits of fasting well covered by many authors and enthusiasts, who have also brought wealth's of functional healing and nutritional truths to the forefront.

Metaphysical guru's claim that with prolonged fasting one can achieve relief from mental traumas and emotional nightmares.

All nature experiences various droughts and also cloudy times. We must learn to dance both in the rain and in the drought, with the intention, the water structure of gratitude and the realization that these time scan benefit us should we choose them too. Daily morning fasts, can contribute to a clean digestive track, which is of the utmost importance to overall physical and mental health.

I do every other day, but I don't forget as I can do what I want and that it is best to go by feel. Morning fasts are very much a staple of my own personal nutritional plan. Studies show testosterone increases can be linked to fasting and we know that ketones are produced in the blood by high fat diets and complete starvation, or starvation from carbohydrate energy.

Cold showers by the way have been proven to help healthy testosterone productions, which are very helpful to food absorption, and the complete metabolic process among many other things.

I recommend to everyone, cold showers and fasting for four hours after wake-up, to be ended in at least a ten-minute meditation forcing also the hunger from thought, three times per week at a minimum; as the minimum effective practice dose. Sort of, kind of; every increment between your food intake increment is a fast increment.

One increment is for cleaning and burning excess (fast), and the other is for loading nutrition into the system.

Use good oil such as coconut or olive can be used, and the cultivation of discipline or music should be at the mind's forefront as both of these focuses have rhythms to them.

With fasting, like any eating or consumption related technique is best timed, when the Nutritional Diversifist, decides to use it, because the feeling of need. Improving our relationship with our stomachs and our food and our action based on need or environment is a vital improvement to overall human optimization.

The timing thing is dynamic and seems complicated at first but by tethering decisions to nature and nature's timing and slowly but surely developing a few rhythms and routines to the wheel house; in time the timing thing becomes quite simple and routine.

At this time many users find, that their being will graduate to new levels of performance, and so this timing, practice time, is a good time to really take on new, diverse and heavier challenges.

"Nutritional Blasting, Blender Bandit Recipes or super smoothies are a great way to end the fast, as your body is hungry and ready to burn up in a moment what it's given.

Pack a great drink full of herbs, greens and fruits for good solid blood building."

I try to get a good 12 to 45 different things in one Nutritional Blast Shake. It takes a bit to know your Nutritional Diversity pallet and become a mixologist at the ND level but once you get it, you've got it and you are good to go. At this point smoothies become amazing!

It's an easy way especially when working solo, to get a good Nutritional Diversity going in your busy routine. It is usually the starting place for new folks implementing the diet, and trying to climb the diversity mountain.

Stick with these selected things, these same species throughout the day. Each species has a minimum effective dose relative to the consuming system and it takes various amounts of time for that to build in many cases usually no more than size weeks. The nutritional diversity diet plan matures to optimal performance enhancing abilities; for that physical training plan, that particular hydration and diet plan design, in that specific gut-culture it creates from where the culture was at start, at that specific time, in that specific environment where the six weeks was passed.

The richness of the meals and shakes will have you suddenly desiring no modern restaurants (as a vegetarian, anyway) and excited as ever for the next day of packed nourishment as you hone your shakemaking and cooking skills. Remember that you are trying to achieve a total of 60 or more different species, and optimally all of them at a minimum effective dose. From there you refine, and refine and refine. Practitioners are always amazed in our classes when asked have they have received messages from self, about maybe "a little less of this herb's flower, or a little more of this tree leaf?"

Stomach gardens and earth plants have a telepathic language, and we will learn more about dynamic telepathy in biological nature in a bit. A full spec, Nutritional Diversity can take a full days or weeks work easily to achieve just in its organization.

There are great taste tricks if that is your thing but, for starters leave big pieces of material. This material brooms the stomach of build ups from bad foods and cooking oils that we really need to get rid of to have this pure experience.

I love and recommend the Vitamix only for sauce making. I will use it at the various farms I work and visit. This routine practice quickly

puts the practitioner in a much better place all around. It is so

effective I want to try to cure addicts with 60-day ND diet farming programs, because they would be so high at the end, coming from where they were they would never want to go back to where they were for anything.

I make shakes for my plants too in the blender. Sometimes I add fresh shakes to my gardens, thrown in the Biodynamic Agriculture (Steiner) quarts directive, and sometimes I take the blended material and mix with other stuff.

After a couple years doing this the plants really love what I am doing with these practices that use the kitchen scraps we don't. Try it out, I guarantee you your plants will love it also and you may even learn which items they prefer.

The get fat and tired plan. Increments should be large, entire plate sized, all cooked, eaten at once. You'll probably be able to

sustain this at only three servings per day for a while. I don't recommend eating this way at all, and it will lead to toxic formations, and various forms of gut rot.

To refine and consider a minimum effective dose with our nutritional or medicinal elements, which I have concluded most solidly is done by maintaining a meal schedule for 6 to 12 weeks at a time; each specie should be logged each day, and each week the feelings of energy should be added to the log with vitals' information such as blood pressure, oxygen blood level, weight, etc.

New home blood testing technologies are on the horizon which will allow our gardeners of the future ecology to get a more scientific grip on their diets and performance, while they go out as the most powerful, positive reforestation effort imaginable.

For example, red meat increments are very filling, at the same time, the feaster loves a large portion of it and likely it was a feast for most of human existence because it was a hunt.

Likely this group of humans were on a foraging schedule, only to maintain until the hunt or catching of fish could more adequately nourish. At the same, for long travels we know jerky's and dried meats and fats were used. It's dynamic the way we are able to eat, trash, and things in excess or lack of their particular most correct increment, I think anything natural and not naturally toxic (an issue of amount/dose) is okay.

Paying better attention to, and interacting with species in the garden, in the wild, on the permaculture, and slowly assessing the particular life in relation to you and your farm, could be very telling regarding how and how much to use it for.

Go with Your Gut

Jesse Cornplanter commented on the Iroquois philosophy of Muskrat Root also Known as Water Hemlock,

"The old people say that Muskrat Root is like any other herbal medicine you want. When you want it, it stands up where it grows calling to you. That is why it is easy to find a medicine you seek."

In this case, interestingly it is those who want to die that is being referred to here, as this plant is highly toxic and just little bits will kill. It is recognized by the tribe as a plant with this aim only, and for this particular species, they may argue with the idea that all things are both healing and toxic, and that this difference is keyed by the dose. This teaching, that comes from many of life's experiences, contains the message that intention is very important in all things.

That nature is here for us even if we are ready to pass on. That

passing on is when its decidedly so, if we are in this dynamic relationship with nature. Really knowing plants, and food items is to clear your stomach on a one day fast.

If you want respect in nature you must give nature the respect she deserves. If your nature is to appreciate beautiful things and blessings you have all the support in the world in nature.

Go ahead and clear the mind while you are at it. Mind and stomach clear.

Stand with the plant, talk to the plant, treat the plant(s) as if it is a member of your family. Bring it water, play music for it, touch it, hug it and kiss it and protect it from the bad guys that might want to hurt it. Sound crazy? I visit about 90 plants each week like this and with an offering to some sort of fertilizer, or treat. The process takes about hours as I take care of several garden chores in the path.

There is evidence that chemical production for the farmer and his family can become richer in response to better treatment.

Nurture nature to nurture self. The best way to be selfish is to be selfless. It happens within yes, but it also comes from out – the ecology can totally decide how to support its animal residents. Nature is patient, tactful and torturous at times. This is a cycle in all biological life. A cosmic function that is dependable. The roller coaster of life goes up and down, and it's good to time certain attentions accordingly. Timing is everything.

With a more dynamic relationship to these ups and downs, and tides and water levels and moons, and seasons the more an artist, warrior, gardener and healer alike is to become.

Nature is likewise an opportunist of support and help for the

chemically empowered. In other words, to deny adequate time in nature to an individual as 90% of modern men do (cultural issue) is insane because this is where the biological re-charge comes from. A person will remain younger and stronger with more time in nature. Immune systems are likely to be at more optimal functionality with time in nature. Arguably for sure, however a logical theory; is that ethical character, respect for all nature would contribute somewhere to the functionality also.

A true diversifists, takes only what he needs, wastes nothing, appreciates everything and gives dedicated intentional love to the ecology. To ask a question in modern language; would there be a return on this investment? Likely so. Would you recognize it when received? If you were a special individual you may.

There is a large unknown space that should be elementary school knowledge about natural process such as compost. For example, "urea" is a main ingredient in commercial and home fertilizers and many medications for humans. More pills than you think contain this "urea." Seriously examine the medications you take now, and you will likely see this on ingredients list. This is urine. You take piss pills. It's not a lot to learn, if we had a valid education system run by loving educators that are tested for Narcissistic Personality Disorders.

A breathing mantra practice for yourself there in front of the plant that loves on your CO_2's wouldn't hurt you or the plant. Believe in the Backster science and add intention to that breath mantra and don't be surprised when those same species just across the way from others, that did not get that love from, take a serious growth lead begging for the same attention.

Bring new species in to the garden and see new bees and butterflies never seen before see the greater cycle of diverse workings and nutrients churns into the beautiful life we know as ours.

Remember this biology in front of you in your bio-dependence. Go figure it will like you are breathing with it but pay attention there is an un-measure able information exchange in front of you. The receptacle for this data must be built in the modern office worker.

I know this all sounds a little hippy-dippy but stay with me, it's pretty scientific actually. The breath mantra is a military training designed for combatant to be able to be in the air, get on land move large distance, then get in the water and mover large distances and be able to persevere. I have taken it to the next level. Many people have a version of what I am writing right now, most endurance athletes for sure. I have for this early revision; and introduction to the combining of next level intention, alternatively sourced high-diversity diet, and an overview of physical practice.

Okay here is where it really gets hard to swallow, and believe me the image you have of the person writing this could not be more far off.

There is an opportunity in nature to cultivate a really important empowering love and appreciation of plants. If a naturalist can manage to do this so the plant will communicate a new level of truths to a body which is able to receive them both in telepathy and in nutritional substance at harvest time (for sufficient time given current health); he will find himself in a position very near to his best level of health ever.

I am sure this will work in every case I have seen more than a few times now. My personal testimony to this diet, and this relationship with nature as a cure all, a self-optimizer is without doubt. I am 100% looking to take the right people on this journey and it does not take long.

The Nutritional Diversity diet concept as it stands now has been focused mostly on edible plant species largely, although arguably, all plants are edible considering a proper dose is known for it. Ultimately, we believe now it will be through advanced and intelligent ALL-NATURAL procreation and extremely high diversity of ingredients that the most effective and optimal diet plans will be concocted.

This should be done at small sustainable spaced out home and small community "labs" of no more than 180 users. I use the word lab, just to keep us always testing and focused and experimenting and bettering systems.

Just imagine that at least five of these things go out and happen and have some decent funding from community liquidation or smart governments or whatever. In five year's what will they have come up with. I tell you what in ten years no doubt about it they are going to need armed security.

On your clear stomach, now having spent time clearing that stomach with the particular plant specimen of study, eat one small serving (of one plant) by itself at a time get a clear message to the brain about this food.

After doing this you will be rightfully hungry with a dynamic choice of what next to do. This kind of study is initial groundwork for another diet experiment. Dedicated and constant diet exploration and experimentation is the key to optimal ND learning.

"Should I go ketogenic?" It is one likely response in modern diet culture people, at least is in the minds of many new farm hands I work with. I could do something like this just to build a little metabolic dexterity.

"Should I fast again and really put my metabolic engine to selfcleaning mode on my system?" Many scientific studies, and diet authors say yes, you should for as long as you can. Many metaphysical practitioners and authors agree. It is a decision that does not have much opposition except from the body building communities that realize muscle destruction comes with it.

Too much fasting will cause the body to "store carbs. In other words, it will put a little tire on you for the next time you go without giving it what it needs.

Cutting out the bad foods is number 1. Not 1 bad food, not one soda, not for 1 year. Not till you are number 1.

Nutritional Diversity

Another decision could be "Let us get some red meat going in this monster animal of a human system I have here!" Carnivore dieters, will be some of the ND practitioner's rank and in this case "nose-to-tail" should be the anthem.

Many others will go back to the high school wrestlers' main dish of chicken fish and rice, which was a pretty functional personal favorite of mine for a long, long time. Rice has gone way down in quality since then, but we don't know about that, and it does hurt us.

Vegan's and vegetarians have a hearty standpoint and using the

narrow grocery store supply they have a well-studied regimen. Its impressive they are alive at all. Just kidding. If they go outside the grocery and up their diversity as I am saying they will be also feeling the best a vegan can.

For the most part, I must say to leave all of this information in the background, as none of these diets have anything real to do with knowing your food, or the nature you come from. They don't explain sufficient diversity that miss that completely, and most of it is still rooted in ill-educated people, and ill-manufacturing of produce.

People will hate me for saying it but the Carnivore diet movement has more of the bases covered for human performance.

The real magic uses natural ingredients the real majesty is using natural ingredients don't get yourself as twisted as the modern culture who thinks lab-built products are the most powerful ones. I am right behind the strength of crazy steroid freaks, and sometimes ahead of them. What I offer here is in its infancy. I have so much to learn. We have so much learned, and as we do we will start to see a more clean, balanced power that surpasses that of the steroid freaks. I have done some initial work. Enough to see the horizon.

The publication of this being post-Coronavirus-timed is also an interesting dynamic to me. Had it not been for the black magic (metaphorical reference for something much worse) of the narc in my life this information could have been sent off in mass back where more applicable. If it is ever reviewed at all by who it should I don't know now, but my gut feeling is our immune health challenges are not over.

I myself believe that all knowledge is out there, accessible through imagination and experience.

"Imagination is more important knowledge." - Albert Einstein

The idea that nature can wipe us all out is tangibly in front of us. Maybe now people will listen.

I would recommend that the diversify practitioner use this moment of fasting and hunger as an opportunity for discipline building. Push yourself to see how long you can take it for. Push yourself to see how much you can do on nothing.

This time in cultivating divine discipline, will be spent by your body releasing ketones, that start burning off fat as running fuel, and this will also help Nutritional Diversifist's getting into the ketogenic diet which most humans do not have an operational mechanism for right away, at least not in a sustainable fashion.

I myself get the idea mostly that while ketogenic release is a healing mode, it's not necessary to be a constant continuous mode, although that said it does not seem to have risk as a continuous mode generally, but for some people.

Assumable is this smaller group of difficulty with prolonged ketogenic tolerance has just been generationally conditioned by epigenetic changes throughout the persons ancestry.

A spectrum of diverse functionality lives in, a dynamic I refer to as metabolic dexterity. Metabolic dexterity can be exampled as the pivotal performance output that comes from going from carb-based fuels to fat-based fuels and back again.

Eating and fasting alike can be more dynamic processes than simply chewing and swallowing things or abstaining from doing so for a time if you think of them in dynamic context. Low and behold continual dynamic thinking leads to more dynamic digestion. I feel like the more I change it up and the more I take things out and put new things in, I am receiving a higher rate of learning.

These ideologies come back up latter in the section entitled Karmic Reforestation (maybe). Keep in the back of your mind throughout this getting to know your ND process that certain plants and food items have both helping and inhibiting elements to them. It is always a double-edged sword in the plant world. That is a difference from the new carnivore movement for sure.

As a Nutritional Diversity community, we cannot at this time answer the question, "If they grow well together do they consume well together?" The answer is no.   The answer is yes. The answer depends on such a dynamic set of factors.

The most functional and well-covered special combination today is turmeric root, and black pepper, which is a pivotal discovery out there in the world if you ask me. Thousands of products have been based on his combination and people are applying the "activator" title to our age-old seasoning that seems to be applicable to more than enhanced taste. The fact is this process of enhanced nutritional activity is potentially thousands of species deep to include species and fungal and cultural growths that don't even exist yet.

Practically, ginger and salt come to mind. A knowledgeable plantsman knows this means that cassava is out because of the ginger. Damiana and mix well with turmeric based dishes in my past and are generally mixable with everything so I will try those two a few days. If I have a well describing log form, I can really refine feelings and do intensive accurate focal work on what I am doing which will help me to clarify these types of physical readings in the future.

Through this very practice, most users begin to develop an appreciation with nature so much they can no longer throw a seed in a trash bag while finding that there is so much for them in the plant and nature world they have been missing that their heart opens up and their body floods with the love chemicals.

Activation of love chemicals is going to be one of the vibrant fluctuating compositors of our new miracle machine self. Like a permanent installation that needs routine maintenance we will routinely check on her and make sure she is there. We do this by being thankful, and putting that thanks into your nutrition.

New diet explorer and result wanting athletes may find themselves picking up trash when they see it in nature, or anywhere they may have done this before but now it is with a new attitude and commitment.

To see proposals to cut down thousands of trees for whatever purpose may come up on the job, and the once well-acclaimed pro now has emotional problems making the big new construct if a price is involved that nature will pay. He may become defensive even violent.

May I recommend simple karmic reforestation.

I see that need for intense upgraded adaptation coming for all my brothers and sisters. Prepare yourself. To get to know nature, in a deeply personal way, according to my suggestions, is an extreme thing only to extremely stupid modern culture that we have now.

On all other forms of comparison and measurement it is the most perfect and balanced thing whose result is everything you see. Any of us familiar with Sean Penn's movie "Into the Wild," based on the book, and story of Christopher McCandless's early 1990's adventures into the wild eventually dying on his last a deepest trip from starvation and toxic plant consumption of a look-a-like to something in one of his books.

If he had used a different method of plant identification and better planning, developed better more one knowledge of those surrounding he was a so-called expert of he could have met different ends.

That is not to say the story is an accurate depiction of real events or knowledge at that time especially being no account was given of the Deadman who died by himself.

Also, if he had been consuming a full range Nutritional Diversity Diet, he likely would have been just fine consuming the toxic plant. But plant identification books don't give you that ideology.

Zoology has been good library of study reference because they want to know about natural consumption. To really know a plant, is to grow a plant, so get out there and do that.

Without the 25 million square miles of leaf, humans, and livestock we don't eat and we don't breathe.

If used correctly it is plant essences at the base of all healing and providing for every need of the human and the animal.

Nutritional Diversity

"All life is brought through the sweetness of photosynthesis," as so eloquently put by Peter Tompkins and Christopher Bird, in the book

"The Secret Life of Plants."cclxxxix This book was a fundamental metaphysical science concept underpinning the peace revolution movement of the 1960's that no one has heard of today, not even many young permaculturists. It contains experiments and data that have become vital and fundamental knowledge in my own progression in the diet.

I have two old schoolers I picked out to love here in Panama as they are both wizards in their own right, highly intelligent beings who tell me things for my benefit, not for theirs. One is named Bruce, and the other is named Lee and they are both "Masters Bruce" and "Master Lee" to you. Black belts of life you can see them as. Thanks to Master Lee for this piece of the puzzle.

Agriculture for most people in pre-machine history, and for most of the time till now has determined the wealth of the nation or state or encampment. Uphof did a six hundred and some page "Dictionary of Economic Plants," which has remained a good reference on the subject of plant economics.ccxc

Carl von Linne, the grandfather of modern botany declared that plants only differentiate from other species in movement, or lack of. Charles Darwin smacked that down when he proved each tendril could move independently, later citing the observation that only when it is of great advantage to them, they will display the movement which is so slow that most will not notice.

Cleve Backster a 1966 expert lie-detector examiner, and teacher to the world of polygraph examiners around the U.S., and the world, one day in sheer curiosity hooked the machine up, to small palm in the office chosen by his secretary, happening to be a very sacred, but popular house plant known as the Dracaena.

A red fluid secreted by several plant species from the genera

Daemonorops, Dracaena, Croton, and Pterocarpus is known as "dragon's blood." They are endemic to different regions of the world. Depending on its manner of secretion and its speciesspecific chemical composition, it is categorized as either a resin or a latex. This red material has a protective function and is either

created (a) naturally and stored in anatomical structures that have already been developed, or (b) is induced in reaction to stressful events such mechanical trauma, pathogen attack, or insect invasion. Dragon's blood, which also plays a protective role in plants, is a priceless natural resource valued for its many therapeutic benefits and artistic applications dating back to antiquity. Considering the crucial role dragon's blood plays, our knowledge of the biological basis for its secretion is still incomplete.ccxci

The plant secretion has many homeopathic medicinal uses and many homeopaths claim it is a miracle. The red sap with medicinal properties goes for about eight dollars for half an ounce worth.

Long story short, Backster discovered that the plant knew when he was a threat to it, and knew when he was faking threat to it. Under real intention of damaging the plant just before actually doing it, he was able to create electronic surges in his machine concluding the plant knew he was going to attack it and released a response. This is now a term in botany called the "Backster Effect" and it refers to the recognition that plants have a very perceptive intelligence, and the likely communicate with these very electric pulses to other plants.

2013 research from the University of California, Davis showed that couples in love did not only skip a beat when seeing each other, but their hearts and respiration cycles would also synchronize with one another. Being in love releases healthy young hormones. That's why a newly fallen-love person appears to be glowing. Fall in love with things, and really mean it is a lesson here. Fall in love with your plants and really mean it. Get to know them. Get to grow them, and get a specific blessing just for you from the highest and longest-living biologically connected intellect in return.

Lew Childre Jr., did some interesting research like this which he called 'tapping into coherence,' which he described as a sort of personal fluency or attention to being calm and happy at all costs, and inner peace of mind in which people are able to synchronize themselves and their heart rhythms with a worldwide happy, healthy frequency.

Nutritional Diversity

Today his Heart Math Institute has focused on stress management techniques and identified life stressor's and the permitted effectiveness on us that they have to be a leading cause of illness both physical and mental.

Dr. Ricky who introduced me to Ozone therapy a powerful tool, also practiced a physical form of tapping specific body parts and areas as nervous system reset medicine. It involved tail bone and some uncomfortable taps at the beginning as a protocol of access, sort of ritualistically; like the starting protocol in hypnotics, followed by

anatomic location taping to tell the body where next to access and

then other taps to try and program a nervous shocking of sorts initiating a resistance-based effect. There is so much about healing physiology packed in this wild Wizard-of-Oz-like tropical adventure that I have been on down here treatments like this one didn't make the cut. I mention it though because acupuncture, massage, pressure point massage and other treatments have similar ideas of accessing health. Health is certainly more dynamic than it is given credit for by the mainstream administrators.

Professor Backster continued his research, living out his day with various plants connected to the galvanometer, when the making of his breakfast started triggering a response in one of the plants, as he cracked his eggs open; accidentally finding out that an unhatched egg, which he eventually hooked up to his galvanometer had a faint impulse at 160 to 180 beats per minute, matching the heart rhythm of a one to four-day old chick.

New Jersey cytologist Dr. Miller concluded that some sort of "cellular consciousness" must be common to all life.

Backster eventually found that across all living things near to the local, there is a reaction to dying tissue, and intentional murder of the living thing, realized from real examples such as small as mixing a jam preservative into a pure recently made yogurt that was killing some of the micro-bacteria in the yogurt.

Marcel Vogel, an expert in luminescence picked up the study and in the interesting realization of quantum physics' role in the newly discovered dynamic ability, determined that one plant reacted to the pain of another plant more so when Vogel was paying attention to it.

Little did he know at that time, that his journey would eventually theorize that plants were able to read minds; not just intentions, but attentions which increased the response level.

I see some level of this in my dogs.

Vogel an also expert interest in Native American knowledge and culture, said that the American Indians knew very well about these facilities and would go into nature, putting their back against the pine trees to rejuvenate themselves with the tree's power.

Finally, Vogel demonstrated to the producers of a TV show called

"You Asked for It," the plants abilities to read his mind and emotions, their minds, and emotions and then showed how they can tune back to nature. MythBusters and various comic experiments for show ratings have duplicated similar results, very easy to duplicate but curiously are completely ignored by mainstream science.

Furthermore, Vogel felt that there was realm of essence we could not detect, without organs or with our science, based on the new scientific discovery - that held an instant form of intelligent communication all its own.

Other scientific expressions of this modality also imagine this example as the innate and perception of certain dogs, who can tune into a person's intentions, character, spiritual consistency or fears. Also, of certain ants and other biological creatures. It is a realm of perception we are yet to experience.

Another lack of experience that maybe, that we believe to be attributed to do lack of sufficient diversity, lack of adequate gut culture to interpret.

Mr. Vogel was able to determine this, by exhalation strongly, from first one foot away to later one hundred feet away, achieving the same response in the plant. At 100 feet away, it became very clear that there was some other force of energy or communication with the plant that doubles with reparation. Vogel theorizes that possibly with a concentrated thought made while holding the breath in, could make the communication more specific and complete.

After tons of experiments Backster went on to form elaborated theories such as that plants and maybe certain animals, wish to be eaten, and assimilated into life forms but only under a communicative relation like that of a kosher ceremony or something akin to the Christian rite of Communion, or the Ancient Asian self-donation of self to nature at old age. The want to go out and get an honorable death lives in most all cultures of old. The achievement of Valhalla, is through a selfless act of fighting for principal and greater good.

Dr. Vogel observed that the plants would give a calm if not a

response at all when this type of communication happened without Backster or someone able to read the results of the plants hooked up to the meters.

Wow a dynamic intellect that can read the mind to this level to know whether or not the person can read the test, and to give a result then that may be only given because of the test that they administered!

They know us beyond us beyond secrets and output, the skeletons in our closet, the intentions behind our acts!

An ultimate athlete and nutritionist would know this!

He continued to favor the Dragon plant for many tests, and realized that mindless brutal slaughter of living specie did provoked a very emotional reaction from her, a reaction unseen the minute a repentance and self-made ritual of apology and thanks and honor would be performed.

Another plant's ability of physical perception and changed based on said perception can be easily tested by any Gardner and that is when they plant a vine, near to a pole or stem. Any observer will notice the vine crawl ever so slowly towards the pole over a few days. Then just before the vine reaches that pole, move the pole and notice the vine also changes its direction to find the newly placed pole.

The conflict of interest could be another pole near to the example. But the results of the test of moving the pole with the conflict will also produce an important result for the observing gardener. You will have to do it to get this level, as it is too hard for me to describe in a fullness. Most "next-level" things our current modern culture is unable to grapple with are like this.

I keep harping away in this region of thought because you basically need to accept that much of your optimal nutritional and performance experience will be far outside of the English language and should remain this way.

I pose the question and idea that the plant can speak to birds and birds can deliver their seed for them to certain nearby or worldwide locations as we have seen happen to many species.

Human is the only things that live outside of nature, that have lost the message, the way and has followed his ego rather than nature thinking that he is nature, and that nature is him - which is also a dynamic truth. It is the basis for quantum physics. What is a divine access point should not become an extremely dominant lifestyle point, but a balanced focus that contains the vast diversity of dynamics included in its considerations.

Should we regain this dynamic communication, we will no doubt find empowerment at the level we see in the animal residents who have it.

I mean as to take pills, develop chemicals, take those, and building cities and structures where most biology dies or weakens could rationally be somehow the link to our separation.

If so would this type of future development style would be to our benefit or demise? Obviously if this is in fact the case, that we are lacking something and missing something that all other biology has, that can't be to our benefit.

It must contribute to our loosing. Certain studies in permaculture have well illustrated that if we live in harmony with nature we can support, many billions more humans, animals, fish and trees.

Nutritional Diversity

It seems like I have started writing really basic stuff here, which is in the fact of really basic error that makes no sense to be featured in a culture that sends rockets to space.

It almost seems as though right now the earth is in communication to try and rebuild itself and utilizing well the few resources we have left her with to maintain a perfect balance of gases and local constituents to save a life in the face of our odd and drastic efforts to kill it.

From me, now having read this information if you believe you can know your plants better, that's a fun experience. One that I myself am most thankful for.

I definitely am a stupid belief, the city idea itself, the central distribution idea itself, lack of diversity or focus on mono-anything itself, and stupid ignorance regarding diet and nature that has killed the human soul, physiology and potentially dynamic, rich and free life experience.

The whole result of the psychedelic experience is the understanding that nature wants to communicate with us. -Terence McKenna

ND Biodiverse Food Study, Panama

The ND Biodiverse Food Study has been ongoing over the last 9 years here in the beautiful Republic of Panama.

We discovered a whole new design structure for diet and nutrition and it is so much more functional and advanced than our existing routine and nutrient supply that we have recorded athletic performance increases of up to one hundred and sixty percent in eight-week test cycles.

We have recorded performance increases of 70 to 90% regularly at 15 days of implementation at it keeps getting better every time and in every category for every case from there.

We are still here all year long every year doing this.

We do this. This Nutritional Diversity discovery and optimization data will revolutionize the way we consume, think and perform in every way moving forward. We continue our research   self - funded today.

For this and for the fact that we have real data that shows a real allnatural way to increase performance beyond limits previously reached in diet and nutritional athletic sciences; we are selling our complete report including over 6 years of test data, a significant amount of data related to new and exotic diet species and important special combinations, recipes and complete with macronutrient   equation guides, several relevant 'do it yourself' instructions plus access to the online always growing and refining application guide a now 100+ page indexed guide to "complete all-natural human optimization."

Everything needed to reach the next step in personal self-human performance on the job, in the gym, in the bed, and in your head.

Get on the cutting edge today!

The ND Biodiverse Food Study, has been an ongoing high variety species diet performance study since 2011 primarily in the Republic of Panama, "Bridge of the Americas."

•This is a fairly, technical explanation of the study. If you are looking for a simpler Introduction to Nutritional Diversity Science, click here . •This following study is a draft write, it is by no means in final form. I have no college degree or license of any kind. While we do have repeatable results, our grossly underfunded operation is currently ongoing and open for further peer review, etc. To get on the cutting edge with updated reports and performance special diversities and recipes, please get access to our live-time-updated cutting edge diet report .

This revision includes sufficient test data to present the abstract. Anyone can use this revision and be highly beneficiated by it and the learning curve to be able to use it can be severely shortened by its mentioned applications.

ABSTRACT

Nutritional Diversity Diet Study is a biodiverse food study currently based in the Republic in Panama, with certain examinations in other areas of Latin America. This study examined the Nutrient Adequacy Ratio (NAR) and the Mean Adequacy Ratio (MAR) of diet, nutrient, and agricultural food diversity, availability, consumption in 5 different communities and individual athletic and healing performance in these comminutes as well as a diverse range of other related observations

and trials. The study observed and worked in the wild, and worked with less domesticated and wild species as it's primary focus.

PREFACE: Poor nutrition can start before birth and continue on for generations, and this is what we see in most people today. The rising health   crisis and younger ages of sick people, parallel the rise and continued   evolution   of   chemical   and   machin - edependent, modern agriculture systems. These same systems are directly linked to the mass killing of wildlife   that   pollinates   and operates the trillions of mechanisms that make up the great cycle of life that facilitates our world. ccxcii ccxciii ccxciv ccxcv ccxcvi ccxcvii

Observing other animals in our ecology it was noticed that the ranges of biodiverse food species in each observed creature's diet were significantly higher than ours. This lack in biodiverse nutrition is also likely   underpinning   the   generational   decline   in   overall human health.ccxcviii ccxcix ccc

Certain organizations offer intricate, aesthetically designed books and pdfs detailing plenty of figures on the points of diversity in diet using flawed modern standards, and points in agriculture although no one involved is actually working with a food biodiversity today. In rare geographical locations where the ecology is well known or a permaculture has been nurtured before are bio-diverse nutrition sources even available. Some agencies, researchers and 'diet pros are as bold as to study wild edible plants (WEP's) so they say, yet we have no actual information from them on the symptomatic, essential effects of the food, let alone any notices of cumulative research results with other species.

The obvious dietary principle of biodiverse food, or should I say general principle of biological nature is completely avoided in modern diet and there is even, questionably, opposition to the idea that a diverse diet is any better than a narrow one. We, instead, have a toxic, manufactured and fake modern diet that promotes disease and suffering in play. What I am saying is, we know these truths, but masterfully we do not employ them not even when we publish pages and pages on it. It's been my hope to try and put together and actual practice, and real results outside of the disappointing modern science methodology completely. Just a simple, straight forward evaluation of new species, and those species in combinations with others in highly diverse ratio's, to the point that a clear athletic and healing power is realized. Diet information today is so rudely and ridiculously wrong and then the wrong is regurgitated and research pools are so polluted, and no doctor or specialist in this field can really be seen with that much credibility.

Dietary Diversity (DDI) guidelines, do not make recommendations, or model solutions, nor do we feel it make any adequate measure of any health or performance status. In short many suffer purely because of the misinformation, and inadequate information and culture from all of the diet and agricultural experts and diet information sources of our day.

BASIS: This study stems from one experimenter who cured his depression with a blend of 50 herbs he learned of and worked with. The story goes that the original idea was that lack of chlorophyll and other substances in living plants, absent in the modern diet, could contribute to fatigues and depression.

While studying permaculture farming models in Costa Rica (2012) the subject was able to accumulate a high diversity of foods and if he was to stray from that diversity the symptoms would return.

Nutritional Diversity

It is now, after 6 years testing believed a certain amount of this result and conclusion to be from (1) using species outside of the normal modern diet which are many times a toxic risk (homeopathy), and (2) from using a high diversity of species far outside the normal modern diet, that cover more of a full spectrum of these vital nutritional elements (3) using dynamic agriculture and wild harvesting methods, that highly enrich the quality of the harvested food (4) using specific known special combinations that are known or have been found through our study to be rich nutrition and (5) gaining a more complete picture through actual; experience and our own research. The individual experienced incredible loss, and circumstantially a depression for a time would be natural.

Statistically, considering the types of loss experienced, it would seem that this depression cycle was successfully treated as much as it can be. Many comparable cases at even double the length of intense suffering time of 4 years and then an "easier" suffering period of about 4 more years, could likely really use this information.

Finally, after several repeat tests we started notice a clear performance increase at around 60 species of diverse plant food.

Later we found with a few different combinations of foods this minimum remained functional to a degree.

Clearly a refinement and intelligent design of this high diversity dieting could result in further increased performance. Supporting Nutrition and Health Information

Stereotypes and cultural norms, as well as modern dietary information is misleading, unhealthy, and modern diet research methods make too many errors, and inaccurate conclusions, even regarding historical nutrition points. We have had one piece of bad information after the other, and in continuous loop.

The conventional wisdom holds that the hunter-gatherer lifestyle in general and Paleolithic man in particular are inferior human models. Evidence has now shown that these biased perspectives—of the dumb, primitive caveman, the uninvolved and less, powerful, or capable—are false (Kent 1989; Kelly 1995).

The famous book, The Secret Life of Plants (1973), Peter Tompkins and Christopher Bird, using new technology, were able to clearly measure the perceptibility of plants, and the emotional responses that until this time unknown to man.

Paul Stamens the grand elder of mycology author and advocate of medicinal fungi and mycoremediation ccci, Stephan Harrod Buhner our most current guide through the dynamics of our medicinal earth, and Rudolph Steiner, the Godfather of advanced biodynamic, biodiverse agriculture in the modern age, have all scientifically determined that a larger intelligence is at play in the way that plants and ecology come to be. All of this is diversity dependent, it requires the natural model.

The landmark book "Man the Hunter" by DeVore and RB lee 1968 ccciishowed hunter-gatherers to be rich, knowledgeable, sophisticated and above all unique individuals from one another. There was no single stage of human development, just different adaptations to ecological and social circumstances, that cultures are adapted to localities, and thus are configured with a wide variety of land uses and livelihoods. As a result, foraging and farming across the world are actually 'overlapping, interdependent, contemporaneous, co-equal and complementary' Sponsel 1989ccciii. This suggests that many rural people and their cultures might be better known as variants of cultivator–hunters or farmer–foragers rather than just farmers or hunter-gatherers.

Culture and nature were thus bound together (B erkes 1999 ; Pretty et a l . 2010).ccciv The combination of these points suggests that man may have been a part of this greater intelligence at some point in history. There are many cultures that claim to have a much deeper relationship with nature, and many of these cultures, have displayed deeper models of consumption and practice regarding their health.

Ultimately food supply, dietary diversity, adequate nutrition, and modern agriculture, each remain crisis issues today. While herbal knowledge for cleared land should be obvious, it is non-existent.

Nutritional Diversity

In the first few years of hands-on tropical plant study here, we learned that there is a master system for regrowth of cleared land and in that system is a series of seriously medicinal herbs that will come in. Unclear still is the complete mechanics of the pollination and spread of these species, but these same similar special systems, with the same species, will come in at the clearing of land and then various stages of allowed regrowth.

Grass-fed cattle here for example; are actually diverse herb fed cattle, that does not mean the particular farmer was completely organic in his cattle placement as injectable antibiotics are still often used.

Understanding of the above and of things like, that all biology grows against resistance, and other core principles of the new six-year evolved science (that is still very much infant, oddly), while very clear to a student of nature, are many times lost to the modern mind cultivated in the city. Most other creatures in the natural environment eat grossly more of a dietary diversity than we do. This narrow diet itself, and the troublesome issues within it such as chemical cultivation methods, are results being distributed by big food corporations.

HYPOTHESIS: Modern diets were not adequate in nutritional coverage or dietary diversity and produce and processes alike were of poor quality, and that poor health and performance is underpinned by this poor agriculture, low and non- biodiverse food availability for poor diet. More diverse life in the soil, in the farm, or the wild and likely in the stomach microbiome is what is to stack into biological stardom. That by following a rule of diversity, security and sustainability can be achieved, relieving stresses from, and improving the quality and the growth of the human experience. A more biodiverse diet, coming from community food production models,

will eliminate food supply and security issues as well as much of the health crisis. On an indtividual level person will achieve personal sustainability, health and better performance. Switching to these safer organic providers will save pollinators and wildlife. Concerns that agricultural industries will suffer, are based on the industry's ability to adapt to a more sustainable culture. In contrast the human assisted, possibilities to cultivate vibrant and brilliant biology in a completely natural and whole elements-based approach seems limitless.

METHODS:

Central American tropical regions: Wild edible plants (WEP's), and alternative agriculture select species were employed, as well world market place supplements, and local commercial produce to assemble Nutritional Diversity diet plans of a minimum of 60 food species, and maximums of 120 species.

Panama is the ideal, cost effective, most dense bridge of diversity in plants and wildlife, and also in human traffic, thanks to its extremely diversified resident populations in Panama City, Boquete and Bocas del Toro Province. Over 50 alternative agriculture models, across Latin America were visited, and evaluated, for soil quality, diverse production, organic methods, and sustainable technologies to keep the group up on the cutting edge in this leg of development.

Pollination, bee culturing, and mycology were investigated in relation to certain food state, food delivery, food preservation, and food cultivation modules, and in the possibilities of enhancing processes.

Over the past 6 years here in the Republic of Panama, Colombia and Costa Rica we have unveiled several combinations, and individual species that have wondrous effects and throughout the course of these studies indications are that these nutritional essences and possibilities are of a seemingly endless number. A point of redundancy in the overall study, of a nutritionally diverse diet science today, which is oddly in infancy, and has been dubiously replaced by an industrious health diminishing, mal-nutritional prescription; that is stacking of monoculture crop produce in the human system creates a toxin overload. The study removed this produce from the table of bringing human physiology into optimal condition (except in the test flow case of "modern diet").

These nutritionally diverse diets were tested and evaluated cross small farming comminutes, interest groups, permaculture farming students, and athletic clubs for noticeable, measurable performance improvements and healing of difficult disease or enhanced healing of other certain problems. Age groups ranged from child to elderly.

Polling of local, indigenous, European, American and Australian participants at local language schools, athletic and farming groups, college graduate vacationers and on our study's website, to find their current diet diversity, and food biodiversity supplied by farm and market sources. Certain polls observed the MDDS and HHDS United Nations Food and Agriculture Guidelines, and others we independently created and series of diverse polls were propositioned.

Results indicated insufficient dietary sources (around 16 species) and volume in most cases.

Athletic testing and health examinations of study participants. Use of electronic devices to measure and document physical activity, geographical location, altitudes of training, and other data.

Extensive examination of previous research and ideas, existing documentation on plant knowledge and uses, as well as scientific testing of plant species.

DISCUSSIONS:

Simple reasoning can be a good instrument in diet, also intensive plant feeling, and athletic performance afterwards can often be much more accurate than (1) existing science, and (2) the modern scientific methods.

Undoubtedly, monoculture farming is a major contributor to nutritional deficiency. Look at Nutritional Diversity Diet Based on "Common Sense" People are interested in science and research.

The only study testing a high diversity of food species consumption (human), is ours. However, most wildlife observers can tell you, and most animal information can tell you that in the wild, the diversity in the diet for these animals is very high. For example, in a three-day observation the howler monkey here on our Island study site ate 120 different leaves.

But let's just think about it.

We evolved on a gathered diversity of wild plants. At one point in time our entire day, was plants, critters, and maybe a large animal every now and then when we could track them with a spear. The spear itself is thought to be a step along the evolutionary course.

There was no office, no television, just nature. Nature who never saw or experienced the plague of our very unnatural monoculture agriculture.

Most dentists and paleontologists agree that a large part of our evolution was in plant-eating. Agriculture which in many ways can be looked at as our biggest mistake, came, in theory, as a result of evolved intelligence. The spear also a point in evolutionary intellect but not so many regrets there.

In nature's garden, there are thousands of plants growing together, a clear message. How we got to monoculture farming I will never understand. Certainly, a deception regarding nutrition and health either way.

So, by this rational; today we eat a highly insufficient diet, sprayed with unnatural chemicals, that will cause and is causing us homo sapiens to devolve into a more domesticated species, weaker and ill, who needs, doctors and dentists (the only ones in nature with this need), and have forgotten about the nature we evolved by and now even grossly abuse that nature.

We have come a long way.

We don't like to see or admit it, but we have educated ourselves into a curious position of taking our nature for granted, poisoning ourselves and nature.

One year into the 12-year crisis, things are getting worse. Fires, notin-harmony-with-nature-impacts from the mal-educated populous, have shown to be much more drastic a footprint than what was predicted.

Nutritional Diversity

In this study, we realize the possibilities of an Avatar-movie-like ecology and the co-development of an even more diverse diversity. This even seems the more natural the more intelligent the next step for humanity if that step is to be evolutionary. As intelligent gardeners working with instead of against our biology and nature, possibilities are endless. As we continue to work outside of nature's needs we surely all die. Simply.

At the current level of dietary diversity development and testing, we estimate a 10% to 35% increase in athletic ability. The range depends on particular individual dietary diversity plans and the overall state of current health. Interestingly we estimate at this time healing advantages of 30% to 70%, depending on the severity of the condition, individual, community and household diet diversity, and of course overall current health of the individual. The bio - diverse food study continues.

No doubt about it the real game changer is high diversity and robust species. Refinement seems endless and nuclear...

Without biodiverse food intake, the health and performance are automatically going to be less, for us any other animal and plants, earth and insect. This diversity is a clear and necessary, basic law in nature.

It could be argued that the scientific "direction of dissection, rather than diverse connection," is the reason we keep producing human sicknesses instead of human optimization.

Medicinal Use of the ND Biodiverse Food Diet System

The diet has no place in emergency medicine, nor in treating the advanced critical diagnosis, or advanced mental health trauma, accept in building a better system that can recuperate from crisis better.

This being said the diet also very well may achieve even more phenomenal results with the inclusion of certain "super" plants, such as ambrosia peruviana, or gotu kola for example in more refined and wise states of construction. Across the board higher results.

Special Diversity

Biodiverse food intake for modern comminutes and households mark far below our own Minimum Optimal Effective Range (MOER) of foods. Wild edible plants (WEP) are rarely known or used here even among the indigenous. However, the Kuna and Nogle tribes both had knowledge of dynamic harvesting. There were rumors of individual experts with more extensive plant knowledge but we were unable to locate most. We did however successfully track down several and mined some very use full gems from them. Permaculture farmers were the most diverse consumers observed.

An explosive diverse reclaiming of our nutritional intake could be the reforestation effort that restores balance to our valuable pollinators overall, and with proper consideration for native trees and native

species, a balance to our industrial age seems realized. A simple

question our group has had again and again, is "why are the streets not lined in fruit trees?" In a well-planned permaculture-based design this same effort of planting fruit trees can be planting several species together, in a highly productive even pollution-reducing format.

If a new level of performance and healing is the goal, reasonably a new level of nutrition would be needed.

This means, a new level of plant and creature, a new level of soil, a new level of agriculture and fertilizer making. The most trustworthy guaranteed to please and cure disease method would be an all-natural one. Using God's ingredients, the idea of the Nutritional Diversity Permaculturist is to create optimal nutrition through dynamic allnatural practice. This is a complex schematic, with a practical learning curve, with intensive study now thought to be around six years to obtain.

A new marketplace and new cultural distribution or cultivation is needed to supply the new food type, the food biodiversity - the new level of nutrition.

A new education on the new biodiverse food diet, which for us has been a cumulative curve brand is still in its infancy, and education in permaculture especially for the new generation could provide the job skills needed to usher in the age of human performance, life span and enhanced quality of life that comes with living in harmony with nature in a more perfected way. A nutritional supplement   could help in the delivery of the full spectrum minimum diversity to consumers.

It has also been noticed that these practices can work in the interest of world hunger, poverty, and world food security. There are many digital networking platforms today where diet enthusiasts can share and build this knowledge base broader, together. Under this idea, we have used Naturalist which provides a good index of species for diet logs and knowledge base.

A 2010 study of Ethiopian subculture in exclaimed " high rich diverse nutrition" at "38 species." The study concluded that the wild food resource was in quick popularity and interest decline, likely from the tastier modern foods.cccv

It would seem much of modern culture is a process of getting too tasty and learning the hard way what a too tasty diet gets you.

Many students of nature long for the, "wild redeemer" you could say and an understanding of the goods gathered from God's existing garden.cccvi

RESULTS:

Agriculture methods in the Central American Tropical Region are primarily centrally grocery store available American / European Standard, mono-culture, chemical and machine dependent farming production and distribution models. The Panama province   of Chiriquí provided for most of the agriculture for the entire nation.

Agricultural communities today are very condensed. These

agricultural installations will have lifeless soil inside of a decade that will be difficult to impossible to restore life to, if it is not this way already. In fact, we find that soil with the most diverse number of microorganisms is what grows the best produce.

The ND Biodiverse Food Study has inherently declared that the modern food is not just toxic, but too narrow to be considered a healthy nutritional biodiversity sufficient for a complex organism. The structural picture continues to the stomach microbiome likely.

Related research exams found also that as of 2016 biodynamic techniques were used on 161,074 hectares in 60 countries]. That is nothing inside the agricultural whole.

Also, curiously when we really compare species grown today available in stores, to permaculture favorites, and other known species the nutritional margin is significant. Once again also, we find foods that modern diet cultures are based in to be also harmful to consume on a regular basis, for example night shade family vegetables. These same vegetables are the selects of the harmful lab engineered glyphosate poison.

The ND Diet Biodiverse Food Study has been thus far effective in treating several health conditions such as arthritis, Alzheimer disease symptoms, colitis, erectile dysfunction, severe depression, insomnia, malnutrition, and is believed to be able to treat cancers, and many other physical and mental health issues.

In all test subjects the biodiverse food diet system has shown a healthier physique, mood, bowel function, and athletic performance and a host of other physiological and meta-physiological benefits. The fuller spectrum diet, and stronger set of nutrients make better scientific sense, simply and across now over 300 test subjects results being predictably, better performance and better health in every case.

Biodiverse food, more specifically Nutritional Diversity Science and exercise are equal keys to optimal human performance and healing and therefore end up being the secondary focus of our study. We find that in healing some of the physical practice nutrition can be as or more effective than the biodiverse food intake.

The younger the human optimization begins, the better, by very large, approximate measure.

Nutritional Diversity

To have the Nutritional Diversity diet during growing years, has had a noticeably more potent effect on performance, that was observed in several young people so far, across the state board with ND biodiverse food trials in young athletes and farm hands.

To naturally strengthen any biological specie takes, resistance or a form of exercise, a good source of water, and a diverse nutrient base, simply. The more complex the nutrient base, combined with the experiential or environmental training of the organism and its knowledge of the elements and increments, the stronger the life form will be.

The amount of optimization that is possible in wild nature is alarming, and the possibilities are endless. It is quite curious that we have such a narrow-minded nutrition system for ourselves. We have been in full sprint the other direction!

Diet effects the individual and so this will inspire individuals to make the change to better food systems for themselves and loved ones, and slowly make the transition away from toxic food, and this will render the modern agriculture systems less popular and the threat to our ecology's pollination team is lessened.

The physical work involved with permaculture hits almost every stretch, observes extremely dynamic range of movements, and teaches smart pacing and gradually increased weights, volumes and resistance in the course of practice. Growing the nutrition almost meets the complete programing of the nutrition.

Children eat what they grow, and they really rejoice in growing things. Home composting vegetable restarts and seed planting are perfect jobs, or chores for the children in the household, and it gives them a practiced ability many do not have, regardless of how potently advantageous the experience works in one's life. For this reason, a children's home farming education pilot was also worth experimenting with.

New marketplaces that featured the organic produce of smaller farms in their area, were observed in several locations and were hugely popular, and very successful to all involved, a comment I think the consumers most of all would agree with.

New Data:

Very recently (2018) a group published, the only other examination other than ours, that we know of to include non-monoculture or wild food, their data is from European regions, with similar results as the monoculture method is dominant in both continents. The in-depth analysis pushed for the idea but not include as high diversity of diet testing. cccvii

Conflicts of interest:

Whole seed foods not sprouted, such as corn and beans, actually carry harmful lectins, that create aging and lag in performance of the body. This information is thanks to the quite brilliant compiled works of Dr. Steven Gundry, entitled the "Plant Paradox." cccviii Seeds and bean foods were excluded in the ND diet for testing in 2018.

The nutrition in major mono-culture crop selections oddly insufficient to other possibilities in our performance tests.

Rice may have some value but by no means is it a best food. It was used as a carbohydrate fail safe, and that was not the planned or ideal fail-safe crop during that test period.

There are likely permanent conflicts in modern data, that all food types can be associated with diseases and causing them when ingested outside of what we find the minimum ND Biodiverse Food diversity.

Continuation:

We continue to work with athletes, we are hoping to work with some high-level athletes, and do more intensive, dedicated nutritional performance testing.

As for diet production increases we hope to test new distribution methods, a larger scope of trials, and integration with sports clubs.

As we compile the experiments and work received, and a more precise guide to the employment of the science; the ND Team will continue to document and formulate progress related to human optimization. We will stay on top of what's going on in the switch back to a realistic and sustainable interaction with nature, and keep those interested in subject and in our study apprised of some of the things we are looking at and working on here at the online info-hub.

We have finally started narrow and identify a plethora of advantageous, tested, aspects of refining the performance process that we could make out of a blur were there around 2016 when we started to document the findings. The study has found the deeper gems and minerals and it's really getting interesting now.

Biodiverse food formulation remains an interesting and advantageous pursuit.

ABSTRACT

Athletes today, generally know they will underperform, and experience a higher rate of injury based on nutritionally inadequate diets. They look mostly to supplements to ensure they have what they need. Information about mono-crop farms, agricultural chemicals, and processed food distributions /grocery store products is not accurate. Most are un aware of how food is cultivated.

Supplementation and other lab products are the go-to sources for meeting high caliber nutrition requirements. The effects of a welldesigned Nutritional Diversity diet would be a level up to replace supplementation at times and could also be 'stack-able,' as in; used in combination with supplementation which would also enhance uptake and digestion of supplements.

Hypothesis: With a sufficient full range spectrum of nutrients, from natural, unmolested sources athletes gain a new level of performance, and the body is adequately supported to accomplished trained tasks without injury.

This level of performance using the dynamics of natural nature has limitless possibilities and the effects relative to performanceenhancing can be surprisingly potent.

While athletic and diet coaches as well as modern diet information itself, outweigh valid athletes, and valid results; a cycle of under achievement in human performance proceeds and sickness and injury are human case statistical highs today, a problem we don't see in other biological creatures. This problematic pool of information is all of the dissect nature of breaking down nutritional elements rather than concentrating on whole foods, new foods, and combinations of foods, or even an adequate variety of foods. Not to mention most food sources today are inappropriate for us, the soil and the pollinators to put it lightly. All food information and food businesses of today are inadequate and therefore irrelevant to this examination of athletic performance.

METHODS

A new level of authoritative instruction, administration and diet sourcing with a calculated fuller spectrum of diverse nutrition is to be administered, for a new level of performance.

Local cycling, cross-fit and Ju - Jitsu clubs will be scouted for eligible and dedicated athletes who will be administered a fresh as possible, ND Team sourced diversity of nutrition in the form of fresh shakes and frozen concentrates. We will handpick athletes for six-month sponsorship, where as to document before and after run times and distances, max amounts of certain calisthenic training, while monitoring over time closely monitor any injury and healing, mental aptitude tests, certain blood-work, etc. People who do not exercise regularly will also be evaluated. Certain medical conditions currently being treated with this diet, in more medicinal studies, will produce results valuable to this study.

Ultimately calculate any difference between the specific ND nutritional changes in performance areas. Narrowing in on some special relations between bone health, organ health, brain stimulus, and other performance areas and new species realized from   the principle study ; (N D   ) Biodiverse Food Sciences .

Athletic Performance Exam A:

GPS Tracking devices were used to measure progress and cover complex details in stored data sets allowing for thorough comparison and analysis.

Diverse workouts were conducted, in a simple yet accurately documented fashion to allow for easy progress marker tracking. Running, Calisthenics Basics, and a few heavy strength scores were documented.

GPS track plotting has good plotting with little trouble, and for this device we find the velocity, time, temperature, and altitude is very accurate. These are the most important factors in our study.

The track here to the left is Panama City's Cinta Costera, the most marvelous running track I have ever been on, and host to a world of exiting organized bicycling I have yet to jump into.

It has been a real privilege to run on this thing, and I get my best times at this track.

This particular example is showing three maintenance jogs, from dates, 11-28 to 12-12, one run every five days. The results are combined here for those three, roughly one mile runs.

Statistics of the joined 15-day period are compiled and for example, if this period was on the modern, and the next 15-day period is on a Nutritional Diversity Diet, then we can clearly see at this level, in this case, a user who rarely exercises at a given time; how much physical benefit is realized from the changes in diet alone.

A measurement of strength in basic calisthenic exercise will also be documented along with personal notes from the volunteer and details of ND diet plan ingredients.

Biodiverse food

Here is two days on the Panama Track and two days on the David, Chiriquí, Panama track.

David is about 7 hours driving from Panama, it's the second-largest city in Panama and the fastest growing city in Latin America.

People ask me if I use a sauna. I tell them I cruise through David regularly and that place is a sauna, and I run in it. Now on the data sets example, averages are pulled out of two climates (temperature & humidity), two elevations, etc.

This data is impressive, accurate and informative, and gives us the opportunity to calculate all of the factors, humidity, terrain contour, elevation, velocity, etc., in one shot.

Stop watch can be used when the distance is known, it does not give as much data, but testers in other geographical areas can participate using GPS device or the same track, with a known distance for each run.

CONCLUSIONS:

These same tests would be conducted weekly, during a six-week modern diet cycle, followed by six weeks on the ND diet and performance results from the two diet periods were then compared.

Clearly in all markers, especially sleep and exercise performance the testers displayed significantly better statistical data.

The following chart shows testers' average for 2018 testing data, assimilated into a 20-point scale. the blue diet period also represents more or less general physical statistics from modern culture. Most of the testers were invited from gym or sports circuits and were already athletic to some degree at the start of the examination.

These are cumulative performance measurements on a scale of one to twenty.

Charts are on the website at nutritionaldiversity.com, just find the

"ND Biodiverse Food Study."

We have done a certain amount of testing beyond 15 weeks of consistent ND dieting and logged constant statistical increases to go with it. Athletic Performance Exams below detail certain such extended increases.

Nutritional Diversity

We have also observed further performance decline on the modern diet, weeks after the exam parameters.

The clear performance jump from modern to ND diet was achieved within the first week on an adequately diverse diet (60 or more species regularly-daily). As reviewers can see the performance increases across the board are significant.

Conflicts of Interest: Maintaining the full Nutritional Diversity diet was harder than planned, most of this test data were realized with higher diversity diets than normal but lower diversity diets than originally laid out by this examination method.

Lengths of exam time for diet periods were not always kept as strictly as we would like to see future testing conducted.

. This Exam concluded in 2019 and the supporting data for it is listed below.

[AL1] Notes for Future Examinations:

Strategic special design (multiple).

Self-cultivated dynamic?

Homeopathic training.

Biodiverse Food geographical considerations?

A testers brain power study possibility. note Athletic Performance Exam B, C, D:

The balanced application of the practice and the measurements in the study was a new core focus this round.

We stepped up the performance data with vital information, blood oxidation levels, and would like to implement a 50 / 50 creativity and cognitive test function as a fifth leg of performance observation.

Running and calisthenic performance is measured the same, strength markers also. Sleep performance was this time measured through a sleep log, and morning vitals.

We were not shocked to see that performance markers for 2019 were all up from the previous year of testing, showing steady performance increase, without any level-off. A direct performance and training stack result, as expected.

Biodiverse food lists.

2016-2019 Conflicts:

2016 We ran the same tests again trying to improve our diversity requirements better and using more testers and more gear to get a closer look at the performance increases, and we implemented some food delivery from specific farms to make sure we had a decent supply.

Once again, we ran into supply problems and getting the minimum 60 species on a constant did not happen. Detailed biodiverse food catalogers and strategic diet formulation were cut short by funds shortage.

was rough year started out with two tragic deaths of extended family members back in the U.S., and focus was difficult - we are ready for 2020. So, life stressors were a heavy factor in these performance figures. This really makes the data more promising if anything.

We were also pointed at the importance of giving a balanced focus to the 4 principle modes of performance in the study and maybe trying to implement the observation of brain bower also as a fifth point. Stress a sixth although this is almost the same as strength in many ways.

Testing:

Well, things are certainly becoming clearer this 2020 year in the world, and in the study.

This year we will run several focus workshops and 10-day intensive testing periods with detailed tests, several Triathlons, and CrossFit events to really put performance to the test and collect detailed and precise performance results.

We have assembled a diet for delivery to United States participants who can run, swim and bike the approx. distances in their respective microclimates and contribute their results using GPS watch files and digital file logs.

July 14th and July 28th, we will race a triathlon on our own or together at our best condition and at peak diet plan and August we will compare and publish the results.

We have done a footloose shoeless portion of the run on the beach (below, right). On this beach would could be both confident in our diet and begging for and injury comparison. *

INITIAL RESULTS:

After several initial years of running formal repetitive tests with

grossly inadequate test subjects and funding, we have been able to form ballpark estimates of performance increases. Our largest test cycle is currently running to soon provide data to narrow performance marks.

At the current level of dietary diversity development and increase (premature), we estimate a 10% to 35% increase in athletic ability in a relatively short period of time. The range depends on the particular individual and group biodiverse food plans, and the overall state of current, initial health. Interestingly we estimate at this time healing advantages of 30% to 70%, depending on the severity of the condition, individual, community and household diet diversity marks, and of course overall current, initial health of the individual.

Three years' worth of test flow cycles have enjoyed across the board indications that: performance increases with and when food biodiversity increases (of over 120 species respectively). That is consistent.

The need exists for more testers to test the diet, using the same diet source and preparations specialist.

General biodiverse food and performance data is well achieved and duplicate-able, the scientific reporting function that remains uncompleted. For our camp this is a branch away, the need being more diverse funding.

Mandatory Fitness Component

The "Pee-Fee" or "Toilet Tax" is what my team does, and that is small five minute routine, every time the bathroom is used, followed by half a liter- to a liter of water. The routine changes but the Chinese drum movement from Chi -Gong stays, and for me if I am home and not in business clothes burpees stay in mine to keep explosivity a part of me.

Any experienced gym veteran will tell you that if you warm up right, you will avoid injury and build better muscle form, and muscle ability.

One of the biggest mistakes I see a lot of guys doing is a short warm up, and a long heavy session. Take your time, and build up your physical ability the right way. I say that if you can do the following routine 12 times resting only a short bit per rotation, that you're ready to get into the heavy the stuff. The warm up is the starting place for the serious trainer and it is very important. For me, many times, my starting place is also my ending place, because I find it best to work the warm up, do high rep, and sort of pyramid down from the heavy stuff, to really focus on my stamina and cardiovascular conditioning towards fight time, or game season.

Getting started with the gym, or coming back to it after some time off, you want to do a minimum of two warm-up-weeks first, where the little muscles are trained and made ready to do big muscle stuff. This period is the most important period, of your gym career. It is the vital period of training where the muscular and athletic supportive foundation is laid. The analogy is something like to build a high building, it must be upon a strong foundation. During the 'warm up weeks' period we do the very same warm up illustrated below, two to ten times per day.

To some people this may seem even simple for a warm up, but trust me, it's highly evolved, and covers a lot of important daily stuff.

"The definition of genius is taking the complex and making it simple." — Albert

Einstein

Walking around the gym guys are seen in every direction all wrapped up, carrying muscle but limping around and gelling to the max. They are not accomplishing my definition of fitness in anyway.

New education in fitness is also needed. It is curious how little we know about our own biology and physiology on the norm, but that just gives you a leg up because you are getting the very powerful information few have today.

Rather than using a belt, I do 1000 sit-ups and or leg lifts a day and do tons of high rep dead-lifts. If I am using a wrap on a joint, I am on the bench healing, or at least not using that joint with any heavy resistance. Experience and injury have taught me, that as soon as you feel the slightest tweak, it is time to go home, rest up do the gels and the vitamins most importantly eat a lot of highly diverse foods for the rest of the day and touchdown to the prayer bones to pray for a quick recovery to that area. One of the top causes for injury and bad development is not warming up right. Another is over-doing it in weight or training time. Remember that rest is a big part of play. Sorry to be redundant on this point but it's true and I want to save you the year benched you can get from a minor injury weightlifting.

Back to cycles think in terms of 1. open, healing, resting, nutrition and 2. zone, damaging, resistance and programming.

The modern gym is a great place one builds their muscles strength and size, bone and cartilage density. The specific damage, resistance and programming users are capable of in the gym is no short of scientific spectacle.

Get in the zone they say. Bulk up and get strong, look good and be tough, is the goal of most gym-steers. Many want to lose the pounds and convert fat. Either way, if this warm up is followed not only will body flow stay open and vital, but injuries will be avoided and the gym goer is able to set and develop a supportive ligament and bone system that will in the long run support incredible athletic ability and strength. The warm up will bring better health, larger range functionality, strength, balance and fast twitch muscle dexterity.

All humans should be doing at least this warm up per day. The following warm up should be the gold standard for gym sessions that want to be multiplied from what they were before it.

Working out with exercise bands, can help older or fragile frames become stronger step by step, and drastically accelerate the warm-up and injury prevention power (serious people should go ahead and get a nice set of exercise bands).

Through the gym doors, and before leading up to them, you want to get your breath mantra started. Start using your total lungs. Deep breaths, in through the mouth and nose together, exhaling through the mouth only to be more forceful is okay, and recommended at times.

This should start slow, and intend to speed up towards the end of the warm up where we are going to lock into a hyper drive setting, the warm up is the thing that will dial that in.

About half way through this warm up start focusing in, this breathing to a in through the nose only, out the mouth only breathing posture where your trying to touch the ceiling with your chest on the top of your breaths.

Your torso, namely the abdomen is the core of the human, it supports all the movement and pounding of runners. The region from the leg sockets to the chin represents the complete core.

Starting with the abdomen as the #1 strength importance overall, no less than 50 sit-ups, declined best should be the opening move on the gym floor. I myself do a set of 150, then two more rotations of whatever I can do of them until abdominal muscle failure, in the warm up, super set rhythm.

I constantly come back to sit ups throughout the entire gym session, because 'core first.' Toe touches, seated and standing, legs straight should be well preformed before leaving for the gym, which brings me to some serious stretching.

Not many people in the gym today will feature a workout like this, and that's one place they are really missing power and inviting injury from.

Stretching is one of the most valuable practices in the gym. I wish I had known this importance longer.

Stretching is as important as any of this. It must be done every day. It is necessary to maintain proper vascular, respiratory and muscular function. Yoga, is the most advanced popular (classes and study groups can be found everywhere) and ancient stretching doctrine, that one could study for decades and still have much to learn.

Also, this routine, can be added to your existing Yoga arsenal, as Yoga does not contain all of the following information. The following does not come close to describe Yoga, which again and again I must recommend to the interested human optimist.

The two standard door frames 27", and for bathrooms and closets, 19 inches, can be used for back and pectoral stretches helping beginners work into functional stretched-states using standard household installations. Please do stretch, and modify these ideas yourself more, and to fit you more. For me, there are two trees outside I prefer to use for the 'door-frame stretching exerciser routines.' Pull ups require

a fixed bar or ledge, and while these are calisthenic exercises mostly, some equipment is necessary. I also like to do a heavy breathing mantra with an elevation simulation face mask. Dedicated workout space is very important, I advocate for some exercise at home, but definitely most exercise should take place out of your home. It is in the community gym that you will make most of your progress here.

At rest times in between sets a stretch should be employed for the entire duration of the rest increment.

"Everything should be as simple as possible, but not simpler." -Albert Einstein

Flow is vitality, stagnancy is rot, disaster, sickness, non-function, etc. Flexibility is inherently representative of youth and youthfulness and reasonable stretching, is the programming formula for youth. Yoga is a worldwide dedicated class and group practice where tutelage is available in almost every community.

Top Flow is that which communicates from one hand through the center chest to the other hand. It is the dynamic spread from straight across to the lateral degrees the arms travel for a jumping jack, and three-dimensional motions that take place in front of and behind the straight chest of an individual.

Before leaving out to the gym you want to do a few minutes of door frame stretching. That is using a 26" standard (not bathroom or closet) front door sized door frame, door open, with feet in the middle grab the inside and the outside of the frame and lean in forward and lean back ward, adjusting your stance as necessary and gently stretching your back and chest muscles as the primary muscle groups of the forward and backward leaning stretches.

Cables or tension cords, also known as resistance bands for right side; stand feet shoulder width apart right foot forward, back straight looking at the ceiling. Connect your right elbow to your right rib cage, facing forward of a cable connected directly behind you; move your hand from straight out to your side 90degree perpendicular, rotate the grip point into the center of your chest touching your sternum, using a cable-weight setting or rubber cable tension you can do 25 times. Maintain the connection of your elbow to your ribs throughout the set.

Chi Gong an ancient discipline like Tai Chi, calls for a momentum and flow related exercise that mirrors the small handheld Chinese toy drum whereas by twisting the handle two strings with weights attached to the end smack the drum simultaneously producing a sharp snare-like sound. With feet shoulder length apart, straight across or diagonally (one step forward or one step backward), the shoulder front, that carries an inlay of nerves, acupuncture points and flow

veins and vessels, where the pectoral major meets the deltoid is tapped with the opposite hand while the back of the kidney is tapped by the other hand. alternating head position and feet position should be done in this exercise. I do this all throughout my day every day and definitely before training. Spinal position and straightness are very important and this exercise helps to keep the spine in its groove, to lead the rest of the bodies' structure.

Do the exercise with feet shoulder width apart, straight under the shoulders for a few minutes than switch up between traditional (left foot forward, right foot back, maintaining a shoulder width distance apart) and southpaw (right foot forward) stances.

This exercise is extremely helpful in maintaining spinal correctness, joint and skeletal pliability, and for certain important endocrine system functions. You will notice the hip, and the knee benefit greatly from this exercise also.

These stretches are all about the legs and the lower flow system.

Front to back and side to side, feet as wide as you can take it stance.

Sitting on your feet, knees in front of them on the floor, lean back on to your hands grabbing your feet or the floor behind you. Push your pelvis area as far up and forward as you can arching your back, but keep your knees firmly on the mat. Breath deep and focus on pushing the pelvis up and forward, looking upside down and directly behind you, while deepening the stretch by pushing your shoulders back further and your chest out now. There is a more advanced version of the 'bridge,' that you can graduate to, but this is the starting line.

With these seemingly basic stretches held for 2 to 5 minutes each basic core flexibility is enhanced. A feature which not much gym produce is flashing around these days. It almost seems like a completely lost art to large gym communities across the America's I have noticed.

"If you can't explain it to a sixyear-old, you don't understand it yourself." — Albert Einstein

Bands can help do the inner groin area, in the seated or standing positions, do the hip-flexor's reverse motion, with the band connected to something at least twice your own weight or fixed in concrete. This area is immensely important, and largely ignored, and is area common for hernias.

Calisthenic exercise refers to exercise where the trainer is using his or her own body weight for the exercise, most of the stuff we have covered so far. One armed push up or pull up is still considered calisthenic and is the jumping jack, or the two armed pull up.

The following super set rhythm, involves a rotation of four calisthenic exercises to be performed one set at a time before rotating to the next exercise. The calisthenic warm up rotation should be completed three times without more than 20 seconds of rest between sets.

Pushups - To muscle failure minimum 40 to go to the gym. Your muscle failure number should longer and longer as this goes on, now I do around 100 each time.

Pull ups, you're going for 20 here, that's the optimal body weight set for the optimal warm up, for the optimal athlete. Gym practitioner hopefuls should stick it out on the playground until they can at least warm up with 12 pull ups. Hate to break it to you, but your stepping in the wrong direction if you enter the gym zone before you have passed my calisthenic warm up minimums.

Dips, you're going for 30 here, minimum to be gym worthy is 22 on this first warm up set.

Double (60) or single (20per) leg squats, best opened with 10 box jumps. If your legs are well trained do one legged leg squats.

Sit ups, minimum of 50. I do them now on the super declined sit-up up bench or the wall hanger.

Nutritional Diversity

After the three rotations has been completed its your opportunity to push the line out, and throw some leg lifts on there, and run to the elliptical machine and run out your tank a bit more before a quick rest and the main course of the gym nutrition. Your breathing mantra, should be at rabid dog mode.

Finishing the warm up described above, gym practitioners are ready to rock and roll. If the breathing mantra is done right, 'rock and roll' takes on new meaning.

When I finish this warm up (3x) which takes me about 25 minutes to complete start to finish, because I hold my stretches long; I flip a mental switch that says "now this gym is going to get hurt, not me." Believe it or not after doing this a long time, now I kick into a new gear here at the finish of the warm-up.

Which bring us to the Gym Killer Workouts.

Remember that:

"Great spirits have always encountered violent opposition from mediocre   minds" -Albert Einstein

A Champion is someone who gets up when they can't. - Jack

Dempsey

Grim Reapers have an ugly sounding name because they make you

feel like you want to die, but that is exactly what makes you a

champion for doing them. Jumping up as high as you can, sprawling out as fast and hard as you can to push up position, from here explode to return to standing position as fast as you can and jump again to repeat the process.

With some break beat or old school 50-70 bpm music I get a really groovy rhythm to it, and if I do them every day for week I can into the hundreds fast, people may notice with an impressed look on their face and I just go and go and go.

This is a momentum-based workout made to train muscles used tons in wrestling, military operations, triathletes, and much more, it's really a great one to add in.

This one is outside of your warm up, this is the stay warm, and trust me it could be one of the top optimal things you can be doing. I call this this one the "urination obligation."

This one is a nature synced, rhythmic cycle of important energy and stamina generating movements and is an excellent way of turning up the metabolic throttle to hold a steady optimal state, as well as enhance a super endurance machine.

When you need to urinate, which should come out as clear as it goes in by the way (drink more if not), hold it and do two 2-6-minute stretches and some grim reapers, pushups or isometric resistance, or balance exercises. This also incorporates ideas of erectile performance and urinary track performance, which is more relative to overall system performance than many thinks. If time is limited at urination trips, do clap pushups (explode on your push, jumping up a bit and clap hands together returning to the push up position) or Chinese push-ups.

In the joint fellas in a set, don't let each other piss without doing some workout like this. When things are hard, you need to be harder than those things to make it by, no? All biology grows against resistance.

Morning exercise, bike run and swim together is so powerful. The way I do it on my best days is I go to bed at 1930, I get up at 0330, shower get in my best running gear, maybe quick ND shake and I am on the track no later than 4:30. I thank myself a thousand times

throughout the day, for starting it this way. Brain works better, everything is better. I saw the sunrise every color in nature this

morning, I breathed it, I ran through, I swam in it, I take it with me throughout the day. Incredibly uplifting, huge boost to performance. Turns out the moon and the sun, help me too for being smart enough to get in the right groove, and rhythm with them.

Nutritional Diversity

On the island I would bike up to Bluff beach, the most beautiful beach I have ever seen, and at 5 am there is no one out there I own the whole thing on most every day (a wild truth), then I do sand sprints, swim tons and bike back. I spend two hours out there, and get back at 7am ready to hit the day. Devine.

Stretching and meditative states have dual benefit and are well timed together especially, in such busy lives as those lead by the modern-day men and women of our time.

Other great practices while stretching is reading, watching movies or informational videos, while writing, while waiting, while in between sets at the Gym. I believe myself that stretching should be done with concentration, mood music maybe, and a focus on breathing.

Mental connection with posture should be in function while standing and seating, or holding any position for a sustained duration of time. Thoughts like 'spine straight' can add years to one's life and can make life much more comfortable and enjoyable. I was once diagnosed with scoliosis, but I am convinced that by mentally correcting my spine as I type this and at all times it will correct over time, just as a straight spine could be curved over time do to neglect of this mental concentration.

Remember that we are supposed to be much smarter, and stronger than modern diet has us running today. We have to expel loads of contaminants from eating loads of porquerias. Stretching is a big part of helping detach those contaminants and candida from their resting places in the system, as we use nutritional and other exercises to rid them right out.

I try to be as religious as I can be with my stretching and stretches, sticking to the basics and making sure I get them in daily has been enough to make me feel young again.

Hydration in all things, and certainly in stretching needs to be adequate for an ultimate performance process.

I firstly and fore-mostly recommend the dedicated study of Yoga, different Yoga's and from different Yogi's (the dedicated students and teachers of Yoga).

There are some core rhythms and stretches that I would like done each day by Nutritional Diversifists, that will prevent common injury, open nutritional flow, and can take place with an almost unnoticeable subtraction of time from one's day, in a very supportive to other things in your day; rhythm cycle.

Business Models

To see the Nutritional Diversity science and

Permaculture sciences to drastically improve, integrate and restore health it is important to discuss how business models featuring this concept can quickly go forward.

This ND diet inherently requires that food come from a permaculture or organic gardening source, alternative agriculture source or wild source. This is so that we can consume lots of plants, without the modern agriculture chemicals in them, that build up in our systems and largely also contribute us to the hospital care industry.

There is nowhere near enough of this food in modern distribution to fill the amount of mouths that find this information today. Insanely, this whole planet produces low grade centrally distributed, food domestication that fall far below what the Nutritional Diversity study has come to realize as acceptable "nutrition."

I have loads of people now whereas I can get them the coaching and the info, of course then they want my diet, but growing my ND supply to cater to more individuals and households and my circle of friends should take time and care!

I cannot get them the food in near adequate supply here in Panama City. The market and the demand are much larger than the current supply here in Panama. Right now, Costa Rica is one of several top Permaculture innovation locations on the globe and Panama is turning it up now that the education has bleed in over the years and also because Master Bruce, a pioneer of Costa Rica's permaculture came here and taught for the last 30 years. Like a true wizard in the bosque, he has since ignored most of who he knows an entered into a state of one-ness with nature. One could imagine this maybe very necessary in order to ascend to spiritual levels most men will not pursue in this life.

The demand is there and growing as fast as people are educated about all of this- just as the opportunities for qualified Nutritional Diversity specialists, in both food production and farming as well as in distribution, cooking and retail selling. It's almost liked a Multi-Level Marketing enterprise distributed direct from the earth, a wholesaler who requires work, not money, and offers the highest quality of life. How so many people live in poverty when there is so much dense forest to hide in left, is sort of hard to pull off when you think about it.

The deceptions are well played and most people now depend on the city rather than the biology they did before. We need to be thankful there is dense forest left at all. Very soon possibly because of modern agriculture's effects on our pollinators, there may not be. Regardless of learning about birds and bees as children, we grow into adults that think they know better in a modern Babylonia of a society.

It's hard not to be human in the face of a human. Jesus always reputed to be calm in nature on the high road, freaked out when certain money business was going on in the wrong place at the wrong time. There will come times where fighting for basic freedoms, against certain oppression and deception will become necessary. To fight a stealthy deceptive creature, without those same skills, could be an error.

The other error is to try them in learning, then fall in the pit of using these advantages and become a product of them. The wise-men we once had to teach us these points of importance have all been killed by those who would want us to live as we do today. This is important history to know and to look into. There is a fight of multifaceted forces between these two lifestyles, one dependent on nature and freedom and the other dependent on control and city-technology. While governments now make small farming more and more difficult, the revolutionary, life and planet saving thing for governments to do is 1. disappear, or 2. incentivize small farms with something potent like no taxes first year in business and great breaks from there on out and ban chemical farms that will kill us all. It is no doubt at this time a smart move to invest in farm land at the least. Really, best to go there and live. I have to mention unfortunately that a small farmer faces

lots of opposition in the United States, and here in the tropics Colombia, Panama and Costa Rica, where red tape is less, production is more is a better option today. Thailand has been making some of the most appealing policies and permaculture is a scene there, and I have considered this region also.

I would honestly like to see humans reclaim freedom and land, it may sound crazy now but really if we all go at once out into the forests, and we conscientiously live in harmony with nature what can really be done about it? Solar power is excellent, it's easy to learn to teach yourself. We have all the PVC, and all that. It has never been easier to be self-sustainable. I think these technologies are well inside the line of acceptable, and they carry limited damage to the planet.

One thing is most authorities would not be educated enough to even recognize new species in an area. Essentially with only ones work new species can be cultivated for a small business model to profit from.

The popularity of this nutrition could theoretically solve homelessness as well.

Yet, the opportunity for small businesses related to the diet to open up in this city market is excellent. Take a look at how the supplement market is a gauge on the interest to independently pay more and import to home better nutrients.

Grocery stores have already inflated food costs even for their chemical and machine dependent farming models. With no machine, chemical or technological industry to support, already inflated food prices, little competition and the new healthier Nutritional Diversity business models, and nutrition have plenty of room to work. This type of distribution by this type of consciousnesses, should illuminate one use plastics, one use tins, one use anything, also.

The simple knowledge I am sharing here, should render in the readers mind, that all products in grocery stores should be avoided.

Nutritional Diversity

Who doesn't want to pay more for something that does not have the poison and was grown responsibly with love and care? Charge more it's a niche market, and until these business models become popular, we have a window of opportunity to come up with as poor and oppressed people. Moses, may have simply led us to freedom and health through knowledge like this, from the sickness and slavery we are born into as troubled youth, in a poverty we had no alternative to.

Be smart take the steps today and tomorrow to get yourself in line with good food, and start bringing it to your loved ones. If you treat your karma, your people, and your health with respect, your financial situation will hopefully soon follow.

Good Nutrition in the City as it turns out is far more important now, and complicated to achieve correctly.

Just the other day, me and my close friends in an extremely urban setting, of an elevator had a stunning conversation. I am used to this conversation, so were they. Wild statements, like "we need to get 30 to 60 different species as your minimum but we can't use grocery store products because you'll just fill yourself with chemicals. So, we need new plants, and new growing methods or do we harvest from wild plants, or semi-domesticated plants in areas we clear but not areas that were agriculturally attended to?"

Insanity is buying groceries so then maybe sanity is buying a farm for the better Permaculture-like method?

Maybe just buying from a farm you can trust to have a little bit of a higher standard in food production is enough. In Costa Rica there are tons of permaculture farms, their large population and large land mass combined with great tourism, facilitated one of the first and now one of the biggest, permaculture and organic growing communities. Here in Panama we have a lot of work to do, and we are far behind but a small population, and there are a lot of co-studies and fun studies in human physiological science here in this Republic because of unique laws they have, protecting the rights for alternative medicine practitioners to practice their crafts.

I offer the soon to be, new wave of Permaculture & Nutritional Biodiversity Revolutionaries; an urban model set for homes and small businesses and integration of good produce of a sufficient variety into the city.

The easy one is to form a cooperative supply company from nearby permacultures getting fresh food lists with fresh food deliveries to clients, like the Panama City Nutritional Diversity Supply Company. This will motivate restaurants to make better stuff, and get a good culture going for this age of better nutrition. Households, and athletes can get the real nutrition they need, keeping up with their city lives. An evolved food market, email list or online ordering interface to get fresh stuff that is available at that time could be employed. Right now, eating well is crucial in order for people to detoxify over an extended period of time.

With the diversity of species, it will be fantastic for nutritional diversifists to have a variety of food vendors to choose from. Competition shouldn't be an issue for a very long time; instead, we should see inspiration for creativity and a wider variety of unique food species available to everyone.

It is projected that demand for the New Urban Model Set for Good Nutrition in the City will outpace supply, so growers and organizers who can demonstrate to clients are required. A small distribution strategy might begin with a basic email list because once people are aware of the grocery store / mono-culture money, they will start seeking for the nutritionally sound options.

Getting a good Nutritional Diversity assembled or just good nutrition in the city is impossible right now.

The Urban Model, or really any model for ND dieting, ultimately should be a cultivation-oriented model. To achieve the best nutrition, you want to cultivate most of it. Next it would be great to have foods from a diversity of Nutritional Diversity Diet Science schooled or Certified, Permaculturists in a trade system so that we may all increase our dietary bio diversities with delicious food by using a lot of excellent growing techniques and farmers.

One position in this agenda on the production end, I call the 'Urban ND Guerrilla,' and he can make deals with everything from yards to balconies to come and plant nutritionally diverse gardens, using Nutritional Diversity calculated species sets, including aggressive management automated systems, maintain and service them, halving the harvest with property owner. This can be a high school kid, or whoever and this person can do it all over the city. Then essentially this model covers the cooperative, PCNDSC, type of model covered above.

The Urban ND Permaculture Guerrilla is a great one for people who like to help others, and this position can expand hopefully towards the gardens of the future, high tech high production cutting edge systems and system development.

Ron Finley's story, Los Angeles' "Gangsta Gardner,"   cccix and a few others like him also affected me. In every small town, let alone a large city, there is more than enough room for ten positions like this.

It can complement the hosting of numerous properties on Airbnb very well, in my opinion. Which could be yet another business model of urban health by implementing diverse species.

Working on automated systems to combine liquids and direct them towards a target utilizing piping, spray, flood, and hose systems to put out some of the worst chemical and jet fuel fires was one of my first duties while I was serving in the US Navy back in 2003. I can't help but see the award-winning production designs for the urban gardening setup in the sky, complete with compost teas attached and tilapia or catfish tanks integrated into a kick-butt automatic plant feeding system.

I know many don't like Google Alexa systems, however there is 100$ water valve that can receive rain and humidity information and gauge it's water allowance accordingly to an exact regular dosage for the plants protected by this system.

I myself feel that Automated Systems integration, especially those as intelligent as the one described above or more so, solar power and even things like mirrors pointed for darker areas to increase light delivery during brighter times to certain awkward urban areas are stable, must have farming concepts.

TECHNIQUE :

Materials: Fire hose water pump, that has bildge tank feed end with various stages of sedement filtering around it, PVC piping (various sized), PVC cement, optional hose or soak-err hose, optional spray nozzle(s) or sprinkler heads, electric fence, water timer valve(s), optional food grade tanks for fish farming and water cycling and compost tea (a liquid produced by extracting beneficial microorganisms (microbes)—bacteria, fungi, protozoa, nematodes, and micro arthropods—from compost using a brewing process), and fertilizer.

Systems can go from as simple as a timer-ed sprinkler on a hose to more intense based on budget. I myself like the time-red sprinkler. I can design all the mixing into a system that needs no sprinklers also.

Smart timer water valves range from 22$ to around 100$ and are easy to install. The one that impresses me is the B-Hyve, WIFI, Alexa compatible timer that can consider weather conditions enabling it to provide more effective, balanced operation. PVC piping is around 10$ a 1/2 diameter, 11-footlong section. 55-gallon food grade plastic drums here will cost around 30$. Systems can be as simple as maintenance watering, and advanced to include tilapia and catfish tanks, also compost tea makers. Multi-timing can be used to facilitate both foliage spray and soil feeding. Bio-char coverings and intense plant food development systems to include soil creatures and fungi are drastic focuses especially when using the right species. The fungi part is something I really want to explore more.

Premier One Portable Solar Powered Electric Fencing for land-based gardens is an easy option to employ, I am a fan. Here except the roof top location I will get to soon, I will require using this otherwise the small critters will get in. For a good fence its around 200$ and for an energizer that hooks up

to the house about $120, and there are some solar ones that I think are the better investment because of mobility and I have seen how good they work for about 250$. I can estimate a flashy set up with all of this from around 1000$, and smaller set up for around 200$

For difficult land areas nutrients can be restored to soil cultures through strategic underground buried waist areas. I recently

Nutritional Diversity

inspected housing area all fill no water layer for 5 feet, solid red fill grade stuff. The trees back there found their way most for surely, but the conditions not ideal for a revolution in this yard. Using my inspection hole, I will dump the trash can located food scrap for composting in the hole bury it and let it do its thing. This particular house can go on for a decade filling a normal 30-quart trash can with solid food scrap and disposing of it in a hole like this strategically selected. No doubt about it, this will make the yard much more nutritious and attractive to worms and plants. It saves the animals from tearing the trash across the street and it's one right way to deal with those organic food waist items.

Home composting can be taught, and blending of food scraps in the normal blender can a great way to speed this up. Compost piles will be safe inside the electric fence.

If you want you can read up on the Rural Permaculture Guerrilla.

Another important position in revolutionizing health for communities is the green roof expert. That's right folks it takes a bit more concentration and some welding, roofing / carpentry skills but food can grow on roof tops, and this kind of thing can apply for

government subsidization. It couples great with solar as a skill and community energy saving, or producing effort. There are lots of different installation and management styles for these roofs, but they provide great cooling, and can be world class production systems. Automated and solar powered automated systems can be easily integrated. These can very easily point towards extremely

sophisticated and being on the roof are ripe and ready for high production. An operation like this could employ permaculture experts, automated systems engineers, architects, artists and materials experts

The Neighborhood Retail Dealer for Good Nutrition in the City, Get the product, put the word out keep building your clientele. Most troubled youth in the city are all checked out on this one but basically what you want to do is go find Permacultures, and start offering everything they have.

Refrigeration will be the only mandatory overhead here, and I don't think to deal with your friends and family any sort of business or professional license or inspection is necessary. Print out the free .PDF version of this text or simply share the link so people can understand and better deal with their nutrition once dealing with you.

Get a diversity going, get rare species, get species that are strong, that grow good, think about growing some in the guerilla permaculture manner.

For each of these models ND will learning course and certification, possibly even inspection of procedures, that I find to satisfaction and dynamically appropriate. I will work with businesses on a yearly certification basis to help them become better and keep a Nutritional Diversity standard, that everyone can trust in. We built an online food ordering model in Panama City.

The Nutritionally Diverse Cafe is an important feature of the Urban Model, I think gym cafes are a great starting place. The Nutritionally Diverse burrito man could be just as popular as any cafe type, especially if he delivers.

NutritionalDiversity.com will be offering a few supplements, and seed kits very soon to help provide complete bio-diverse nutrition directly to homes.

Timing is everything with these niche markets cause eventually everyone's doing it and the competition just saturates the market place. Now is the time to get going in this health revolution!

The Bio diverse, or Nutritionally Diverse Cafe concept is great because it is a place where the family can go not just nourish their

bodies with better Nutrition but a great way to learn about key principles in life and hydration. Eating should be like this as much as possible!

The moment customers come in they offered a glass of water from our water diversity stock; ozone water, distilled water, filtered water, or vitamin water. With a Nutritionally Diverse Meal, a Nutritionally Diverse shake is a great compliment.

Nutritional Diversity

Developing recipes with a larger range of ingredients, is just as it seems, it is more complicated, but can provide more nutritional coverage and we believe it is the key to the next level of health and performance. I recommend having a few complicated fuller spectrum recipes for later in the day and then having the keep it simple combinations as I call them, or even one plant at a time during the workday, although this method requires sort of all-day snacking. Smoothies and blended drinks, are a great way to make the Nutritional Diversity concept more convenient.

Nutritional Diversity diet is developed across several permaculture farms and wildlife areas, and in a study and education center in Panama. The educational center is equipped with a cafe, and a few models for permaculture gardens that supply the bio-diverse foods to try there "garden to table." This is the way food should come to the table, same day harvest fresh, and five-minute harvest fresh is the best. Refrigeration does prolong freshness time.

The sustainable cafe with the Ultimate Nutrition.

We have several drink recipes at the cafe with around 15 species, all organically grown and totally comprised of our own stuff here at our farm, grown by us. These drinks can be combined with our meal options, to grant near 60 organic species to the consumer with outstanding taste! We do to-go boxes also so that friends can come in, eat a Nutritional Diversity meal and take a few with them to re-heat later and keep the diverse nutrition going.

It has been a successful venture so far with a lot of healing and a lot of interest. This is a great small business model being that as the food toxicity information gets out there more and more, demand will grow for this kind of nutrition. Imagine if tomorrow an existing food outlet, such as the Subway food franchise started offering these greens at even a small increase in price, the lines would be very long there. The grocery stores right now do not carry these things. They carry the centrally distributed food that is toxic.

We plan soon to do a fine-r dining, nature model of a reservation only breakfast, dinner and lunch place. Breakfasts that really wake you up and give you the fuel for the day. The breakfast part of the day is great for those looking to switch off of coffee a bit, and those who are off to seriously hardcore output day. Discounts for those running or biking in of course, we will have showers for the sweat covered audience to ready right there for work. Here in Panama you can do these things, no red tape.

We will have warm towels and a pool to do laps in. A Sauna and hot tub, and we will open at 4 am. What kind of life can we make here? The ND Diet doctrine and texts, tend to be fans of intermittent fasting which is consuming only water till mid-day or later. This does not have to be every day, but maybe every day that a ND Breakfast cannot be consumed/ scheduled.

Eating at our nice little cafe or restaurant here in Panama folks can get to know what better nutrition is from the front lines. The cutting edge of nutrition can be in a business you start just like ours here. New Nutritional Diversifists, chef's and developers of the diet can link with us now on social media as well as right here in our own forum - that one is for serious interests that we can talk to a bit and feel out. We are building quite the team behind all of this and if you are interested in working on this more please advise how.

The Menu development realizes the availability of different like tasting things so the menu can stay tasting good while swapping ingredients.

Burritos are a good way to hold a bunch of stuff together without trying to have so much in the recipe that sticks it together such as with the veggie burger or multiple meat burger.

Stir Fry is the next obvious one that, could be easy to build on.

Sheppard's pies and the like, but the best for me is the fresh salad.

Hostels and permaculture farms alike many times feature positions at work away sites, and volunteer for cheaper travel cost outlets. The farm or hostel will offer lodging and possibly food for people's hours of volunteer work in exchange.

Could this be a good model to start a food exchange with also. Food and lodging can have their values, while hours in different lines of work can have their respective value also. Experienced and inexperienced versions of work would have different values as well as permaculture versus modern agriculture grown foods do too. This would be an interesting experiment, and one that could logically help determine more fair values for produce and service.

Could the exchange rate with farm work find a value system that is sustainable? Of course, it could. Could we value work at such a rate where our produce could provide for five more? Surely.

Certainly, a hostel with a market and a full produce section, would make for a drastic increase in the quality of the hostel's guests' lives but also in the surrounding community. Should a resident earn to stick around for a while and get the learning curve of richer cooking, then the popularity of this concept could become explosive.

Some permaculturists believe that farms practicing the "fair share" core principle of permaculture, in a move to set a basic bar of selfless care and operation, produce food with an intrinsic imprint grown into the living plants in their growth and in their own intentions that other produce does not have. Several cultures throughout human existence have taken very seriously certain growing and harvesting functions for food they are willing to eat. This work for food and shelter model plays well into a community equality and functional operation to these ends. Learning and experience is always gained.

The Anarchist Commune in the Rainforest: Poole's Land a presentation I watched on YouTube produced by VICE Published 19 November, 2018, was a great expose of a work exchange communal success. Just like an old schooler of mine, a Chiriquí located hotel owner, was the thing that worked for the hippies in the 60s, Poole's Land's success and security are based on the cannabis crop, in Poole's case this is extended to all plant-based medicines, like magic mushrooms. Drugs, such as cocaine or heroin are not allowed there.

This nutritional exchange for work concept is really something I want to explore more, and I think this kind of community has lots of potential, and a much better quality of life.

Supplements are good. Some are really good. Modern nutritional supplement science, while much of is synthetic, I don't feel that is as harmful or risky as grocery store food is. Sport supplements can contribute to health, there are some of course that could be- harmful.

My doctor friend here in the mountains of Chiriquí, believes too much of protein supplementation can mean bowel destruction. I believe the ratio is the same as with meats or potatoes, that getting five times this weight in plants is what is necessary to keep health, performance, digestion and gut track optimal. I encourage anyone to take advantage of the sport supplements market, you can get healthier and get a fuller spectrum of nutrients this way. It is equally important that five times the taken volume of supplement matter, is taken in plant matter.

A complete or high spectrum Nutritional Diversity is so hard to put together. Formulation of nutritionally diverse supplements, and can be a great answer, and business model.

As a brand, Nutritional Diversity is recognized as study in Panama, as way of eating, an athletic performance enhancer, and soon as a lifestyle trend.

Inflation is causing all product prices to rise. Back in 73, a world elite meeting went down (Bilderberg) and there it was decided to raise the gas price over night by 400%. It happened. Popularity for the Nutritional Diversity diet, could propel community permaculture operations and investment, which maybe the way to curtail these inflating prices on common goods. Common goods which will also continue to fall in quality and nutritional value.

The global dietary supplements market size was valued at USD 133.1 billion in 2016 and has been projected to accelerate at a CAGR of 9.6% from 2016 to 2024. Predictably, this represents a market size worth $278.02 billion by 2024, according to the Grand View Research

Company. Everyone is using supplements today, and with our modern diets, there is good reason for that.

Even in competition with other such "diverse" supplements, of which there are now none, this Nutritional Diversity Science offers countless combination and experimentation is needed, the market can take as many good biodiverse supplements as creators can create, may the best team of qualified Nutritional Diversifists win.

To provide a strong foundation, we have developed a Nutritional

Diversity Certification Program to help maintain a certain set of standards and wisdom behind new supplement developments, the produce that doesn't sell can be used in permaculture to create supplements. No doubt revolutionary supplements will come from this Nutritional Diversity design formula.

We are starting to develop a few good supplements of our own. We have done the formulation on several supplements, and we have the company and the sourcing all ready to go, including Amazon listing. These supplements are sourced, mixed, and to be sold in the United States Only Market, first. But these products will soon be wanted worldwide. The market for ND supplements will start to move once successful combinations are identified and developed.

This Nutritional Diversity Science and Standard, is a realization that applies to all humans, this new need for much higher diversity in our nutrition, is the first step in a long global narrative to better food security, better nutrition and quality of life, and possibly helping problems noted in global climate changes.

This new playbook is going to be just as more inspiring as it is supportive to the actual deed, of doing for nature what is needed for a heavy return in self. In other words, the knowledge immediately lights the path to the potential, and this kind of motivation is one of a kind, effective, powerful motivation.

Once a person applies the knowledge and begins to cultivate a diverse set of nutrition for himself or herself, and ingests it regularly, the nutritional support is unmatched in diet on the planet today and the feelings are just the way you would expect – phenomenal. The momentum if uninterrupted for a good time becomes pretty much unstoppable. We will hopefully, for the sake of our ecology as well, never eat again the way we once did and take a new level of importance when it comes to enhancing and repairing ecological damages that have been done is a new-advanced food-producing way.

Carbon Conversation

Elon Musk has organized "XPRIZE," an enterprise hosting worldwide competitions to save the planet. Competitions such as "Feed the Next Billion," a proteinfocused search for better and more abundant food production, and "Carbon Removal," aimed to see carbon removed from the atmosphere. Our proposal can be called "Ecological Enhancement." [X,X]

Well, we, the 'Biodiverse Food Study here in Panama,' already possess knowledge of the existing solution to both of these issues ("so we think in our crazy heads" – interview below start at 2:45). Now we just need to demonstrate the all-natural climate change solution.

Our team has developed a few tech concepts like our digital 'gangmaker' platform rough-draft that has laid dormant the last year, and a few old-schoolers just getting our hands dirty with the internet.

This platform creative outburst from 2019, "the Gangmaker App," was originally an in-house beta experiment to help organize labor and student groups to tackle all of the farm responsibilities in a robust and dynamic ecological enhancement operation. The idea was also to work towards automated systems integration and dynamic real-time climate, even water ph level and other statistical inputs.

The app now works for a perfect place to organize and develop the BioTribe Carbon Removal agenda, carry out experiments among the interns from our tropical research and study center, along with our principal team who is traveling from farm to farm every 11 days here in Central and South America; always on the move, and also between alumni interns who now work their own models of this stuff

[x].

"Excess carbon is an excellent opportunity to reforest and repair the damage we have done."

What we are working to do now is integrate two excellent concepts into an effective moving force and then "move out."

The "crypto" NFT (non-fungible token) space has a well-tested robust and exciting full world-scale economy creation. This non-central bank is "blockchain" code-based, so it is completely transparent and more dependable and concrete than that what we have now. [x,x,x]

To boot, they have created a mock world platform that goes all the way to complete replicas and variations of natural life in what they call the digital "metaverse."

This is the very perfect technology to show our "dimension of ecological restorations" and compensate participants in very clear, transparent direct-to-worker performance payments of source funds.

New "Polygon" blockchain technology going into play over the last several months allows for the very low-cost NFT creation allowing anyone to participate.

This is big news for blockchain and within the natural coming sharp raise in the blockchain tech-popularity that is expected by a large number of today's brilliant minds, and increased computer time for people; it could be argued that implementing as many real-nature-based influences into the "crypto culture" would be a good thing on its own, giving people new incentives that could bring new would-be purely tech printed youth into more nature-tethered and dynamic life experience.

The blockchain system can allow us to create an economy around tree planting, natural enhancements and restorations, animal repopulation, and balance work and provide the organizational structure for advancing natural enhancements in a calculated fashion. A "sweat-based" economy is not yet a popular mode of operation in the crypto culture space at this time, but it should be.

This new blockchain technology is expected to facilitate better voting and democracy, documenting of history within agendas and product developments as well as in governments and it could certainly offer these features to this important health direction as well as promote quick visibility for new innovations.

Education and modus operandi updates can b quickly distributed and received through this economy.

For starters, we plan to attach valuable NFTs and cryptocurrencies for GPS-mapped ecological enhancements. Funds can go directly into the hands of anyone who puts the work in.

This functionality is timed very well; for a time when people don't want a boss and don't want to work in a soulless company anymore as well as a serious wave of homelessness issues. I have always found "the most problemed to be the most solving." [x,x,x]

"Guerilla Permaculture" is a theory and experimentation system that seeks the enhancement of our ecology via a unique human-to-nature-nurturing program. The BioTribe has been doing these concept sites and experiments for about 6 years now.

As a counterweight to deforestation and urbanization, Guerilla Permaculture is a contemporary work aimed at overall personal and ecological health with new climatechange awareness technical efforts. We feel this approach will exceed that of a carbon-neutral system for healthy behavior and a sustainable planet.

This program is a diverse nature nurturing system, that offers various deployment options and business models that can be scaled from subsistence levels to help economicallychallenged populations.

In the pursuit of ecological health for all, our official system calls on much more than just individual market persons, however, to provide the functionality to needed scale -in the proper format is incredibly important.

We are proud of our work on this concept that we feel is the best Carbon Removal and food crisis solution that is more than 60 recent years in the making on "Permacultures" everywhere, that do improve all aspects of life around them, that curiously remains unknown to the masses.

We invite all groups globally to participate where individual efforts can be developed in their respective locales. We have built the interfaces necessary to map and catalog biological efforts, species, and climatic data in realtime worldwide.

The next step of human progression will require a more symbiotic tie with nature, the reason being that we have reached a critical line of demarcation, not in population size but in our cultural practices. In other words, it is not our life, but our way of life that is harmful.

BioTribe Team, Panama

The whole thing should really tie into one of these plant identification applications to expedite our group experimentations and education.

Our facilities and talents so far in the journey have been remarkable. To be able to use our blessings and developed and create a real presentation that submits to the scientific community and answers all of the requirements outlined in the competition guidelines – which are intense; would complete the very important mission here of bringing an extreme positive from the extreme negative. More importantly, unlocking and demonstrating natural methods of enhanced carbon conversion and quality of life is paramount today.

In the spirit of 'permaculture' (that is a search term folks) a dedicated observation of nature's functionality; a rule of "each selection in the organism must function for at least two purposes," exists.

Sincerely

Brandon E.

Carbon Conversion Concept - 'Ecological

Enhancement'

What we propose is enhancing the capacity of current farmland and other lands toincrease carbon capture using fungi's insects, animals, and specialized plant selections,diverse growing constructions, the techniques of permaculture and regenerative agriculture systems, and biodynamic agriculture preparations and soil treatments.

In the words of Bill Mollison, who designed the

"Permaculture Design Manual,"

"Permaculture is a philosophy of working with, rather than against nature; of protracted and thoughtful observation rather than protracted and thoughtless labor; and of looking at plants and animals in all their functions, rather than treating any area as a single-product system." Our motivation for deciding to work on farmland is manifold. Agriculture is currently responsible for about a quarter of net greenhouse gas emissions and thus significantly contributes to climate change [1]. This is due to the use and production of synthetic fertilizers, the use of fossil fuel-intensive machinery, soil degradation, and livestock [2,3c]. Furthermore, land conversion from natural ecosystems to agricultural land is linked to the loss of biomass above and below the ground [4]. A recent study [5] predicts 240 GtC uptake on 2020 Mha of land, a rate of 0.12 GtC Mha−1 over a 50-year period. At this rate, we'd need to convert around 83 Mha of agricultural land every year to reach the 10 GtC per year goal. At the end of the 50 year period, around 4.1 billion of the available 5 billion hectares used for agricultural land [4] would need to be converted.

The solution has also an indirect impact on CO2 emissions from decreased fossil-fuelintensive machinery in agriculture, the industrial processes involved in the creation ofsaid machinery, and chemical fertilizers. Since permaculture works with animals too, the meat, dairy, and egg industries will diminish their emissions.

We can extend the idea to not only use agricultural land. Another recent study [6] suggests that the planet can support an additional 900 Mha of forest without using agricultural land or living environments. If designed to

be permacultural food forests, this new land could capture an additional 108 GtC at our

estimated rate, and help feed the

2.2 estimated billion additional humans the United Nations estimates will live by 2050.

Literature to Support Approach

Edenhofer, O.; Pichs-Madruga, R.; Sokona, Y.; Farahani, E.; Kadner, S.; Seyboth, K.;

Adler, A.; Baum, I.; Brunner, S.; Eickemeier, P.; et al. (Eds.) Climate Change 2014:

Mitigation of Climate Change; IPCC: Geneva, Switzerland, 2014; Contribution of

Working Group III to the Fifth Assessment Report of the Intergovernmental Panel on Climate Change.

Hathaway, M.D. Agroecology and permaculture:

Addressing key ecological problems by rethinking and redesigning agricultural systems. J. Environ. Stud. Sci. 2016, 6, 239–250.

Rojas-Downing, M.M.; Nejadhashemi, A.P.; Harrigan, T.; Woznicki, S.A. Climate change and livestock:

Impacts, adaptation, and mitigation. Clim. Risk Manag. 2017,

16,

145–163.

Food and Agriculture Organization of the United Nations. Land use in agriculture by the numbers.
http://www.fao.org/sustainability/news/detail/en/c/12742

19/. Accessed 30 Sept. 2021.

V. K. Arora, A. Montenegro, Small temperature benefits provided by realistic

afforestation efforts. Nat. Geosci. 4, 514–518 (2011).

Bastin, J.-F., Finegold, Y., Garcia, C., Mollicone,

D., Rezende, M., Routh, D., Zohner,

C. M., & Crowther, T. W. (2019). The global tree restoration potential. Science,

365(6448), 76–79.

https://doi.org/10.1126/science.aax0848

[7] Smith, P, Soussana, J-F, Angers, D, et al. How to measure, report and verify soil carbon change to realize the potential of soil carbon

sequestration for atmospheric greenhouse gas removal. Glob Change

Biol. 2020; 26: 219– 241.

https://doi.org/10.1111/gcb.14815

There is the potential for the most significant and smartest information creation in ecological enhancement sciences to function as a mainframe to global automated biodynamic systems management (example) or (infinite possibilities).

We take the opportunity to look at sustainable human culture support systems in what we are doing. Private innovation should be incentivized and easily distributed and integrated into the "worldwide Bio-team,"

These application platforms are also great opportunities to develop our group-work concept site, and other technical resources especially those that bridge the gap and create a harmonious balance between tech and nature – which really could be a serious part of the solutions to both protein and carbon issues.

Developing real natural human-managed solutions will take cultural changes, and simply, "lots of real humans." Our project plans account for this manpower and propose a simple switch of existing job place duties.

We have engineered and used engineered protoenhancements that use existing agricultural machines, facilities, and associations, by strategic changes in materials, direction, and process.

We aim to bring valid natural solutions at insanely low cost by way of improving existing societal and cultural formulas and large-scale education.

Thanks to my good friend Dennis (whats up D-man!) the carbon conversation has yet a new miracle in it known to the team, and that is a new algae injection that could restore damaged soils.

Ref - Saudi J Biol Sci. 2022 May; 29(5): 3083–3096.

Published online 2022 Mar 19. doi:

10.1016/j.sjbs.2022.03.020 PMCID: PMC8961072 PMID:

35360501

Nutritional Diversity

Algae could be the cure to many afflictions even cancer.

Ref - Yue Qiao et al. ,Engineered algae: A novel oxygengenerating system for effective treatment of hypoxic cancer.Sci.

Adv.6,eaba5996(2020).DOI:10.1126/sciadv.aba5996

iReferences

Parke, Donna, and L. Nicholas Ornston. "Nutritional diversity of Rhizobiaceae revealed by auxanography." Microbiology 130.7 (1984): 1743-1750.

Yari, Zahra et al. "Dietary diversity and its relationship with nutritional adequacy in 24 to 59 months old children in Iran: study protocol." BMC

nutrition vol. 8,1 118. 23 Oct. 2022, doi:10.1186/s40795-022-00616-6

Clausing, Peter. "Thoughts on agricultural transformation." Degrowth conference Leipzig. 2014.

ivhttps://www.sciencedirect.com/referencework/9780 444641304/encyclopedia-of-ecology#book-description

vhttps://www.sciencedirect.com/referencework/97804 44641304/encyclopedia-of-ecology#book-description

https://gangmaker.org/A1/xprize-carbonremoval/

https://gangmaker.org/A1/xprize-carbonremoval/

viiihttps://www.sciencedirect.com/science/article/pii/ B9780120884582500278

Isaak CK, Siow YL. The evolution of nutrition research.

Can J Physiol Pharmacol. 2013 Apr;91(4):257-67. doi:

10.1139/cjpp-2012-0367

Epub 2013 Jan 18. PMID: 23627837.

https://nutritionaldiversity.com/vegan/

Isaak CK, Siow YL. The evolution of nutrition research. Can J Physiol Pharmacol. 2013 Apr;91(4):257-67. doi: 10.1139/cjpp-2012-0367. Epub 2013 Jan 18. PMID: 23627837.

Russell, Jonathan R et al. "Biodegradation of polyester polyurethane by endophytic fungi." Applied and environmental microbiology vol. 77,17 (2011): 6076-84. doi:10.1128/AEM.00521-11

First Report of Pestalotiopsis microspora Causing Leaf Spot of Hidcote (Hypericum patulum) in Japan M. Zhang, H. Y. Wu, T. Tsukiboshi, and I. Okabe Plant Disease 2010 94:8, 1064-1064

Muhamad Hafiz Abd Rahim, Nur Hazlin HazrinChong, Hanis Hazeera Harith, Wan Abd Al Qadr Imad Wan-Mohtar, Rashidah Sukor, Roles of fermented plant-, dairy- and meat-based foods in the modulation of allergic responses, Food Science and Human Wellness, 10.1016/j.fshw.2022.09.002, 12, 3, (691-701), (2023).

Jeniffer Ferreira de Miranda, Giulia Martins Pereira Belo, Laís Silva de Lima, Kelly Alencar Silva, Thais Matsue Uekane, Alice Gonçalves Martins Gonzalez, Vanessa Naciuk Castelo Branco, Nayla Souza Pitangui, Fabrício Freitas Fernandes, Adriene Ribeiro Lima, Arabic coffee infusion based kombucha: Characterization and biological activity during fermentation, and in vivo toxicity, Food Chemistry, 10.1016/j.foodchem.2023.135556, 412, (135556), (2023).

Lefebvre P, Letois F, Sultan A, Nocca D, Mura T, Galtier F. Nutrient deficiencies in patients with obesity considering bariatric surgery: a cross-sectional study. Surg Obes Relat Dis. 2014 May-Jun;10(3):540-6. doi: 10.1016/j.soard.2013.10.003. Epub 2013 Oct 14. PMID: 24630922.

Black RE. Zinc deficiency, infectious disease and mortality in the developing world. J Nutr. 2003 May;133(5 Suppl 1):1485S-9S. doi: 10.1093/jn/133.5.1485S. PMID:

12730449.

https://makah.com/makah-tribal-info/

Paull, John (2011). "Attending the First Organic Agriculture Course: Rudolf Steiner's Agriculture Course at Koberwitz, 1924" (PDF). European Journal of Social Sciences. 21 (1): 64–70.

Sender R, Fuchs S, Milo R. Revised Estimates for the Number of Human and Bacteria Cells in the Body. PLoS Biol. 2016 Aug 19;14(8):e1002533. doi:

10.1371/journal.pbio.1002533. PMID: 27541692; PMCID: PMC4991899.

Qin J, Li R, Raes J, Arumugam M, Burgdorf KS, Manichanh C, Nielsen T, Pons N, Levenez F, Yamada T,

Mende DR, Li J, Xu J, Li S, Li D, Cao J, Wang B, Liang H,

Zheng H, Xie Y, Tap J, Lepage P, Bertalan M, Batto JM,

Hansen T, Le Paslier D, Linneberg A, Nielsen HB, Pelletier

E, Renault P, Sicheritz-Ponten T, Turner K, Zhu H, Yu C,

Li S, Jian M, Zhou Y, Li Y, Zhang X, Li S, Qin N, Yang H,

Wang J, Brunak S, Doré J, Guarner F, Kristiansen K,

Pedersen O, Parkhill J, Weissenbach J; MetaHIT Consortium; Bork P, Ehrlich SD, Wang J. A human gut microbial gene catalogue established by metagenomic sequencing. Nature. 2010 Mar 4;464(7285):59-65. doi:

10.1038/nature08821. PMID: 20203603; PMCID:

PMC3779803.

https://nutritionaldiversity.com/digestive-enzymes/

Belkaid, Yasmine, and Timothy W Hand. "Role of the microbiota in immunity and inflammation." Cell vol. 157,1 (2014): 121-41. doi:10.1016/j.cell.2014.03.011

"ATTRA – National Sustainable Agriculture Information Service". Archived from the original on 26 May 2011. Retrieved 23 May 2006.

Mark Pilkington (June 10, 2004). "Primary perception". The Guardian. Retrieved 2013-08-05.

The Art of War. Translated by Michael Nylan. W.W. Norton & Company, Inc. 2020. ISBN 9781324004899. xxvii

https://nutritionaldiversity.com/kombucha/

xxviii Schultz, T. R.; Brady, S. G. (2008). "Major evolutionary transitions in ant agriculture". Proceedings of the National Academy of Sciences of the United States of America. 105 (14): 5435–5440.

xxix

https://www.drphil.com/slideshows/brainwashedby-my-parents/

Holick MF. Vitamin D deficiency. N Engl J Med. 2007 Jul 19;357(3):266-81. doi: 10.1056/NEJMra070553. PMID: 17634462.

Hunt JR. Bioavailability of iron, zinc, and other trace minerals from vegetarian diets. Am J Clin Nutr. 2003 Sep;78(3 Suppl):633S-639S. doi: 10.1093/ajcn/78.3.633S. PMID: 12936958.

Garner, Dwight (March 13, 2005). "TBR: Inside the list". The New York Times Book Review. p. 30. ProQuest 217307067

Matthews, Robert (April 8, 2006). "Water: The quantum elixir". New Scientist (2546)

Wu G, Wu Z, Dai Z, Yang Y, Wang W, Liu C, Wang B, Wang J, Yin Y. Dietary requirements of "nutritionally nonessential amino acids" by animals and humans. Amino Acids. 2013 Apr;44(4):1107-13. doi: 10.1007/s00726-0121444-2. Epub 2012 Dec 18. PMID: 23247926.

Pfeiffer B, Stellingwerff T, Hodgson AB, Randell R, Pöttgen K, Res P, Jeukendrup AE. Nutritional intake and gastrointestinal problems during competitive endurance events. Med Sci Sports Exerc. 2012 Feb;44(2):344-51. doi:

10.1249/MSS.0b013e31822dc809. PMID: 21775906.

DeMars, Laura L., and Gregory R. Ziegler. "Texture and structure of gelatin/pectin-based gummy confections." Food hydrocolloids 15.4-6 (2001): 643-653.

Dickinson, Eric. "Properties of emulsions stabilized with milk proteins: overview of some recent developments." Journal of Dairy Science 80.10 (1997): 26072619.

Gu, Yeun Suk, Eric A. Decker, and D. Julian McClements. "Influence of pH and carrageenan type on properties of β-lactoglobulin stabilized oil-in-water emulsions." Food Hydrocolloids 19.1 (2005): 83-91.

Tareke E, Rydberg P, Karlsson P, Eriksson S, Törnqvist M. Analysis of acrylamide, a carcinogen formed in heated foodstuffs. J Agric Food Chem. 2002 Aug 14;50(17):49985006. doi: 10.1021/jf020302f. PMID: 12166997.

United States Food and Drug Administration (FDA) (2017). Questions & Answers about Acrylamide. the information was collected from

https://www.fda.gov/food/chemicals/acrylamidequestions-and-answers.

https://www.goodreads.com/en/book/show/1845 xlii Calisher, Charles H. "Taxonomy: what's in a name? Doesn't a rose by any other name smell as sweet?." Croatian medical journal vol. 48,2 (2007): 268-70.

oan D'Arc (1 November 2000). Phenomenal World: Remote Viewing, Astral Travel, Apparitions, Extraterrestrials,

Lucid Dreams and Other Forms of Intelligent Contact in the Magical Kingdom of Mind-at-Large. Book Tree. pp. 191– 192. ISBN 978-1-58509-128-7. Retrieved 7 August 2013.

Bhuyan, Deep Jyoti et al. "The Odyssey of Bioactive

Compounds in Avocado (Persea americana) and Their Health

Benefits." Antioxidants (Basel, Switzerland) vol. 8,10 426. 24 Sep. 2019, doi:10.3390/antiox8100426

Rubinstein, Mor et al. "Genetic diversity of avocado (Persea americana Mill.) germplasm using pooled sequencing." BMC genomics vol. 20,1 379. 15 May. 2019, doi:10.1186/s12864-019-5672-7

Flores, Marcos et al. "Avocado Oil: Characteristics, Properties, and Applications." Molecules (Basel, Switzerland) vol. 24,11 2172. 10 Jun. 2019, doi:10.3390/molecules24112172

Kilaru, Aruna et al. "Oil biosynthesis in a basal angiosperm: transcriptome analysis of Persea Americana mesocarp." BMC plant biology vol. 15 203. 16 Aug. 2015, doi:10.1186/s12870-0150586-2

https://www.aspca.org/pet-care/animal-poisoncontrol/toxic-and-non-toxic-plants/avocado

Salehi, Bahare et al. "Medicinal Plants Used in the Treatment of Human Immunodeficiency Virus." International journal of molecular sciences vol. 19,5 1459. 14 May. 2018, doi:10.3390/ijms19051459

Robles-Zepeda, Ramón Enrique et al. "In vitro antimycobacterial activity of nine medicinal plants used by ethnic groups in Sonora, Mexico." BMC complementary and alternative medicine vol. 13 329. 25 Nov. 2013, doi:10.1186/1472-6882-13-329

Moraes Neto, Roberval Nascimento et al. "Asteraceae Plants as Sources of Compounds Against Leishmaniasis and Chagas Disease." Frontiers in pharmacology vol. 10 477. 8 May. 2019, doi:10.3389/fphar.2019.00477

Lans, Cheryl. "Ethnomedicines used in Trinidad and Tobago for reproductive problems." Journal of ethnobiology and ethnomedicine vol. 3 13. 15 Mar. 2007, doi:10.1186/1746-4269-3-

Alonso-Castro, Angel Josabad et al. "Medicinal Plants from North and Central America and the Caribbean Considered Toxic for Humans: The Other Side of the Coin." Evidence-based complementary and alternative medicine : eCAM vol. 2017 (2017): 9439868. doi:10.1155/2017/9439868

Deocaris, Custer C et al. "Merger of ayurveda and tissue culture-based functional genomics: inspirations from systems biology." Journal of translational medicine vol. 6 14. 18 Mar. 2008, doi:10.1186/1479-5876-6-14

Kurapati, Kesava Rao Venkata et al. "Ashwagandha (Withania somnifera) reverses β-amyloid1-42 induced toxicity in human neuronal cells: implications in HIV-associated neurocognitive disorders (HAND)." PloS one vol. 8,10 e77624. 16 Oct. 2013, doi:10.1371/journal.pone.0077624

Dutta, Kallol et al. "Withania somnifera Reverses Transactive Response DNA Binding Protein 43 Proteinopathy in a Mouse Model of Amyotrophic Lateral Sclerosis/Frontotemporal Lobar Degeneration." Neurotherapeutics : the journal of the American Society for Experimental NeuroTherapeutics vol. 14,2 (2017): 447-462. doi:10.1007/s13311-016-0499-2

Lopresti, Adrian L et al. "An investigation into the stressrelieving and pharmacological actions of an ashwagandha (Withania somnifera) extract: A randomized, double-blind, placebo-controlled study." Medicine vol. 98,37 (2019): e17186. doi:10.1097/MD.0000000000017186

Kaushik, Mahesh K et al. "Triethylene glycol, an active component of Ashwagandha (Withania somnifera) leaves, is responsible for sleep induction." PloS one vol. 12,2 e0172508. 16 Feb. 2017, doi:10.1371/journal.pone.0172508

Ahmed, Wafaa et al. "Antioxidant activity and apoptotic induction as mechanisms of action of Withania somnifera (Ashwagandha) against a hepatocellular carcinoma cell line." The Journal of international medical research vol. 46,4 (2018): 1358-1369. doi:10.1177/0300060517752022

Shah, Jigna Samir, and R K Goyal. "Usage trends for memory and vitality-enhancing medicines: A pharmacoepidemiological study involving pharmacists of the Gujarat region." International journal of Ayurveda research vol. 1,3 (2010): 138-43. doi:10.4103/0974-7788.72484

Shah, Jigna Samir, and R K Goyal. "Usage trends for memory and vitality-enhancing medicines: A pharmacoepidemiological study involving pharmacists of the Gujarat region." International journal of Ayurveda research vol. 1,3 (2010): 138-43. doi:10.4103/0974-7788.72484

Pratte, Morgan A et al. "An alternative treatment for anxiety: a systematic review of human trial results reported for the Ayurvedic herb ashwagandha (Withania somnifera)." Journal of alternative and complementary medicine (New York, N.Y.) vol. 20,12

(2014): 901-8. doi:10.1089/acm.2014.0177

Wadhwa, Renu et al. "Water extract of Ashwagandha leaves has anticancer activity: identification of an active component and its mechanism of action." PloS one vol. 8,10 e77189. 10 Oct.

2013, doi:10.1371/journal.pone.0077189

Dongre, Swati et al. "Efficacy and Safety of Ashwagandha

(Withania somnifera) Root Extract in Improving Sexual Function in Women: A Pilot Study." BioMed research international vol. 2015 (2015): 284154. doi:10.1155/2015/284154

Nasimi Doost Azgomi, Ramin et al. "Effects of Withania somnifera on Reproductive System: A Systematic Review of the Available Evidence." BioMed research international vol. 2018 4076430. 24 Jan. 2018, doi:10.1155/2018/4076430

Deshpande, Abhijit et al. "Study protocol and rationale for a prospective, randomized, double-blind, placebo-controlled study to evaluate the effects of Ashwagandha (Withania somnifera) extract on nonrestorative sleep." Medicine vol. 97,26 (2018): e11299. doi:10.1097/MD.0000000000011299

Choudhary, Dnyanraj et al. "Body Weight Management in Adults Under Chronic Stress Through Treatment With Ashwagandha Root Extract: A Double-Blind, Randomized, Placebo-Controlled Trial." Journal of evidence-based complementary & alternative medicine vol. 22,1 (2017): 96-106. doi:10.1177/2156587216641830

Konar, Arpita et al. "Protective role of Ashwagandha leaf extract and its component withanone on scopolamine-induced changes in the brain and brain-derived cells." PloS one vol. 6,11 (2011): e27265. doi:10.1371/journal.pone.0027265

Lobo, V et al. "Free radicals, antioxidants and functional foods: Impact on human health." Pharmacognosy reviews vol. 4,8 (2010): 118-26. doi:10.4103/0973-7847.70902

Iguchi T, Kuroda M, Ishihara M, Sakagami H, Mimaki Y. Steroidal constituents isolated from the seeds of Withania somnifera. Nat Prod Res. 2021 Jul;35(13):2205-2210. doi: 10.1080/14786419.2019.1667351. Epub 2019 Sep 20. PMID: 31538506.

Choudhary D, Bhattacharyya S, Bose S. Efficacy and Safety of Ashwagandha (Withania somnifera (L.) Dunal) Root Extract in

Improving Memory and Cognitive Functions. J Diet Suppl. 2017 Nov 2;14(6):599-612. doi: 10.1080/19390211.2017.1284970. Epub 2017 Feb 21. PMID: 28471731.

Pingali U, Pilli R, Fatima N. Effect of standardized aqueous extract of Withania somnifera on tests of cognitive and psychomotor performance in healthy human participants. Pharmacognosy Res. 2014 Jan;6(1):12-8. doi: 10.4103/09748490.122912. PMID: 24497737; PMCID: PMC3897003.

Singh, Narendra et al. "An overview on ashwagandha: a Rasayana (rejuvenator) of Ayurveda." African journal of traditional, complementary, and alternative medicines : AJTCAM vol. 8,5 Suppl

(2011): 208-13. doi:10.4314/ajtcam.v8i5S.9

Kataria, Hardeep et al. "Water extract from the leaves of Withania somnifera protect RA differentiated C6 and IMR-32 cells against glutamate-induced excitotoxicity." PloS one vol. 7,5

(2012): e37080. doi:10.1371/journal.pone.0037080

Kumar, Gajendra et al. "Efficacy & safety evaluation of

Ayurvedic treatment (Ashwagandha powder & Sidh

Makardhwaj) in rheumatoid arthritis patients: a pilot prospective

study." The Indian journal of medical research vol. 141,1 (2015): 100-

6. doi:10.4103/0971-5916.154510

Grover, Abhinav et al. "Ashwagandha derived withanone targets TPX2-Aurora A complex: computational and

experimental evidence to its anticancer activity." PloS one vol. 7,1

(2012): e30890. doi:10.1371/journal.pone.0030890

Choudhary D, Bhattacharyya S, Bose S. Efficacy and Safety of Ashwagandha (Withania somnifera (L.) Dunal) Root Extract in Improving Memory and Cognitive Functions. J Diet Suppl.

2017 Nov 2;14(6):599-612. doi:

10.1080/19390211.2017.1284970. Epub 2017 Feb 21. PMID: 28471731.

Almalki, Daklallah Ahmed. "Renoprotective Effect of Ocimum Basilicum (Basil) Against Diabetesinduced Renal Affection in Albino Rats." Materia sociomedica vol. 31,4 (2019): 236-240. doi:10.5455/msm.2019.31.236-240

Rabbani, Mohammed et al. "Evaluation of anxiolytic and sedative effect of essential oil and hydroalcoholic extract of Ocimum basilicum L. and chemical composition of its essential oil." Research in pharmaceutical sciences vol. 10,6 (2015): 535-43.

Bassolé, Imaël Henri Nestor et al. "Composition

and antimicrobial activities of Lippia multiflora Moldenke, Mentha x piperita L. and Ocimum basilicum L. essential oils and their major monoterpene alcohols alone and in combination." Molecules (Basel, Switzerland) vol. 15,11 782539. 3 Nov. 2010, doi:10.3390/molecules15117825

Behbahani, Mandana. "Evaluation of in vitro

anticancer activity of Ocimum basilicum, Alhagi maurorum, Calendula officinalis and their parasite Cuscuta campestris." PloS one vol. 9,12 e116049. 30 Dec. 2014, doi:10.1371/journal.pone.0116049

Noor, Zoy I et al. "In Vitro Antidiabetic, AntiObesity and Antioxidant Analysis of Ocimum

basilicum Aerial Biomass and in Silico Molecular Docking

Simulations with Alpha-Amylase and Lipase Enzymes." Biology vol. 8,4 92. 4 Dec. 2019, doi:10.3390/biology8040092

Zhang, Ji-Wen et al. "The main chemical

composition and in vitro antifungal activity of the essential oils of Ocimum basilicum Linn. var. pilosum (Willd.) Benth." Molecules (Basel, Switzerland) vol. 14,1 273-8. 8 Jan. 2009, doi:10.3390/molecules14010273

Sarahroodi, Shadi et al. "The effects of green Ocimum basilicum hydroalcoholic extract on retention and retrieval of memory in mice." Ancient science of life vol. 31,4 (2012): 185-9. doi:10.4103/0257-7941.107354

Gucwa, Katarzyna et al. "Investigation of the Antifungal Activity and Mode of Action of Thymus vulgaris, Citrus limonum, Pelargonium graveolens, Cinnamomum cassia, Ocimum basilicum, and Eugenia caryophyllus Essential Oils." Molecules (Basel, Switzerland) vol. 23,5 1116. 8 May. 2018, doi:10.3390/molecules23051116

Sakr, Saber A, and Hanna Z Nooh. "Effect of Ocimum basilicum extract on cadmium-induced testicular histomorphometric and immunohistochemical alterations in albino rats." Anatomy & cell biology vol. 46,2 (2013): 122-

30. doi:10.5115/acb.2013.46.2.122

Nascimento, Simone S et al. "Cyclodextrin-

complexed Ocimum basilicum leaves essential oil increases Fos protein expression in the central nervous system and produce an antihyperalgesic effect in animal models for fibromyalgia." International journal of molecular sciences vol. 16,1 547-63. 29 Dec. 2014, doi:10.3390/ijms16010547

Sakr, Saber A, and Hanna Z Nooh. "Effect of Ocimum basilicum extract on cadmium-induced testicular histomorphometric and immunohistochemical alterations in albino rats." Anatomy & cell biology vol. 46,2 (2013): 12230. doi:10.5115/acb.2013.46.2.122

Joseph, Baby, and D Jini. "Antidiabetic effects of Momordica charantia (bitter melon) and its medicinal potency." Asian Pacific Journal of Tropical Disease vol. 3,2 (2013): 93–102. doi:10.1016/S2222-1808(13)60052-3

Marisol Cortez-Navarrete, Esperanza Martínez-Abundis, Karina G. Pérez-Rubio, Manuel González-Ortiz, and Miriam Méndez-del Villar.Momordica charantia Administration Improves Insulin Secretion in Type 2 Diabetes Mellitus.Journal of Medicinal Food.Jul 2018.672-677.

Alam, Md & Uddin, Riaz & Subhan, Nusrat & Rahman, Md. Mahbubur & Jain, Preeti & Reza, Hasan. (2015). Review Article Beneficial Role of Bitter Melon Supplementation in Obesity and Related Complications in Metabolic Syndrome. Journal of Lipids. 2015. 10.1155/2015/496169.

Joseph, Baby, and D Jini. "Antidiabetic effects of Momordica charantia (bitter melon) and its medicinal potency." Asian Pacific Journal of Tropical Disease vol. 3,2 (2013): 93–102. doi:10.1016/S2222-1808(13)60052-3

Li, Chia-Jung et al. "Momordica charantia Extract Induces Apoptosis in Human Cancer Cells through Caspase- and Mitochondria-Dependent Pathways." Evidence-based complementary and alternative medicine : eCAM vol. 2012 (2012): 261971. doi:10.1155/2012/261971

Rebultan SP. Bitter melon therapy: an experimental treatment of HIV infection. AIDS Asia. 1995 Jul-Aug;2(4):6-7. PMID: 12346831.

https://www.naturalmedicinejournal.com/journal/nutrientprofile-bitter-melon-momordica-charantia

Mardani, Saeed et al. "Impact of Momordica charantia extract on kidney function and structure in mice." Journal of nephropathology vol. 3,1 (2014): 35-40. doi:10.12860/jnp.2014.08 xcvii Marangoni, Franca et al. "Role of poultry meat in a balanced diet aimed at maintaining health and wellbeing: an Italian consensus document." Food & nutrition research vol. 59 27606. 9 Jun. 2015, doi:10.3402/fnr.v59.27606

Choct M, Naylor AJ, Reinke N. Selenium supplementation affects broiler growth performance, meat yield and feather coverage. Br Poult Sci. 2004 Oct;45(5):677-83. doi:

10.1080/00071660400006495. PMID: 15623223.

Maurin, Olivier et al. "Towards a Phylogeny for Coffea (Rubiaceae): identifying well-supported lineages based on nuclear and plastid DNA sequences." Annals of botany vol. 100,7 (2007): 1565-83. doi:10.1093/aob/mcm257

Vaughan, Michael Joe et al. "What's Inside That Seed We Brew? A New Approach To Mining the Coffee Microbiome." Applied and environmental microbiology vol. 81,19 (2015): 6518-27. doi:10.1128/AEM.01933-15

Samoggia, Antonella, and Bettina Riedel. "Consumers' Perceptions of Coffee Health Benefits and Motives for Coffee Consumption and Purchasing." Nutrients vol. 11,3 653. 18 Mar. 2019, doi:10.3390/nu11030653

Haskell-Ramsay, Crystal F et al. "The Acute Effects of Caffeinated Black Coffee on Cognition and Mood in Healthy Young and Older Adults." Nutrients vol. 10,10 1386. 30 Sep. 2018, doi:10.3390/nu10101386

Gunter, Marc J et al. "Coffee Drinking and Mortality in 10 European Countries: A Multinational Cohort Study." Annals of internal medicine vol. 167,4 (2017): 236-247. doi:10.7326/M16-2945

Gunter M.J., Murphy N., Cross A.J., Dossus L., Dartois L., Fagherazzi G., Kaaks R., Kühn T., Boeing H., Aleksandrova K., et al. Coffee Drinking and Mortality in 10 European Countries: A Multinational Cohort Study. Ann. Intern. Med. 2017;167:236– 247. doi: 10.7326/M16-2945.

Bułdak, Rafał J et al. "The Impact of Coffee and Its Selected Bioactive Compounds on the Development and Progression of

Colorectal Cancer In Vivo and In Vitro." Molecules (Basel, Switzerland) vol. 23,12 3309. 13 Dec. 2018, doi:10.3390/molecules23123309

Higdon JV, Frei B. Coffee and health: a review of recent human research. Crit Rev Food Sci Nutr. 2006;46(2):101-23. doi: 10.1080/10408390500400009. PMID: 16507475.

Motamayor, Juan C et al. "Geographic and genetic population differentiation of the Amazonian chocolate tree (Theobroma cacao L)." PloS one vol. 3,10 e3311. 1 Oct. 2008, doi:10.1371/journal.pone.0003311

Katz, David L et al. "Cocoa and chocolate in human health and disease." Antioxidants & redox signaling vol. 15,10 (2011): 2779-811. doi:10.1089/ars.2010.3697

Katz, David L et al. "Cocoa and chocolate in human health and disease." Antioxidants & redox signaling vol. 15,10 (2011): 2779-811. doi:10.1089/ars.2010.3697

Jaramillo Flores, Maria Eugenia. "Cocoa Flavanols: Natural Agents with Attenuating Effects on Metabolic Syndrome Risk Factors." Nutrients vol. 11,4 751. 30 Mar. 2019, doi:10.3390/nu11040751

Jaramillo Flores, Maria Eugenia. "Cocoa Flavanols: Natural Agents with Attenuating Effects on Metabolic Syndrome Risk Factors." Nutrients vol. 11,4 751. 30 Mar. 2019, doi:10.3390/nu11040751

cxii Pucciarelli, Deanna L. "Cocoa and heart health: a historical review of the science." Nutrients vol. 5,10 3854-70. 26 Sep. 2013, doi:10.3390/nu5103854 cxiii Mirković, Milica et al. "The Sensory Quality and Volatile Profile of Dark Chocolate Enriched with Encapsulated Probiotic Lactobacillus plantarum Bacteria." Sensors (Basel, Switzerland) vol. 18,8 2570. 6 Aug. 2018, doi:10.3390/s18082570

Cavarretta, Elena et al. "Dark Chocolate Intake Positively Modulates Redox Status and Markers of Muscular Damage in Elite Football Athletes: A Randomized Controlled Study." Oxidative medicine and cellular longevity vol. 2018 4061901. 21 Nov. 2018, doi:10.1155/2018/4061901

Baharum, Zainal et al. "Theobroma cacao: Review of the Extraction, Isolation, and Bioassay of Its Potential Anti-cancer Compounds." Tropical life sciences research vol. 27,1 (2016): 21-42.
cxvi Allen, Robert W et al. "Cinnamon use in type 2 diabetes: an updated systematic review and meta-analysis." Annals of family medicine vol. 11,5 (2013): 452-9. doi:10.1370/afm.1517

Butler, Kurt; Rayner, Lynn. (1985). The Best Medicine: The Complete Health and Preventive Medicine Handbook. Harper & Row, Publishers, San Francisco. pp. 133-135. ISBN 0-06-250123-2

Sartorius, Tina et al. "Cinnamon extract improves insulin sensitivity in the brain and lowers liver fat in mouse models of obesity." PloS one vol. 9,3 e92358. 18 Mar. 2014, doi:10.1371/journal.pone.0092358

Erdem, Sinem Aslan et al. "Blessings in disguise: a review of phytochemical composition and antimicrobial activity of plants belonging to the genus Eryngium." Daru : journal of Faculty of Pharmacy, Tehran University of Medical Sciences vol. 23 53. 14 Dec.

2015, doi:10.1186/s40199-015-0136-3

Magee AR, van Wyk B-E, Tilney PM, van der Bank M. A Taxonomic Revision Of the South African Endemic Genus Arctopus (Apiaceae, Saniculoideae) 1. Ann Missouri Bot Garden. 2008;95(3):471–86. doi: 10.3417/2005174.

Thomas PS, Essien EE, Ntuk SJ, Choudhary MI. Eryngium foetidum L. Essential Oils: Chemical Composition and Antioxidant Capacity. Medicines (Basel). 2017 Apr 28;4(2):24. doi: 10.3390/medicines4020024. PMID: 28930239; PMCID: PMC5590060.

Dawilai, Suwitcha et al. "Anti-inflammatory

activity of bioaccessible fraction from Eryngium foetidum leaves." BioMed research international vol. 2013 (2013):

958567. doi:10.1155/2013/958567

Kouitcheu Mabeku LB, Eyoum Bille B, Nguepi E. In Vitro and In Vivo Anti-Helicobacter Activities of Eryngium foetidum (Apiaceae), Bidens pilosa (Asteraceae), and Galinsoga ciliata (Asteraceae) against Helicobacter pylori. Biomed Res Int. 2016;2016:2171032. doi: 10.1155/2016/2171032. Epub 2016 Aug 18. PMID: 27631003; PMCID: PMC5007343.

Price, Joseph A 3rd. "An in vitro evaluation of the Native American ethnomedicinal plant Eryngium yuccifolium as a treatment for snakebite envenomation." Journal of intercultural ethnopharmacology vol. 5,3 219-25. 4 May. 2016, doi:10.5455/jice.20160421070136

Rojas-Silva P, Graziose R, Vesely B, Poulev A, Mbeunkui F, Grace MH, Kyle DE, Lila MA, Raskin I. Leishmanicidal activity of a daucane sesquiterpene isolated from Eryngium foetidum.

Pharm Biol. 2014 Mar;52(3):398-401. doi:

10.3109/13880209.2013.837077. Epub 2013 Oct 23. PMID: 24147866.

Simon OR, Singh N. Demonstration of anticonvulsant properties of an aqueous extract of Spirit Weed (Eryngium foetidum L.). West Indian Med J. 1986 Jun;35(2):121-5. PMID: 3739342.

Paul JH, Seaforth CE, Tikasingh T. Eryngium foetidum L.: a review. Fitoterapia. 2011 Apr;82(3):302-8. doi: 10.1016/j.fitote.2010.11.010. Epub 2010 Nov 6. PMID: 21062639. cxxviii Lans C. Ethnomedicines used in Trinidad and Tobago for reproductive problems. J Ethnobiol Ethnomed. 2007 Mar 15;3:13. doi: 10.1186/1746-4269-3-13. PMID: 17362507; PMCID: PMC1838898.

Janwitthayanuchit K, Kupradinun P, Rungsipipat A, Kettawan A, Butryee C. A 24-Weeks Toxicity Study of Eryngium foetidum Linn. Leaves in Mice. Toxicol Res. 2016 Jul;32(3):231-7. doi: 10.5487/TR.2016.32.3.231. Epub 2016 Jul 30. PMID: 27437090; PMCID: PMC4946421.

Panda, Ashok Kumar, and Kailash Chandra Swain. "Traditional uses and medicinal potential of Cordyceps sinensis of Sikkim." Journal of Ayurveda and integrative medicine vol. 2,1 (2011): 9-13. doi:10.4103/0975-9476.78183

Yi, X., Xi-zhen, H. & Jia-shi, Z. Randomized double-blind placebo-controlled clinical trial and assessment of fermentation product of Cordyceps sinensis (Cs-4) in enhancing aerobic capacity and respiratory function of the healthy elderly volunteers. Chin. J. Integr. Med. 10, 187–192 (2004).

Lin B, Li S. Cordyceps as an Herbal Drug. In: Benzie IFF, Wachtel-Galor S, editors. Herbal Medicine: Biomolecular and Clinical Aspects. 2nd edition. Boca Raton (FL): CRC Press/Taylor & Francis; 2011. Chapter 5. Available from: https://www.ncbi.nlm.nih.gov/books/NBK92758/

Xu YF. Effect of Polysaccharide from Cordyceps militaris

(Ascomycetes) on Physical Fatigue Induced by Forced Swimming. Int J Med Mushrooms. 2016;18(12):1083-1092. doi:

10.1615/IntJMedMushrooms.v18.i12.30. PMID: 28094746.

Yi Liu, Jihui Wang, Wei Wang, Hanyue Zhang, Xuelan Zhang, Chunchao Han, "The Chemical Constituents and

Pharmacological Actions of Cordyceps sinensis", Evidence-Based

Complementary and Alternative Medicine, vol. 2015, Article ID 575063, 12 pages, 2015. https://doi.org/10.1155/2015/575063

https://www.mskcc.org/cancer-care/integrativemedicine/herbs/cordyceps

Guangxin Yuan, Liping An, Yunpeng Sun, Guangyu Xu, Peige Du, "Improvement of Learning and Memory Induced by Cordyceps Polypeptide Treatment and the Underlying

Mechanism", Evidence-Based Complementary and Alternative Medicine, vol. 2018, Article ID 9419264, 10 pages, 2018.

Chisenga, Shadrack Mubanga et al. "Progress in research and applications of cassava flour and starch: a review." Journal of food science and technology vol. 56,6 (2019):

2799-2813. doi:10.1007/s13197-019-03814-6

Boukhers I, Boudard F, Morel S, Servent A, Portet K, Guzman C, Vitou M, Kongolo J, Michel A, Poucheret P. Nutrition, Healthcare Benefits and Phytochemical Properties of Cassava (Manihot esculenta) Leaves Sourced from Three Countries (Reunion, Guinea, and Costa Rica). Foods. 2022 Jul 8;11(14):2027. doi: 10.3390/foods11142027. PMID: 35885268; PMCID: PMC9315608.

Ma ZF, Lee YY. Virgin Coconut Oil and its Cardiovascular Health Benefits. Nat Prod Commun. 2016 Aug;11(8):1151-1152. PMID: 30725578.

Law, Kim Sooi et al. "The effects of virgin coconut oil (VCO) as supplementation on quality of life (QOL) among breast cancer patients." Lipids in health and disease vol. 13 139. 27 Aug.

2014, doi:10.1186/1476-511X-13-139

cxli

https://www.washingtonpost.com/news/morningmix/wp/2015/07/20/can-pot-heal-broken-bones-theanswer-is-yes-study-finds/?noredirect=on

cxlii

https://www.epilepsy.com/treatment/alternativetherapies/medical-marijuana

cxliii https://www.diabetes.co.uk/recreational-drugs/cannabis.html

cxlivgoogle.com.pa/books?id=ALaEeOkAGKAC&printsec=frontcover&dq=Medical+Marijuana+Cannabis+Cultivation:&hl=en&sa=X&ved=0ahUKEwjN64PL6PXoAhXNUt8KHVoTBT8Q6AEIJjAA#v=onepage&q=Medical%20Marijuana%20Cannabis%20Cultivation%3A&f=false

https://healthland.time.com/2012/01/10/study-smoking-marijuana-not-linked-with-lung-damage/

Wirngo, Fonyuy E et al. "The Physiological Effects of Dandelion (Taraxacum Officinale) in Type 2 Diabetes." The review of diabetic studies : RDS vol. 13,2-3 (2016): 113-131. doi:10.1900/RDS.2016.13.113

Schütz, K., Carle, R., & Schieber, A. (2006). Taraxacum--a review on its phytochemical and pharmacological profile. Journal of ethnopharmacology, 107(3), 313–323. https://doi.org/10.1016/j.jep.2006.07.021

Williams, C. A., Goldstone, F., & Greenham, J. (1996). Flavonoids, cinnamic acids and coumarins from the different tissues and medicinal preparations of Taraxacum officinale. Phytochemistry, 42(1), 121–127.

https://doi.org/10.1016/0031-9422(95)00865-9

Feistel, Bjoern & Walbroel, Bernd & Benedek, B. (2010). Damiana (Turnera diffusa Willd.) - A traditionally used aphrodisiac as modern PDE-5 inhibitor. Planta Medica - PLANTA MED. 76. 10.1055/s-0030-1264300.

Willer J, Jöhrer K, Greil R, Zidorn C, Çiçek SS. Cytotoxic Properties of Damiana (Turnera diffusa) Extracts and Constituents and A Validated Quantitative UHPLC-DAD Assay. Molecules. 2019; 24(5):855. https://doi.org/10.3390/molecules24050855 cli Schäffer, Marion & Gröger, Thomas & Pütz, Michael & Zimmermann, Ralf. (2013). Assessment of the presence of damiana in herbal blends of forensic interest based on comprehensive two-dimensional gas chromatography. Forensic Toxicology. 31. 10.1007/s11419-013-0186-5.

Ana María DB, Rosa María VV, Lilian MN, Lucía MM, Oscar GP, Rosa ER. Neurobehavioral and toxicological effects of an aqueous extract of Turnera diffusa Willd (Turneraceae) in mice. J Ethnopharmacol. 2019 May 23;236:50-62. doi: 10.1016/j.jep.2019.02.036. Epub 2019 Feb 25. PMID: 30818006.

Yakubu MT, Akanji MA, Oladiji AT. Aphrodisiac potentials of the aqueous extract of Fadogia agrestis (Schweinf. Ex Hiern) stem in male albino rats. Asian J Androl. 2005 Dec;7(4):399-404. doi: 10.1111/j.17457262.2005.00052.x. PMID: 16281088.

D, J. (2022). 6 Amazing Benefits of Fadogia Agrestis |.

Google.com. Retrieved 3 October 2022, Fadogia Agrestis:

Definition, Benefits, Side Effects & more. Turkesterone.

(2022). Retrieved 3 October 2022,

FADOGIA AGRESTIS: Overview, Uses, Side Effects, Precautions, Interactions, Dosing, and Reviews. Webmd.com.

(2022). Retrieved 3 October 2022,

Munteanu C, Schwartz B. The Effect of Bioactive

Aliment Compounds and Micronutrients on Non-Alcoholic Fatty Liver Disease. Antioxidants. 2023; 12(4):903. https://doi.org/10.3390/antiox12040903

Bylka, Wiesława et al. "Centella asiatica in cosmetology." Postepy dermatologii i alergologii vol. 30,1 (2013): 46-9. doi:10.5114/pdia.2013.33378

Ratz-Łyko, A et al. "Moisturizing and Antiinflammatory Properties of Cosmetic Formulations Containing Centella asiatica Extract." Indian journal of pharmaceutical sciences vol. 78,1 (2016): 27-33. doi:10.4103/0250-474x.180247

Lokanathan, Yogeswaran et al. "Recent Updates in Neuroprotective and Neuroregenerative Potential of Centella asiatica." The Malaysian journal of medical sciences : MJMS vol. 23,1 (2016): 4-14.

Gray, Nora E et al. "Centella asiatica modulates antioxidant and mitochondrial pathways and improves cognitive function in mice." Journal of ethnopharmacology vol. 180 (2016): 78-86. doi:10.1016/j.jep.2016.01.013

Jiang, Hui et al. "Identification of Centella asiatica's Effective Ingredients for Inducing the Neuronal Differentiation." Evidence-based complementary and alternative medicine : eCAM vol. 2016 (2016): 9634750. doi:10.1155/2016/9634750

Soumyanath, Amala et al. "Centella asiatica Extract Improves Behavioral Deficits in a Mouse Model of Alzheimer's Disease: Investigation of a Possible Mechanism of Action." International journal of Alzheimer's disease vol. 2012 (2012): 381974. doi:10.1155/2012/381974

Gray, Nora E et al. "Centella asiatica attenuates Aβ-induced neurodegenerative spine loss and dendritic simplification." Neuroscience letters vol. 646 (2017): 24-29. doi:10.1016/j.neulet.2017.02.072

Lokanathan, Yogeswaran et al. "Recent Updates

in Neuroprotective and Neuroregenerative Potential of Centella asiatica." The Malaysian journal of medical sciences : MJMS vol. 23,1 (2016): 4-14.

Gray, Nora E et al. "Caffeoylquinic acids in Centella asiatica protect against amyloid-β toxicity." Journal of Alzheimer's disease : JAD vol. 40,2 (2014): 359-73. doi:10.3233/JAD-131913

Farooqui, Akhlaq A et al. "Ayurvedic Medicine

for the Treatment of Dementia: Mechanistic

Aspects." Evidence-based complementary and alternative medicine : eCAM vol. 2018 2481076. 15 May. 2018, doi:10.1155/2018/2481076

James, Jacinda T, and Ian A Dubery.

"Pentacyclic triterpenoids from the medicinal herb,

Centella asiatica (L.) Urban." Molecules (Basel, Switzerland) vol. 14,10 3922-41. 9 Oct. 2009, doi:10.3390/molecules14103922

Puttarak, Panupong et al. "Effects of Centella

asiatica (L.) Urb. on cognitive function and mood related outcomes: A Systematic Review and Meta-

analysis." Scientific reports vol. 7,1 10646. 6 Sep. 2017, doi:10.1038/s41598-017-09823-9

Gohil, Kashmira J et al. "Pharmacological Review

on Centella asiatica: A Potential Herbal Cure-all." Indian journal of pharmaceutical sciences vol. 72,5 (2010): 546-56. doi:10.4103/0250-474X.78519

Choi, Myung-Joo et al. "Protective effects of Centella asiatica leaf extract on dimethylnitrosamine-induced liver injury in rats." Molecular medicine reports vol. 14,5 (2016): 4521-4528. doi:10.3892/mmr.2016.5809

Gray, Nora E et al. "Centella asiatica attenuates Aβ-induced neurodegenerative spine loss and dendritic simplification." Neuroscience letters vol. 646 (2017): 24-29. doi:10.1016/j.neulet.2017.02.072

Orhan I. E. (2012). Centella asiatica (L.) Urban:

From Traditional Medicine to Modern Medicine with Neuroprotective Potential. Evidence-based complementary and alternative medicine : eCAM, 2012, 946259. https://doi.org/10.1155/2012/946259

Renner, S. S., H. Balslev & L. B. Holm-Nielsen. 1990. Flowering plants of Amazonian Ecuador—A checklist. AAU Rep. 24: 1–241.

Jørgensen, P. M. & S. León-Yánez. (eds.) 1999. Catalog of the vascular plants of Ecuador. Monogr. Syst. Bot. Missouri Bot. Gard. 75: i–viii, 1–1181.

Belén Branchiccela, Loreley Castelli, Sebastián DíazCetti, Ciro Invernizzi, Yamandú Mendoza, Estela Santos, Carlos Silva, Pablo Zunino, Karina Antúnez. (2023) Can pollen supplementation mitigate the impact of nutritional stress on honey bee colonies?. Journal of Apicultural Research 62:2, pages 294-302.

Valido, A., Rodríguez-Rodríguez, M.C. & Jordano, P. Honeybees disrupt the structure and functionality of plantpollinator networks. Sci Rep 9, 4711 (2019).

Samarghandian, Saeed et al. "Honey and Health: A Review of Recent Clinical Research." Pharmacognosy research vol. 9,2

(2017): 121-127. doi:10.4103/0974-8490.204647

Ahmed, Sarfraz et al. "Honey as a Potential Natural Antioxidant Medicine: An Insight into Its Molecular

Mechanisms of Action." Oxidative medicine and cellular longevity vol. 2018 8367846. 18 Jan. 2018, doi:10.1155/2018/8367846

Erejuwa, Omotayo O et al. "Effects of honey and its mechanisms of action on the development and progression of cancer." Molecules (Basel, Switzerland) vol. 19,2 2497-522. 21 Feb. 2014, doi:10.3390/molecules19022497

https://nutritionaldiversity.com/hot-peppers/ clxxxi 1-Leal P., I. Figueiredo, F. B. Pimentel, L. Almeida, and R. Monteiro. Current Knowledge on the Mechanisms, Pain Treatment, and Other Pre-Clinical and Clinical Applications of Capsaicin. Molecules (online). 2021 January 26;26(3):625 (accessed 2023 March 15). You can get this at:

https://www.ncbi.nlm.nih.gov/pmc/articles/PMC786 2287

Kang JH, Yu R, Kawada T, Han IS, Goto T, and Kim YM. In obese mice fed a high-fat diet, dietary capsaicin lessens the insulin resistance and hepatic steatosis brought on by obesity. [Internet] Obesity (Silver Spring). 2010 Apr 18(4):780-7 [cited 2023 Mar 15]. You can get this at:

https://www.ncbi.nlm.nih.gov/pmc/articles/PMC282658 9

Whiting S, Derbyshire E, Tiwari BK. Capsaicinoids and capsinoids. A potential role for weight management? A systematic review of the evidence. Appetite. 2012 Oct;59(2):341-8. doi: 10.1016/j.appet.2012.05.015. Epub 2012 May 22. PMID: 22634197.

https://nutritionaldiversity.com/jackfruit/

Khoo, Hock Eng & Azlan, Azrina & Ismaila, Amin. (2015). Sauropus androgynus Leaves for Health Benefits: Hype and the Science. The Natural Products Journal. 5. 10.2174/2210315505021507021142028.

Bunawan, Hamidun et al. "Sauropus androgynus (L.) Merr. Induced Bronchiolitis Obliterans: From Botanical Studies to Toxicology."

Evidence-based complementary and alternative medicine : eCAM vol. 2015 (2015): 714158. doi:10.1155/2015/714158

Mustarichie, Resmi et al. "Determination of the Major Component of Water Fraction of Katuk (Sauropus androgynous (L.) Merr.) Leaves by Liquid Chromatography-Mass Spectrometry." Journal of pharmacy & bioallied sciences vol. 11,Suppl

4 (2019): S611-S618. doi:10.4103/jpbs.JPBS_205_19

clxxxviii Salehi, Bahare et al. "Antidiabetic Potential of Medicinal Plants and Their Active Components." Biomolecules vol. 9,10 551. 30 Sep. 2019, doi:10.3390/biom9100551

Unuofin, Jeremiah Oshiomame, and Sogolo Lucky Lebelo. "Antioxidant Effects and Mechanisms of Medicinal Plants and Their Bioactive Compounds for the Prevention and Treatment of Type 2 Diabetes: An Updated Review." Oxidative medicine and cellular longevity vol. 2020 1356893. 13 Feb. 2020, doi:10.1155/2020/1356893

Prakoso, Yos Adi et al. "The Role of Sauropus androgynus (L.) Merr. Leaf Powder in the Broiler Chickens Fed a Diet Naturally

Contaminated with Aflatoxin." Journal of toxicology vol. 2018 2069073. 1 Oct. 2018, doi:10.1155/2018/2069073

Bunawan, Hamidun et al. "Sauropus androgynus (L.) Merr. Induced Bronchiolitis Obliterans: From Botanical Studies to Toxicology." Evidence-based complementary and alternative medicine : eCAM vol. 2015 (2015): 714158. doi:10.1155/2015/714158

Lauricella, Marianna et al. "Multifaceted Health Benefits of Mangifera indica L. (Mango): The Inestimable Value of

Orchards Recently Planted in Sicilian Rural Areas." Nutrients vol. 9,5 525. 20 May. 2017, doi:10.3390/nu9050525

Nadeem, Muhammad et al. "Promising features of mango (Mangifera indica L.) kernel oil: a review." Journal of food science and technology vol. 53,5 (2016): 2185-95. doi:10.1007/s13197-015-2166-8

Morton, J. 1987. Mangosteen. p. 301–304. In: Fruits of warm climates. Julia F. Morton, Miami, FL.

Gutierrez-Orozco, Fabiola, and Mark L Failla. "Biological activities and bioavailability of mangosteen xanthones: a critical review of the current evidence." Nutrients vol. 5,8 3163-83. 13 Aug. 2013, doi:10.3390/nu5083163

Gutierrez-Orozco, Fabiola, and Mark L Failla. "Biological activities and bioavailability of mangosteen xanthones: a critical review of the current evidence." Nutrients vol. 5,8 3163-83. 13 Aug. 2013, doi:10.3390/nu5083163

Krishnamachary, B., Subramaniam, D., Dandawate, P., Ponnurangam, S., Srinivasan, P., Ramamoorthy, P., Umar, S.,

Thomas, S. M., Dhar, A., Septer, S., Weir, S. J., Attard, T., & Anant, S. (2019). Targeting transcription factor TCF4 by γMangostin, a natural xanthone. Oncotarget, 10(54), 5576–5591.

https://doi.org/10.18632/oncotarget.27159

Lee, K. X., Shameli, K., Mohamad, S. E., Yew, Y. P.,

Mohamed Isa, E. D., Yap, H. Y., Lim, W. L., & Teow, S. Y. (2019). Bio-Mediated Synthesis and Characterisation of Silver Nanocarrier, and Its Potent Anticancer Action. Nanomaterials (Basel, Switzerland), 9(10), 1423.

https://doi.org/10.3390/nano9101423

Mitbumrung, W., Suphantharika, M., McClements, D. J., & Winuprasith, T. (2019). Encapsulation of Vitamin D3 in

Pickering Emulsion Stabilized by Nanofibrillated Mangosteen Cellulose: Effect of Environmental Stresses. Journal of food science, 84(11), 3213–3221. https://doi.org/10.1111/1750-3841.14835

Sugiyanto, Z., Yohan, B., Hadisaputro, S., Dharmana, E., Suharti, C., Winarto, Djamiatun, K., Rahmi, F. L., & Sasmono, R. T. (2019). Inhibitory Effect of Alpha-Mangostin to Dengue Virus Replication and Cytokines Expression in Human Peripheral Blood Mononuclear Cells. Natural products and bioprospecting, 9(5), 345–349. https://doi.org/10.1007/s13659-019-00218-z

Tjahjani, S., Biantoro, Y., & Tjokropranoto, R. (2019). Ethyl acetate Fraction of Garcinia Mangostana L Rind Study as Antimalaria and Antioxidant in Plasmodium berghei Inoculated Mice. Open access Macedonian journal of medical sciences, 7(12), 1935–1939. https://doi.org/10.3889/oamjms.2019.480

Waranuch, N., Phimnuan, P., Yakaew, S., Nakyai, W., Grandmottet, F., Onlom, C., Srivilai, J., & Viyoch, J. (2019). Antiacne and antiblotch activities of a formulated combination of Aloe barbadensis leaf powder, Garcinia mangostana peel extract, and Camellia sinensis leaf extract. Clinical, cosmetic and investigational dermatology, 12, 383–391. https://doi.org/10.2147/CCID.S200564

Larsuprom, L., Rungroj, N., Lekcharoensuk, C., Pruksakorn, C., Kongkiatpaiboon, S., Chen, C., & Sukatta, U. (2019). In vitro antibacterial activity of mangosteen (Garcinia mangostana Linn.) crude extract against Staphylococcus pseudintermedius isolates from canine pyoderma. Veterinary dermatology, 30(6), 487–e145. https://doi.org/10.1111/vde.12783

Li, P., Yang, Z., Tang, B., Zhang, Q., Chen, Z., Zhang, J., Wei, J., Sun, L., & Yan, J. (2019). Identification of Xanthones from the Mangosteen Pericarp that Inhibit the Growth of Ralstonia solanacearum. ACS omega, 5(1), 334– 343. https://doi.org/10.1021/acsomega.9b02746 ccv Rana, M. N., Tangpong, J., & Rahman, M. A. (2019). Xanthones protects lead-induced chronic kidney disease (CKD) via activating Nrf-2 and modulating NF-kB, MAPK pathway. Biochemistry and biophysics reports, 21, 100718. https://doi.org/10.1016/j.bbrep.2019.100718

Rana, M. N., Tangpong, J., & Rahman, M. A. (2019). Xanthones protects lead-induced chronic kidney disease (CKD) via activating Nrf-2 and modulating NFkB, MAPK pathway. Biochemistry and biophysics reports, 21, 100718. https://doi.org/10.1016/j.bbrep.2019.100718

Chen, T. H., Tsai, M. J., Fu, Y. S., & Weng, C. F. (2019). The Exploration of Natural Compounds for Anti-Diabetes from Distinctive Species Garcinia linii with Comprehensive Review of the Garcinia Family. Biomolecules, 9(11), 641.

https://doi.org/10.3390/biom9110641

Vellapandian, Chitra et al. "A Comparative Study of Actinidia deliciosa and Garcinia mangostana in Ovariectomy-Induced Osteoporosis in Female Wistar Rats." BioMed research international vol. 2017 (2017): 5349520. doi:10.1155/2017/5349520

Tjahjani, Susy. "Antimalarial activity of Garcinia mangostana L rind and its synergistic effect with artemisinin in vitro." BMC

complementary and alternative medicine vol. 17,1 131. 28 Feb. 2017, doi:10.1186/s12906-017-1649-8

See, Irene et al. "Two new chemical constituents from the

stem bark of Garcinia mangostana." Molecules (Basel,

Switzerland) vol. 19,6 7308-16. 4 Jun. 2014, doi:10.3390/molecules19067308

Konda, Manikyeswara Rao et al. "Combined extracts of Garcinia mangostana fruit rind and Cinnamomum tamala leaf supplementation enhances muscle strength and endurance in

resistance trained males." Journal of the International Society of Sports

Nutrition vol. 15,1 50. 22 Oct. 2018, doi:10.1186/s12970-018-0257-4

Turner, Alyna et al. "Protocol and Rationale: A 24-week Double-blind, Randomized, Placebo Controlled Trial of the Efficacy of Adjunctive Garcinia mangostanaLinn. (Mangosteen) Pericarp for Schizophrenia." Clinical psychopharmacology and neuroscience : the official scientific journal of the Korean College of Neuropsychopharmacology vol. 17,2 (2019): 297-307. doi:10.9758/cpn.2019.17.2.297

Ashton, Melanie M et al. "The Therapeutic Potential of Mangosteen Pericarp as an Adjunctive Therapy for Bipolar Disorder and Schizophrenia." Frontiers in psychiatry vol. 10 115. 13 Mar. 2019, doi:10.3389/fpsyt.2019.00115

Ashton, Melanie M et al. "Efficacy of adjunctive Garcinia mangostana Linn (mangosteen) pericarp for bipolar depression: study protocol for a proof-of-concept trial." Revista brasileira de psiquiatria (Sao Paulo, Brazil : 1999) vol. 41,3 (2019): 245-253. doi:10.1590/1516-4446-2018-0114

ccxv Carvalho-Silva, Ronaldo et al. "DNA Protection against Oxidative Damage Using the Hydroalcoholic Extract of Garcinia mangostana and Alpha-Mangostin." Evidence-based complementary and alternative medicine : eCAM vol. 2016 (2016): 3430405. doi:10.1155/2016/3430405

ccxvi Gonzales, G., Cordova, A., Vega, K., Chung, A., Villena, A., & Gonez, C. (2003). Effect of Lepidium meyenii (Maca), a root with aphrodisiac and fertility-enhancing properties, on serum reproductive hormone levels in adult healthy men, Journal of Endocrinology, 176(1), 163-168. Retrieved Apr 20, 2023, from https://doi.org/10.1677/joe.0.1760163

https://womeninbalance.org/2012/10/26/discoveringthe-health-benefits-of-maca/

Antoine, E., Chirila, S., & Teodorescu, C. (2019). A Patented Blend Consisting of a Combination of Vitex agnus-castus Extract, Lepidium meyenii (Maca) Extract and Active Folate, a Nutritional Supplement for Improving Fertility in Women. Maedica, 14(3), 274–279. https://doi.org/10.26574/maedica.2019.14.3.274

L. Stojanovska, C. Law, B. Lai, T. Chung, K. Nelson, S. Day, V. Apostolopoulos & C. Haines (2015) Maca reduces blood pressure and depression, in a pilot study in postmenopausal women, Climacteric, 18:1, 69-78, DOI: 10.3109/13697137.2014.929649

Fei, W., Hou, Y., Yue, N. et al. The effects of aqueous extract of Maca on energy metabolism and immunoregulation. Eur J Med Res 25, 24 (2020). https://doi.org/10.1186/s40001-020-00420-7

Huarancca Reyes, T., Esparza, E., Crestani, G. et al. Physiological responses of maca (Lepidium meyenii Walp.) plants to UV radiation in its high-altitude mountain ecosystem. Sci Rep 10, 2654 (2020). https://doi.org/10.1038/s41598-020-59638-4

Simona Tafuri, Natascia Cocchia, Anastasia Vassetti, Domenico Carotenuto, Luigi Esposito, Lucianna Maruccio, Luigi Avallone & Francesca Ciani (2021) Lepidium meyenii (Maca) in male reproduction, Natural Product Research, 35:22, 45504559, DOI: 10.1080/14786419.2019.1698572

ccxxiii

https://www.hindawi.com/journals/ecam/2015/949036/

ccxxivhttps://www.sciencedirect.com/science/article/abs/pii/S03 78874109005728

ccxxv

https://onlinelibrary.wiley.com/doi/full/10.1111/j.17555949.2008.0 0052.x

https://webprod.hc-sc.gc.ca/nhpid-bdipsn/monoReq.do? id=1903&lang=eng

Perumalla Venkata, Rekhadevi, and Rajagopal

Subramanyam. "Evaluation of the deleterious health effects of consumption of repeatedly heated vegetable oil." Toxicology reports vol. 3 636-643. 16 Aug. 2016, doi:10.1016/j.toxrep.2016.08.003

Gaforio, José J et al. "Virgin Olive Oil and Health:

Summary of the III International Conference on Virgin Olive

Oil and Health Consensus Report, JAEN (Spain) 2018." Nutrients vol. 11,9 2039. 1 Sep. 2019, doi:10.3390/nu11092039

Banks, Leah D et al. "Olive oil prevents benzo(a)pyrene [B(a)P]-induced colon carcinogenesis through altered B(a)P metabolism and decreased oxidative damage in Apc(Min) mouse model." The Journal of nutritional biochemistry vol. 28 (2016): 37-50. doi:10.1016/j.jnutbio.2015.09.023

Ramsden C E, Zamora D, Majchrzak-Hong S, Faurot K

R, Broste S K, Frantz R P et al. Re-evaluation of the traditional diet-heart hypothesis: analysis of recovered data from Minnesota

Coronary Experiment (1968-

73) BMJ 2016; 353 :i1246 doi:10.1136/bmj.i1246

Guasch-Ferré, Marta et al. "Olive oil intake and risk of cardiovascular disease and mortality in the PREDIMED Study." BMC medicine vol. 12 78. 13 May. 2014, doi:10.1186/1741-7015-12-78

Rinaldi de Alvarenga, José Fernando et al. "Using Extra Virgin Olive Oil to Cook Vegetables Enhances Polyphenol and Carotenoid Extractability: A Study Applying the sofrito Technique." Molecules (Basel, Switzerland) vol. 24,8 1555.

19 Apr. 2019, doi:10.3390/molecules24081555

Rigacci, Stefania, and Massimo Stefani. "Nutraceutical Properties of Olive Oil Polyphenols. An Itinerary from Cultured Cells through Animal Models to Humans." International journal of molecular sciences vol. 17,6 843. 31 May. 2016, doi:10.3390/ijms17060843

Rodríguez-Morató, Jose et al. "Potential role of olive oil phenolic compounds in the prevention of neurodegenerative diseases." Molecules (Basel, Switzerland) vol. 20,3 4655-80. 13 Mar.

2015, doi:10.3390/molecules20034655

Reboredo-Rodríguez, Patricia et al. "State of the

Art on Functional Virgin Olive Oils Enriched with Bioactive Compounds and Their Properties." International journal of molecular sciences vol. 18,3 668. 20 Mar. 2017, doi:10.3390/ijms18030668

Cougnard-Grégoire, Audrey et al. "Olive Oil Consumption and Age-Related Macular Degeneration:

The Alienor Study." PloS one vol. 11,7 e0160240. 28 Jul. 2016, doi:10.1371/journal.pone.0160240

Norahmad, Nor Azrina et al. "Effect of freeze-dried Carica papaya leaf juice on inflammatory cytokines production during dengue virus infection in AG129 mice." BMC complementary and alternative medicine vol. 19,1 44. 11 Feb. 2019, doi:10.1186/s12906-019-2438-3

Mohd Abd Razak, Mohd Ridzuan et al. "Preliminary study on the expression of endothelial cell biology related genes in the liver of dengue virus infected mice treated with Carica papaya leaf juice."

BMC research notes vol. 12,1 206. 3 Apr. 2019, doi:10.1186/s13104-019-4242-z

Anjum, Varisha et al. "Antithrombocytopenic

and immunomodulatory potential of metabolically characterized aqueous extract of Carica papaya leaves." Pharmaceutical biology vol. 55,1 (2017): 2043-2056. doi:10.1080/13880209.2017.1346690

Chandrasekaran, Rajkuberan et al. "Carica

papaya (Papaya) latex: a new paradigm to combat against dengue and filariasis vectors Aedes aegypti and Culex quinquefasciatus (Diptera: Culicidae)." 3 Biotech vol. 8,2 (2018): 83. doi:10.1007/s13205-018-1105-6

Gheith, Ibtsam, and Abubakr El-Mahmoudy. "Novel and classical renal biomarkers as evidence for the nephroprotective effect of Carica papaya leaf extract." Bioscience reports vol. 38,5 BSR20181187. 20 Sep.

2018, doi:10.1042/BSR20181187

Juárez-Rojop, Isela Esther et al. "Hypoglycemic

effect of Carica papaya leaves in streptozotocin-induced diabetic rats." BMC complementary and alternative medicine vol. 12 236. 28 Nov. 2012, doi:10.1186/1472-6882-12-236

Miranda-Osorio, Pedro H et al. "Protective

Action of Carica papaya on β-Cells in Streptozotocin-

Induced Diabetic Rats." International journal of environmental

research and public health vol. 13,5 446. 27 Apr. 2016, doi:10.3390/ijerph13050446

Kugo, M et al. "Fortification of Carica papaya

fruit seeds to school meal snacks may aid Africa mass deworming programs: a preliminary survey." BMC complementary and alternative medicine vol. 18,1 327. 7 Dec. 2018, doi:10.1186/s12906-018-2379-2

Nguyen, Thao T et al. "Chemical Characterization and in Vitro Cytotoxicity on Squamous Cell Carcinoma Cells of Carica papaya Leaf Extracts." Toxins vol. 8,1 7. 24 Dec. 2015, doi:10.3390/toxins8010007

Jayasinghe, Chanika Dilumi et al. "Mature leaf concentrate of Sri Lankan wild type Carica papaya Linn. modulates nonfunctional and functional immune responses of rats." BMC complementary and alternative medicine vol. 17,1 230. 26 Apr. 2017, doi:10.1186/s12906-017-1742-z

Santana, Lidiani F et al. "Nutraceutical Potential of Carica papaya in Metabolic Syndrome." Nutrients vol. 11,7 1608. 16 Jul. 2019, doi:10.3390/nu11071608

Santana, Lidiani F et al. "Nutraceutical Potential of Carica papaya in Metabolic Syndrome." Nutrients vol. 11,7 1608. 16 Jul. 2019, doi:10.3390/nu11071608

Prado, Samira Bernardino Ramos do et al. "Ripening-induced chemical modifications of papaya pectin inhibit cancer cell proliferation." Scientific reports vol. 7,1 16564. 29 Nov. 2017, doi:10.1038/s41598-017-167093

Saliasi, Ina et al. "Effect of a Toothpaste/Mouthwash Containing Carica papaya Leaf Extract on Interdental Gingival Bleeding: A Randomized Controlled Trial." International journal of environmental research and public health vol. 15,12 2660. 27 Nov. 2018, doi:10.3390/ijerph15122660

ccli Fiber and Prebiotics: Mechanisms and Health Advantages, Slavin J. Nutrition [Online]. 2013 Apr 22;5(4):1417-35. You can get this at: https://www.ncbi.nlm.nih.gov/pmc/articles/PMC3705355

Weaver CM, Martin BR, Clavijo A, Nakatsu CH, and Armstrong AP. In both normal and ovariectomized rats, dietary prebiotics enhance calcium absorption and bone mineralization. 2019 May 1 [cited 2023 Mar 15];149(5):840-7.

The Journal of Nutrition [Internet]. Disponible à partir de: https://www.ncbi.nlm.nih.gov/pmc/articles/PMC6470833.

Hiel S, Gianfrancesco MA, Rodriguez J, Portheault D, Leyrolle Q, Bindels LB, Gomes da Silveira Cauduro C, Mulders MDGH, Zamariola G, Azzi AS, Kalala G, Pachikian BD, Amadieu C, Neyrinck AM, Loumaye A, Cani PD, Lanthier N, Trefois P, Klein O, Luminet O, Bindelle J, Paquot N, Cnop M, Thissen JP, Delzenne NM. Link between gut microbiota and health outcomes in inulin -treated obese patients: Lessons from the Food4Gut multicenter randomized placebo-controlled trial. Clin Nutr. 2020 Dec;39(12):3618-3628. doi: 10.1016/j.clnu.2020.04.005. Epub 2020 Apr 13. PMID: 32340903.

Goodarzi A, Mozafarpoor S, Bodaghabadi M, Mohamadi M. The potential of probiotics for treating acne vulgaris: A review of literature on acne and microbiota. Dermatol Ther. 2020 May;33(3):e13279. doi: 10.1111/dth.13279. Epub 2020 Apr 7. PMID: 32266790.

Wang YY, Hsieh YH, Kumar KJS, Hsieh HW, Lin CC, Wang SY. The Regulatory Effects of a Formulation of Cinnamomum osmophloeum Kaneh and Taiwanofungus camphoratus on Metabolic Syndrome and the Gut Microbiome. Plants (Basel). 2020 Mar 20;9(3):383. doi: 10.3390/plants9030383. PMID: 32244889; PMCID: PMC7154906.

Calero CDQ, Rincón EO, Marqueta PM. Probiotics, prebiotics and synbiotics: useful for athletes and active individuals? A systematic review. Benef Microbes. 2020 Mar 27;11(2):135-149. doi: 10.3920/BM2019.0076. Epub 2020 Feb 19. PMID: 32073297.

- Gibson GR, Sanders ME, Hutkins R, Reimer RA, Salminen SJ, and others. The consensus declaration on the definition and application of prebiotics by the International 4- Scientific Society for Probiotics and Prebiotics (ISAPP). 2017 August [cited 2023 Mar 15];14(8):491-502. Nature Reviews Gastroenterology & Hepatology [Internet]. NRGASTRO.2017.75 is accessible at: https://www.nature.com/articles

Aggarwal D, Garg A, Kaur IP. Development of a topical niosomal preparation of acetazolamide: preparation and evaluation. J Pharm Pharmacol. 2004 Dec;56(12):1509-17. doi: 10.1211/0022357044896. PMID: 15563757.

Nirale N. M., Menon M. D. Topical formulations of serratiopeptidase: development and pharmacodynamic evaluation. Indian Journal of Pharmaceutical Sciences. 2010;72(1):65–67. doi: 10.4103/0250-474X.62246

Kee W, Tan S, Lee V, Salmon Y. The treatment of breast engorgement with Serrapeptase (Danzen): a randomized doubleblind controlled trial. Singapore Med J 1989;30:48–54

Prasad S, Aggarwal BB. Turmeric, the Golden Spice: From Traditional Medicine to Modern Medicine. In: Benzie IFF, Wachtel-Galor S, editors. Herbal Medicine: Biomolecular and Clinical Aspects. 2nd edition. Boca Raton (FL): CRC Press/Taylor & Francis; 2011. Chapter 13. Available from: https://www.ncbi.nlm.nih.gov/books/NBK92752/

Skiba, Meghan B et al. "Curcuminoid Content and Safety-Related Markers of Quality of Turmeric Dietary Supplements Sold in an Urban Retail Marketplace in the United States." Molecular nutrition & food research vol. 62,14 (2018): e1800143. doi:10.1002/mnfr.201800143

Ravindran, Jayaraj et al. "Curcumin and cancer

cells: how many ways can curry kill tumor cells selectively?." The AAPS journal vol. 11,3 (2009): 495-510. doi:10.1208/s12248-009-9128-x

Park, Wungki et al. "New perspectives of

curcumin in cancer prevention." Cancer prevention research (Philadelphia, Pa.) vol. 6,5 (2013): 387-400. doi:10.1158/1940-6207.CAPR-12-0410

Hewlings, Susan J, and Douglas S Kalman. "Curcumin: A Review of Its Effects on Human

Health." Foods (Basel, Switzerland) vol. 6,10 92. 22 Oct.

2017, doi:10.3390/foods6100092

Sharma S, Tanwar A, Gupta DK. Curcumin: an

adjuvant therapeutic remedy for liver cancer. Hepatoma Research. 2016; 2:62-70. http://dx.doi.org/10.20517/2394-

5079.2015.59

Kusmayadi, Andri et al. "The effects of

mangosteen peel (Garcinia mangostana L.) and Turmeric (Curcuma domestica Val) flour dietary supplementation on the growth performance, lipid profile, and abdominal fat content in Cihateup ducks." Veterinary world vol. 12,3

(2019): 402-408. doi:10.14202/vetworld.2019.402-408

Gupta, Subash C et al. "Therapeutic roles of

curcumin: lessons learned from clinical trials." The AAPS journal vol. 15,1 (2013): 195-218. doi:10.1208/s12248-012-

9432-8

Pearson, Wendy, and Laima S Kott. "A

biological extract of turmeric (Curcuma longa) modulates response of cartilage explants to lipopolysaccharide." BMC complementary and alternative medicine vol. 19,1 252. 11 Sep. 2019, doi:10.1186/s12906-019-2660-z

McCann, Mark J et al. "The effect of turmeric (Curcuma longa) extract on the functionality of the solute carrier protein 22 A4 (SLC22A4) and interleukin-10 (IL10) variants associated with inflammatory bowel disease." Nutrients vol. 6,10 4178-90. 13 Oct. 2014, doi:10.3390/nu6104178

Lee, Hwa-Young et al. "Turmeric extract and its active compound, curcumin, protect against chronic CCl4induced liver damage by enhancing antioxidation." BMC complementary and alternative medicine vol. 16,1 316. 26 Aug. 2016, doi:10.1186/s12906-016-1307-6

Baliga, M. S., Joseph, N., Venkataranganna, M. V., Saxena, A., Ponemone, V., & Fayad, R. (2012). Curcumin, an active component of turmeric in the prevention and treatment of ulcerative colitis: preclinical and clinical observations. Food & function, 3(11), 1109–1117. https://doi.org/10.1039/c2fo30097d

cclxxiii Santos, P A S R et al. "Assessment of Cytotoxic Activity of Rosemary (Rosmarinus officinalis L.), Turmeric (Curcuma longa L.), and Ginger (Zingiber officinale R.) Essential Oils in Cervical Cancer Cells (HeLa)." TheScientificWorldJournal vol. 2016 (2016): 9273078. doi:10.1155/2016/9273078

cclxxiv Kim, Sang-Wook et al. "The effectiveness of fermented turmeric powder in subjects with elevated alanine transaminase levels: a randomised controlled study." BMC complementary and alternative medicine vol. 13 58. 8 Mar. 2013, doi:10.1186/1472-6882-13-58

Choi, Yohan et al. "Puffing as a Novel Process to Enhance the Antioxidant and Anti-Inflammatory Properties of Curcuma longa L. (Turmeric)." Antioxidants (Basel, Switzerland) vol. 8,11 506. 23 Oct. 2019, doi:10.3390/antiox8110506

Peterson, Christine T et al. "Effects of Turmeric and Curcumin Dietary Supplementation on Human Gut Microbiota: A Double-Blind, Randomized, Placebo-Controlled Pilot Study." Journal of evidence-based integrative medicine vol. 23 (2018): 2515690X18790725. doi:10.1177/2515690X18790725

de Souza Tavares, Wagner et al. "Turmeric powder and its derivatives from Curcuma longa rhizomes: Insecticidal effects on cabbage looper and the role of synergists." Scientific reports vol. 6 34093. 2 Nov. 2016, doi:10.1038/srep34093

Flores, Gonzalo. "Curcuma longa L. extract improves the cortical neural connectivity during the aging process." Neural regeneration research vol. 12,6 (2017): 875-880. doi:10.4103/1673-5374.208542

Kunnumakkara, Ajaikumar B et al. "Curcumin, the golden nutraceutical: multitargeting for multiple chronic diseases." British journal of pharmacology vol. 174,11 (2017): 1325-1348. doi:10.1111/bph.13621

Kim, Yoona, and Peter Clifton. "Curcumin, Cardiometabolic Health and Dementia." International journal of environmental research and public health vol. 15,10 2093. 24 Sep. 2018, doi:10.3390/ijerph15102093

Ravindran, P.N. & Babu, K. & Shiva, KN.

(2007). Botany and crop improvement of turmeric. Turmeric: The Genus Curcuma. 15-70.

Skiba, Meghan B et al. "Curcuminoid Content and Safety-Related Markers of Quality of Turmeric Dietary Supplements Sold in an Urban Retail Marketplace in the United States." Molecular nutrition & food research vol. 62,14 (2018): e1800143. doi:10.1002/mnfr.201800143

Fanelli Kuczmarski, Marie et al. "Aspects of Dietary Diversity Differ in Their Association with Atherosclerotic Cardiovascular Risk in a Racially Diverse US Adult Population." Nutrients vol. 11,5 1034. 8 May. 2019, doi:10.3390/nu11051034

Bartlett JD, Hawley JA, Morton JP. Carbohydrate availability and exercise training adaptation: too much of a good thing? Eur J Sport Sci. 2015;15(1):3-12. doi: 10.1080/17461391.2014.920926. Epub 2014 Jun 19. PMID: 24942068.

https://michaelpollan.com/books/the-botany-of-desire/

Bachman, J. L., & Raynor, H. A. (2012). Effects of manipulating eating frequency during a behavioral weight loss intervention: a pilot randomized controlled trial. Obesity (Silver Spring, Md.), 20(5), 985–992. https://doi.org/10.1038/oby.2011.360

Leidy, H. J., & Campbell, W. W. (2011). The effect of eating frequency on appetite control and food intake: brief synopsis of controlled feeding studies. The Journal of nutrition, 141(1), 154–157. https://doi.org/10.3945/jn.109.114389

https://www.amazon.com/MucuslessHealing-System-Arnold-Ehret/dp/0879040041

https://www.amazon.com/Secret-PlantsPeter-Tompkins-Christopher/dp/B006L7S55S

https://www.goodreads.com/book/show/3504953dictionary-of-economic-plants

Jura-Morawiec, Joanna, and Mirela Tulik. "Dragon's blood secretion and its ecological significance." Chemoecology vol. 26 (2016): 101-105. doi:10.1007/s00049-016-0212-2

Greim H, Saltmiras D, Mostert V, Strupp C. Evaluation of carcinogenic potential of the herbicide glyphosate, drawing on tumor incidence data from fourteen chronic/carcinogenicity rodent studies. Crit Rev Toxicol. 2015 Mar;45(3):185-208. doi:

10.3109/10408444.2014.1003423. Epub 2015 Feb 26. PMID: 25716480; PMCID: PMC4819582.

Turcotte MM, Araki H, Karp DS, Poveda K, Whitehead SR. The eco-evolutionary impacts of domestication and agricultural practices on wild species.

Philos Trans R Soc Lond B Biol Sci. 2017 Jan 19;372(1712):20160033. doi: 10.1098/rstb.2016.0033. PMID: 27920378; PMCID: PMC5182429.

Duke SO, Lydon J, Koskinen WC, Moorman TB, Chaney RL, Hammerschmidt R. Glyphosate effects on plant mineral nutrition, crop rhizosphere microbiota, and plant disease in glyphosate-resistant crops. J Agric Food Chem. 2012 Oct 24;60(42):10375-97. doi:

10.1021/jf302436u. Epub 2012 Oct 15. Erratum in: J Agric Food Chem. 2013 Dec 26;61(51):12745. PMID: 23013354; PMCID: PMC3479986.

Motta EVS, Raymann K, Moran NA.

Glyphosate perturbs the gut microbiota of honey bees. Proc Natl Acad Sci U S A. 2018 Oct 9;115(41):1030510310. doi: 10.1073/pnas.1803880115. Epub 2018 Sep 24. PMID: 30249635; PMCID: PMC6187125.

Gillezeau C, van Gerwen M, Shaffer RM, Rana I, Zhang L, Sheppard L, Taioli E. The evidence of human exposure to glyphosate: a review. Environ Health. 2019 Jan 7;18(1):2. doi: 10.1186/s12940-018-0435-5. PMID: 30612564; PMCID: PMC6322310.

Tarazona JV, Court-Marques D, Tiramani M, Reich H, Pfeil R, Istace F, Crivellente F. Glyphosate toxicity and carcinogenicity: a review of the scientific basis of the European Union assessment and its differences with IARC. Arch Toxicol. 2017 Aug;91(8):2723-2743. doi: 10.1007/s00204-017-1962-5. Epub 2017 Apr 3. PMID: 28374158; PMCID: PMC5515989.

Myers JP, Antoniou MN, Blumberg B, Carroll L, Colborn T, Everett LG, Hansen M, Landrigan PJ, Lanphear BP, Mesnage R, Vandenberg LN, Vom Saal FS, Welshons WV, Benbrook CM. Concerns over use of glyphosate-based herbicides and risks associated with exposures: a consensus statement. Environ Health. 2016 Feb 17;15:19. doi: 10.1186/s12940-016-0117-0. PMID: 26883814; PMCID: PMC4756530.

Londo JP, McKinney J, Schwartz M, Bollman M, Sagers C, Watrud L. Sub-lethal glyphosate exposure alters flowering phenology and causes transient malesterility in Brassica spp. BMC Plant Biol. 2014 Mar 21;14:70. doi: 10.1186/1471-2229-14-70. PMID: 24655547; PMCID: PMC3998022.

Andreotti G, Koutros S, Hofmann JN, Sandler DP, Lubin JH, Lynch CF, Lerro CC, De Roos AJ, Parks CG, Alavanja MC, Silverman DT, Beane Freeman LE. Glyphosate Use and Cancer Incidence in the Agricultural Health Study. J Natl Cancer Inst. 2018 May 1;110(5):509516. doi: 10.1093/jnci/djx233. PMID: 29136183; PMCID: PMC6279255. Ccci

Ten Speed Press's 2005 book Mycelium Running:

How Mushrooms Can Save the Planet (ISBN 978-1-

58008-579-3)

DeVore, I., Lee, R. B., & De Vore, I. (Eds.). (1968). Man the hunter. Chicago, IL: Aldine Publishing Company.

Kent, S. (Ed.). (1989). Farmers as hunters: the implications of sedentism. CUP Archive.

Bharucha, Zareen, and Jules Pretty. "The roles and values of wild foods in agricultural systems." Philosophical transactions of the Royal Society of London. Series B, Biological sciences vol. 365,1554 (2010): 2913-26. doi:10.1098/rstb.2010.0123

Teklehaymanot T, Giday M. Ethnobotanical study of wild edible plants of Kara and Kwego semipastoralist people in Lower Omo River Valley, Debub Omo Zone, SNNPR, Ethiopia. J Ethnobiol Ethnomed. 2010 Aug 17;6:23. doi: 10.1186/1746-4269-6-23. PMID: 20712910; PMCID: PMC2933608.

Cruz-Garcia GS, Price LL. Gathering of wild food plants in anthropogenic environments across the seasons: implications for poor and vulnerable farm households. Ecol Food Nutr. 2014;53(4):363-89. doi: 10.1080/03670244.2013.808631. PMID: 24884553.

Dietary species richness as a measure of food biodiversity and nutritional quality of diets | PNAS

https://www.amazon.com/Plant-ParadoxDangers-Healthy-Disease/dp/006242713X

cccix

https://www.theguardian.com/environment/2020/apr/2 8/ron-finley-gangsta-gardener-transforming-los-angeles